WOLVES IN SHEEP'S CLOTHING

STEPHEN MARSHALL

disinformation®

for Mia and Poppa,

who taught me that truth in love means loyalty
and perseverance without honor is merely survival

Published by The Disinformation Company Ltd.
163 Third Avenue, Suite 108
New York, NY 10003
Tel.: +1.212.691.1605
Fax: +1.212.691.1606
www.disinfo.com

Library of Congress Control Number: 2007921169

ISBN–13: 978–1932857–42–9
ISBN–10: 1–932857–42–7

Distributed in the USA and Canada by:
Consortium Book Sales and Distribution
1045 Westgate Drive, Suite 90
St Paul, MN 55114
Toll Free: +1.800.283.3572 Local: +1.651.221.9035
Fax: +1.651.221.0124 www.cbsd.com

Distributed in the United Kingdom and Eire by:
Virgin Books
Thames Wharf Studios, Rainville Road
London W6 9HA
Tel.: +44.(0)20.7386.3300 Fax: +44.(0)20.7386.3360
E–Mail: sales@virgin–books.co.uk

Distributed in Australia by:
Tower Books
Unit 2/17 Rodborough Road
Frenchs Forest NSW 2086
Tel.: +61.2.9975.5566 Fax: +61.2.9975.5599
E–mail: info@towerbooks.com.au

Attention colleges and universities, unions and other organizations:
Quantity discounts are available on bulk purchases of this book for educational
training purposes, fund–raising, or gift giving. Special books, booklets, or book
excerpts can also be created to fit your specific needs. For information contact
the Marketing Department of The Disinformation Company Ltd.

Design by Ralph Bernardo

Printed in USA

1   3   5   7   9   10   8   6   4   2

CONTENTS

ACKNOWLEDGEMENTS

I am indebted to my editor Jake Klisivitch, who had the mean job of slicing through the forest to find the branches, arcs and seeds; my fact-checker Alexandra Epstein who made the manuscript legit; my transcribers Rita Liazza, Maya Kramer, Cynthia Helton, Hannah Zander, Griff Foxley, Gerasimos (Jerry) Manolatos, Joseph Huff-Hannon, and Brian Leahy, without whose dedication this book could not have been produced; my consultants Rob Campbell, Jordy Cummings, Randy Thompson, Rebecca Myles, Wilson Becton, Jan Begine, and Savanna Reid whose late night conversations and emails were critical to forming some of the ideas presented here; Ralph Bernardo and Gary Baddeley at Disinfo; and to Emily Haynes, Luca, Sharon Chavez, Ina Howard, Ann Gollin, Ashleigh Banfield, Deirdre English, Peter Florence, Clare Purcell, Ed Rampell, Scott Noble, Andrew Heywood, Jonathan Powell, Milka Stanisic, Richard Falk, Peg Booth, Barbara Glauning, Ulla Rapp, Amy Redford, Chase Kimball, Axel Schmidt, Marko Popovic and Katarina Zivanovic, who helped in ways too varied and numerous to cite here.

And finally, to my parents Jeff and Diana, who kindly pretend to understand the economy of nonfiction; my grandparents, Wels, Dorothy, Stephen and Patricia, who seem to live for ever and have blessed me with their DNA; Nancy Smith, my surrogate consigliere; Kim and Olivia, my spiritual advisors who taught me that faith is something we earn; Paul Mason and Rose Barker, the two teachers at LCS who gave me the seemingly incorruptible desire to write; Ian Inaba, Anthony Lappé and Josh Shore, my three G's at GNN; my surf siblings (Emily, Patrick, and Christopher) who love me like the youngest; and finally, to Lisa Kawamoto Hsu, who carries the rarest alchemy of intellectual depth, spiritual calm and physical beauty; I could not have finished this book without you... *aishite imasu.*

NOTES ON STYLE AND STRUCTURE

I have chosen to write *Wolves* much in the style in which I make my documentaries. While it is nonfiction, the story unfolds as a linear narrative with a primary focus on characters and the scenes within which I encountered them. There are times when the reader is simply placed within the moment of a conversation. In many cases I leave it to their judgment to interpret the deeper connection between the subject's ideas and the book's thesis. At other times, I have injected myself more decisively, delving into the back stories that made this material so compelling for me. I am a firm believer in the slow reveal, that the journey is the destination. And so, while I have surrendered to my editor's wish that I clearly map out the key arguments and goal of this book in its first chapter, I have generally avoided the kind of academic handholding that is found throughout most books of this nature. I want it to be as much as an adventure into the legacy of America's failed liberal project for the reader as it was for me.

Creation Theory

It has been our fate as a nation not to
have ideologies, but to be one.
— Richard Hofstadter

US AND THEM

Americans are facing one of the most important decisions in their history. It is the kind of political moment that very few nations experience in that the outcome will have a tangible impact on the lives of many around the world. Such is the power and influence of citizens in the sole global superpower, that even those who abstain from the American electoral process can determine the fate of people across continents.

I'm not talking about a choice between political parties or presidential candidates. This isn't about *American Idol*. In the new millennium, the destiny of the United States and its role in the world will lie in the hands of a bunch of kids (born between 1980 and 1994) collectively known as Generation Y. The choice to be made now is exactly what kind of country Americans want them to inherit. Will it be one that looks suspiciously beyond its borders, jealously guarding its share of world resources and treating other nations as threatening competitors? Or will it be something entirely different, one that views itself as part of a larger global family, dedicated to leading an authentically globalist political idea which accords the same value and respect to all individuals, in every country?

America at the turn of the century has largely been shaped by our parents' generation (born between 1943 and 1964), the Baby Boomers. It is they who are in the positions of power across the political, economic, and military spectrum. It is they who we can blame or credit for the state of affairs in which we now find ourselves.

My generation, X, has been the subject of much cultural analysis, but will never hold as much influence over American destiny as the Boomers and Gen Y. Those two generations comprise approximately half the U.S. population—24 percent and 26 percent respectively—while we factor in at 17 percent. But that does not mean Gen X doesn't have a role in the destiny of the country.[1] I argue that at this present time, our generation has the most important responsibility of all. And that is to be a bridge between these two dominant generations and attempt to steer the country away from a path that could ultimately lead to the kind of apocalyptic end in which only Muslim and Christian fundamentalists see a silver lining.

It sounds like an exaggeration, but let me explain why we should be worried: In the past few years, I have traveled extensively through the Middle East and Muslim world and the one recurring theme I have heard from moderate and educated Muslims is that the American liberal project is dead. Many of them believe that the '60s era anti-war protesters who gave the world faith in the United States even as their Democratic president dropped napalm on villagers in North Vietnam, have abandoned their ideological post and allowed the country's political axis to slide far from its traditional center. Without that critical balancing force, they argue, America can only be viewed as a threat to the entire world.

As a high-ranking Pakistani intelligence agency official told me in Islamabad, "I believe that great nations have a resonance. They emit power and integrity and everyone else can see that about them. This is how America used to be. But now—there is this Latin term, *argumentum ad baculum*, which basically means violence as a form of argument; that everyone should do as you say or they will be punished with force. Well, that is a fallacious argument. And we know that as soon as a country has to use force in order to get others to comply with its will, it has already lost. And this is what has happened to America. But what is worse is that the liberal side has allowed it. They have bought into the argument as well."[2]

Of course, not all of the liberal Boomers have abandoned their principles. But among those that have turned the corner and backed the U.S. bombing of Yugoslavia, the first Gulf War, and post-9/11 invasions of Afghanistan and Iraq are some of the most eloquent and influential liberals in the country. This book is a journey into the heart of the ideological retreat of that generation. It is a quest to discover what drives people to abandon their youthful anti-militarism and sanction the kind of warfare that ultimately destroys and destabilizes entire communities.

The Boomer rebels were the inheritors of a liberal project born out of the New Deal and Great Society, dedicated to safeguarding the dignity and economic sustainability of the weakest in society and eradicating old existing hierarchies of elitism and exploitation. In the '60s they represented a youth wave so dynamic that it catalyzed a worldwide movement of peace-loving, power-busting hippies who ultimately exposed the most corrupt machinations of state power and hastened an end to the Vietnam War. But as they grew older their views began to change.

Irving Kristol once joked that a neoconservative is a liberal who got mugged by reality.[3] He was referring to those liberals who switched sides back in the 1980s when it became clear that big government was a sham; while it looked great on paper, it didn't work in practice. But what happened after 9/11 is that everyone got mugged. The attacks brought home how vulnerable the whole country had become. And when a nation is presented with a threat to its survival, the first thing it does is lose the idealism and get very tight with reality. Which means sacrificing many of the rights and values that were once considered sacred. The neoconservatives were really just the early adapters in this equation. Their shift away from social liberalism is indicative of the tide that will sweep the American ideological shore.

In a short conversation with former *New York Times* Middle East bureau chief Chris Hedges, the Pulitzer Prize winner told me that we are witnessing the "Weimarization of American society." He does not see the xenophobic, right-wing extremism that put Bush in the White House as a fleeting shift in the political pendulum. Rather, Hedges explains that it is a more permanent result of a downward economic spiral in the country. Over twenty percent of manufacturing jobs were lost between 1995 and 2005, forcing those workers into the service industry or unemployment lines. Where once it was the Democratic Party that would offer shelter to the working class, now it is the Christian right that channels the anger and shame of the economically disenfranchised into what Hedges calls a "politics of despair," one that ultimately clamors for the days when America was God-abiding, racially pure and prosperous. Couple that with analysts' warnings about the limited prospect for a revival of the manufacturing sector and, Hedges warns, it's a recipe for disaster.[4]

Faced with the loss of prestige and influence in the world and the real threat of economic decline, a core group of highly influential Boomer liberals blinked. Realizing they are losing ground in a competition that will not favor those who play by established rules of liberal society, they have thrown in their lot with empire, playing good cop to the neoconservatives' militarized, warmongering bad cop. Worse, they are pimping a system that has been reduced to a memory of its original intent. It is *the idea* of America that they are proposing that soldiers die for. Modern liberalism is not based on the archaic virtues of "individual liberty" as pronounced by its founding philosophies. Modern liberalism is now involved in a mortal struggle for its own survival, giving way to a system that has a tendency to exploit far more than liberate. It is the antithesis of that proscribed by its originators. And yet they are willing to maintain the illusion that America is bringing an evolved, humane political and economic system without acknowledging it's a front for the free market engine that, once implemented, will ensure the short-term strengthening of their own economy. If the neocons are wolves on the hunt for food and territory, then the liberals are wolves in sheep's clothing.

This book is a two-tiered journey. On one level, it beats a path into the minds of these wolves in sheep's clothing. On the other, I travel from Iraq, through the backroom parlor society of London's intellectual jet set, out to the frontier of liberal war-making in Serbia and then across the United States, exploring the history of liberalism, its origins and mutations, its radicals and apostates, its domination of American politics and final surrender to the *realpolitikal* forces that assert themselves when a nation begins to fall from greatness.

My focus is squarely on that powerful group of Boomer liberals who have set the agenda for a new American liberalism. These are not the politicians nor the business leaders who still pretend to champion the cause of a social liberalism. It would be too easy a target to uncover their contradictions and hypocrisies. I am much more interested in our liberal academics, journalists and philosophers who have traditionally channeled and guided the national subconscious. Without understanding why many of these great liberal thinkers, the architects of the greatest social revolution in the world's history, abandoned their vital questioning of governments which seek war as a response to questionable external threats, then we will never know how to avoid that same tendency in ourselves.

AN HONEST BROKER

"You think people want to hear this?" asks the soldier.

I nod, looking past him at the poster of Britney Spears in a football uniform, her arms slung around a pack of NFL players.

"Well, it's about globalization." Pausing, he bends down and spits a stream of brown fluid from his mouth. "We have to stabilize new and emerging markets in order to secure resources. Fifty or a hundred years... it's not about what it can do for us in the short term, it's about what it can do for us in the long term." *

I am standing in the small makeshift headquarters for the Fourth Infantry Division in Samarra, Iraq. Sgt. First Class Robert Hollis is deconstructing the Iraq war and sounding more like Noam Chomsky than a crack M1 Abrams tank commander.

"When Americans say 'liberation,' we mean capitalism," he states matter-of-factly. "That's what we mean when we say 'liberation.' It's our way of life, and we believe in it."[5]

This kind of talk would be unimaginable from a bureaucrat or politician, who excavate economic variables from the discussion about America's presence in the Middle East. But not Hollis, who seems very comfortable in the role of pointing out the Emperor's unconscious nudity.

"Can you tell mothers and daughters and sisters that your sons are dying for the American way of life? Can you say that they're

* Sgt. Hollis appears in GNN's award-winning documentary, *BattleGround: 21 Days on the Empire's Edge.*

dying for capital goods? No, you cannot." Hollis nods confidently, "So you have to make sure that whenever you fight, you fight for moral and ethical reasons. This is what the public buys."

For those on the front lines of Iraq's guerrilla war, clarity of purpose is a critical psychological asset. In many ways, Hollis offers the sanest explanation for the ongoing loss of American and Iraqi lives that I have heard since the invasion of Iraq. It's far more logical than the notion of protecting America from a foreign threat, which very few of the troops are willing to cite. Preferring the less controversial, they stick to the tangible. "It's a war game," one tells me, "every few years America likes to go out and test its fighting force." Another is less crass, explaining, "We're here to help the Iraqis rebuild their society, one school at a time." But Hollis is an anomaly. He sees the conflict through a wider, historical prism: In an age of multinational corporate globalization and fierce compe-tition over dwindling resources, if the protection of American economic power and global hegemony aren't worth fighting for, then what is?

This is the kind of honest, no-guff rhetoric that goes back to the 1950s and the days of Charlie Wilson, the brash, plain-speaking head of General Motors whose nomination to secretary of defense by President Dwight Eisenhower foreshadowed the private-to-public sector vacillations of modern political agents like Vice President Dick Cheney. At first Wilson was reluctant to sell his GM stock, which was valued at over $2.5 million, but then relented under pressure. During his confirmation hearings, Wilson was asked if he would be able to make a decision against the interests of General Motors from his position in the Pentagon. "Yes," he answered, adding the famous caveat that he could not conceive of such a situ-ation "because for years I thought what was good for the country was good for General Motors and vice versa."[6]

It is a mixture of duplicity and pragmatism that prevents our modern business and political leaders from speaking so candidly about the relationship between American corporations and the government that serves them, especially in the realm of foreign policy. Since the violent Seattle protests in 1999, the ideological (and physical) battle between the champions of American-led globalization and its opponents has become too fierce for even the most nuanced references to geostrategic capitalism. We have truly entered the clichéd era of perpetual war and Orwellian *double-speak*, in which government spokespeople stick to a well-rehearsed script, modifying it as they encounter ideological or practical inconsistencies. It's nearly impossible to glean deeper meaning in the vast expenditure of American resources, both capital and human, in Iraq.

What was once presented to the American public as a vital issue of national security has morphed through several incarnations, finding its ultimate iteration in George W. Bush's second inaugural speech, in which he stated:

> *There is no justice without freedom. And there can be no human rights without human liberty.*

The "inalienable" rights of life, liberty and the pursuit of happiness are at the core of American national identity and form the basis for its constitutional republic. You would be hard-pressed to find any American politician or commentator, liberal or conservative, who would deny that a free society is dependent on a free economy. The entire Cold War was fought to prove that democracy and capitalism—not communism and its central, planned economy— represented the ultimate sociopolitical engine, guaranteeing the highest form of human liberty and individual advancement.

And so, at least for the American economic and political elite, there is an inextricable, causal link between the free society advocated by Bush in his inaugural speech and the capitalist system Hollis is fighting for in Iraq. When Americans speak of bringing liberty to the Iraqis, they are also talking about expanding the free market system to their borders, with the implicit understanding that it will extend the reach of American corporate interests into that region. But this aspect of liberalism is almost never mentioned by those who use it to justify the war. Almost.

A few years before the war, one influential mainstream commentator offered a parallel to Hollis's linking of capitalism and militarism. For Thomas Friedman, the *New York Times* columnist who has made himself into the West's preeminent prophet for globalization, the integration of world economies is the central organizing principle of the new millennium. Yet, he understands that for the long arm of globalization to work, it needs the muscle of a thumping heart. Writing in his bestselling *The Lexus and the Olive Tree*, Friedman asserted: "The hidden hand of the market will never work without a hidden fist... McDonald's cannot flourish without McDonnell Douglas. And the hidden fist that keeps the world safe for Silicon Valley's technologies to flourish is called the U.S. Army, Air Force, Navy and Marine Corps."*[7] Like any student of capitalism, Friedman understands that the success of corporate enterprise is based on the continual expansion of markets, extraction of raw materials and development of cheap labor pools.

Thomas Friedman, meet Sergeant Hollis. Standing here, in this embattled outpost of the War on Terror, Hollis is exactly the man for the job. In fact, I wonder if he reads Friedman's column in the *Times* because he uses the language of a corporate internationalist.

"The regime that we are replacing was brutal," he continues. "It was inefficient. It was killing and murdering people. It was not

---

* Anti-globalization activist Arundhati Roy wrote that Friedman's hand/fist analogy was "the most succinct, accurate description of the project of corporate globalisation that I have read." (Arundhati Roy, Lannan Speech, September 29, 2002).

developing its oil efficiently. So what does that mean? With the world being interdependent, if a manager is mismanaging his fiefdom you have to fire him. How do you fire him? You have to go in and take him out."

A small group of soldiers have gathered around us to listen. Hollis grins at them shyly. A few chuckle back. Though articulate, he's not one for the spotlight, which is a good thing for the Pentagon. Can you imagine reading this in the *Washington Post*?

"In clashes of cultures, many have been wiped out. The great problem is that one side must win, one side must lose, because they're two opposites."

I ask him if it's worth risking soldiers' lives and fighting a war for capitalism when that was never the stated goal.

He nods gently. "But the question is: what do you want to do to defend our way of life? We are just doing what we have to do. The war must be won in Afghanistan, it must be won here... to improve our way of life."

The soldiers disperse as a group of Special Forces operatives shuffle past us on their way out to look for militants. Hollis straps on his helmet and picks up his gun. He turns to me and asks of the audience who might hear his words, "Do you think they'll understand?"

I smile at him, uncertain of what to say. He shrugs his shoulders and walks out to rejoin the battle.

Flying home from the Middle East a few days later, I have a lot of time to think about my encounter with Sergeant Hollis. It was the first time I had come face to face with a man who was willing to admit he would kill for the cause of capitalism. Hollis's interpretation of the war's *raison d'etre* is not as radical as it seems. In the morning papers and nightly broadcasts we hear that America is facing serious challenges to its global economic hegemony. In the governmental white papers that preceded the war, the case was made that the United States cannot afford to let other, less-favored nations, nor a handful of unstable dictators, control the last remaining oil reserves which serve as the fuel for the national economy. And yet the war was never connected to these warnings. They did not form a part of an official explanation, perhaps, for the simple reason that America's new millennial architects could not afford to have the invasion presented as a geostrategic goal, whether it was true or not.

In order to galvanize a coalition of willing states, the argument had to be made that a preemptive attack on Iraq was critical to defending America, and the free world, from Islamic terrorism. Or, alternately, for those Americans who desired a military response to 9/11 but could not align themselves with Bush's coercive patriotism, one of liberal interventionism,* in which an alliance of democratic powers presses its military forces into action for the purpose of liberating an oppressed population. Like an arrow in the heel of Achilles, the proposition of the war as a liberal intervention splintered the Left, shifting the axis of American political identity into a new magnetic field altogether. The one-time standard-bearers of American liberalism, whose mass mobilization of society in the 1970s was enough to stop the Vietnam War, caved and bought the rationale of regime change in Iraq. Instead of questioning their own impulses and probing whether they were justifying an unprovoked, unilateral attack to quell the innermost fear of a decline in American fortunes, they stepped out into the public square and became its champions. And in so doing, they provided a crucial flank to Bush's battle-ready neoconservatives. By presenting themselves as the same old defenders of human liberty and freedom instead of frightened First Worlders making a

---

* This idea, which is the brainchild of former '60s radicals who once viewed all state-sponsored military actions as imperialist ventures, came into vogue during the 1999 NATO bombing of Serbia and then reappeared as a major thrust of the institutional liberal argument for invading Iraq.

last-minute grab for resources and territory, these liberals gave the war a softer face. A kinder mask. One that hid the wild eyes and gnarling teeth of a wolf pack on the hunt behind the wooly brow and gentle smile of a protective, but conflicted, herd of sheep.

Nearly one year after my return from Iraq, I would come face-to-face with two of America's most influential proponents of war as a liberal venture, one of whom would say such an astonishing thing that it became the driving inspiration for this book.

MILITANT LIBERALS

On a blustery fall evening, one month before the 2004 presidential election, I stand at a packed reception at the Overseas Press Club in New York. The crowd is diverse. Young college students mingle with greyer, tweed-jacketed types.

We're gathered to hear a discussion between Paul Berman and Michael Ignatieff, two leading liberal intellectuals. The subject: how the War on Terrorism is impacting liberal society. Berman, a journeyman writer of the New Left generation that came of age during the glory days of '60s era student activism, is undoubtedly the star of the event. His latest book, a slim polemic titled *Terror and Liberalism,* quickly emerged as the bible for liberal hawks who were conflicted over the election of George Bush but supported his brisk military response to 9/11. Using the history of radical Muslim icon Sayyid Qutb, a leader of Egypt's Muslim Brotherhood who was hanged in 1966, Berman depicts the Islamist philosophy as one directly borne of a reaction to liberalism. Qutb had studied in the West and had come to believe that the most evil aspect of American society was the separation of church and state; it represented a toxic virus of sacrilegious secularism that would eventually pene-trate and destroy Islam. Moreover, he saw European imperialism and American foreign policy as extensions of the Crusades. Thus, for Qutb, the jihad was defensive. It was the only viable response to the insidious creeping influence of Western culture and ideas, and the all-reaching hand of the exploitative free market. Qutb declared a theological war against liberalism itself, one that found its ultimate heroes in Osama bin Laden and the nineteen suicidal hijackers of September 11.[8]

Given the ferocious nihilism of the terrorists and their jihadi creed, Berman invokes the spirit of the great emancipator, Abraham Lincoln, who warned that a liberal society would have to be warlike in order to endure the challenges of its enemies. Berman calls for a multi-front campaign against the Islamists and chided George Bush for focusing the world's anger and fear on Osama bin Laden, giving the false impression that "our enemy was merely a single person, or a band of desperadoes, and not anything larger." Because the enemy is, he warns, much larger. It is, according to Berman, a totalitarian death cult that has its roots in the "apocalyptic and phantasmogorical movements that have risen up against liberal civilization ever since the calamities of the First World War."[9] This is powerful stuff and you can see why Berman, who watched the smoldering World Trade towers from his Brooklyn apartment, surfed the zeitgeist of the post-9/11 reactionary moment. Imbued in all of his writing is an unmistakable sense of fear, a realization that the War on Terror has nothing to do with left or right, it is simply a battle for the survival of the liberal West.

Mingling with some of the other audience members in the reception hall at the Press Club, I quickly discover that a few of them are Canadian and, despite Berman's high profile, are here to see their fellow countryman Michael Ignatieff "rub one on the nose of the pro-war crowd," as one ostentatiously bejeweled woman tells me. Her remark is surprising. Though Ignatieff, a professor at Harvard, emerged as one of America's leading liberal ethicists and champions of rights-based society, he has been as openly pro-war as Paul Berman. In fact, it was Ignatieff, writing in the *Guardian* on the one-month anniversary of 9/11, who first defined the terrorists as "apocalyptic nihilists" and compared them to European fascists, arguments that later became pillars of Berman's *Terror and Liberalism.*[10] And while most liberals were still grappling with the significance of the attacks and how they should respond to Bush's vengeful militancy, on October 1, 2001, Ignatieff was clear: "Since the politics of reason cannot defeat apocalyptic nihilism, we must fight. Force is legitimate to the degree that it is discriminate, and to the degree that it is discriminate, it is just." [11]

We are suddenly interrupted by the five minute warning. The sparkling woman excuses herself, explaining that she wants to get a good seat. Watching her move cat-like through the crowd, it strikes me that many of the people here may hold similar false conceptions that Ignatieff is anti-war and that they are here to see a debate. For most Canadians, it is a default position, so why wouldn't one of their leading lights bolster the conventional wisdom? But Ignatieff was careful to isolate himself from the critics of American foreign policy who imputed sympathetic justifications to the terrorist attacks, writing "it is an adolescent fantasy to assign the injustice of the world to a single address." [12] Yet he was not so judicious with his alliance to other, equally fantastic claims. A year after 9/11, Ignatieff cautiously pushed the Bush administration's Saddam/Osama hypothesis in the *Financial Times,* cloaking it in a reasonable sounding deliberation over "how much assistance terror receives from rejectionist states, chief among them Saddam Hussein's Iraq." [13]

When the time came for war, however, Ignatieff's measured uncertainty was replaced with hesitant acquiescence. Sounding like a man severely compromised by the pressure Americans were foisting on prominent liberal academics, he described his position as a surrender to "the least bad of the available options." And one year after the invasion, he confessed he was a "reluctant yet convinced supporter" of the war,[14] hardly the full-throated supporter that other pro-war liberals like Paul Berman had become by that time.* But Ignatieff was mining a theme that would become central to his thinking throughout the post-9/11 period. In each successive article and public speech since his original backing of Bush's military response to 9/11, he had increasingly portrayed himself as a philosophic yet embattled participant in the national dialogue; a deep-thinking intellectual, troubled by the dirty prospects of war on terror but conscious of the need for America to defend itself. As a champion of civil liberties, Ignatieff soon found that he had been forced into the difficult position of trafficking in what he termed "lesser evils": the recognition that defeating terror may not only require violence, but also coercion, deception, secrecy, and violation of rights. How would a liberal society maintain its standards when its enemies had none, he asked. It is a question that ultimately became the thesis for his own book, *The Lesser Evil: Political Ethics in the Age of Terror*, and which forms the inspiration for our gathering at the Press Club this night.[15]

Walking into the jammed lecture hall, I take the last seat in the second row reserved for press. I am not surprised to see such a large crowd. Michael Ignatieff and Paul Berman are two of America's most respected liberal intellectuals. Both have written persuasive and provocative books, each identifying a major crisis being faced by American liberal democracy. Scanning the earnest faces, waiting patiently for the intellectuals to make their appearance, I wonder which one is of greater concern to the people

* Even if Ignatieff sounded conflicted over his decision to back the war, he still defended the Bush administration's case for it, vigorously dismissing claims that Americans had been misled by a fabricated case for WMD. Further, he assailed anti-war liberals who had presented, what he considered, a feeble argument against the invasion. "It didn't follow," he wrote in the *Times*, "that America's guilty history made it wrong to go after Iraq. Good deeds are often done by people with bad histories." Quote from Michael Ignatieff, "The Year of Living Dangerously, *New York Times Magazine*, March 14, 2004.

gathered here: the internal conflict described by Ignatieff or the external threat posited by Berman?

All heads turn as the two men enter the room. Had I not seen the photographs on their respective book jackets, I would have confused them. Berman, the nervy dragon-slayer, is diminutive and bookish while Ignatieff, the judicious worrier, resembles a former college quarterback. Ignatieff opens with a soft rebuke to the anti-war movement, which he condescendingly describes as "otherwise well-meaning people protesting against the overthrow of a homicidal, genocidal, maniacal dictator." Beside him, Berman nods approvingly. I feel the audience titter. Ignatieff continues, raising the issue of Abu Ghraib. The crowd nods in unison at the scandalous mark against the invasion. But, again, Ignatieff swerves away from any flat-out condemnation of the American campaign. He describes the revelations of torture as a "catastrophic geostrategic defeat," limiting it to the context of a major PR disaster.* Further, he warns, despite the controversy Americans would need to avoid any kind of "moral perfectionism" that would hinder the war on terror. Behind me, a woman sighs. I feel warm air on the back of my neck.

Like much of the audience, I came to witness the clash of two intellectual titans who see vastly different dangers looming in America's war on terror. But it never comes. Perhaps under some tacit agreement, the men steer away from points of contention in favor of pressing the case that wartime necessarily places strains and poses challenges to liberal democracy. They never question the primary forces that drove America into Iraq, only the failures of the Bush administration in making its case to the public. They

---

* Listening to Ignatieff's lament of the torture at Abu Ghraib, I was astonished that he made the lazy case of compartmentalizing it from the war, isolating it from the character of the invasion. It seems obvious to me that Abu Ghraib was a direct product of the unilateral spirit of the war, indicative of just how little regard its planners held for the Iraqi's lives and future.

shirk any truly radical desire to get to the root of the conflict between Islam and the West, beyond the narrative we have been given by the White House and mainstream press. In this way, they come off more as apologists for the war and its ill effects than incisive political scientists who are charged with the responsibility of exploring every angle.

I keep waiting for Ignatieff and Berman to jump through the mirror and look at the Iraq war from the outside in. But they never do. As the talk wears on, the crowd becomes increasingly agitated. A collective sense of shock starts to set in that, at a time when the world is deeply divided over the disastrous results of the invasion, two of America's top liberal thinkers seem incapable, or unwilling, to question the intent of the war. Not once do they openly consider that the overthrow of Saddam may be linked to the same economic factors that Sergeant Hollis suggested to me in Iraq, even though it has been one of the major contentions of the anti-war crowd. Gone is the kind of liberal radicalism that once would have propelled them to invoke a long legacy of American presidents twisting facts and manipulating fears to produce the necessary political conditions for a military adventure. Instead, the two liberals present a unified front, limiting their focus to the threat that terrorism, and America's response to it, pose to liberal society. And in this way, themselves become the biggest threat to American liberalism.

Instead I scribble notes and steal furtive looks at the crowd, who have woken from their glassy-eyed resignation and suddenly perked up. Berman is in his element, speaking in graven tones about the fascistic nature of the bin Ladenite Islamicists who are the enemies of reason and little more than a glorified "death cult." Ignatieff plays the good cop, expressing a hopeful realism. The West can survive the War on Terror, he explains, but "we have to be very, very tough." In the end, the solution must be political, and for that reason we cannot back out until liberal democracy has been delivered to the Iraqi people. Then, he declares without the slightest hint of irony, "I can think of no more noble a sacrifice than for U.S. soldiers to die defending an Iraqi polling station."

Initially, I just process the words and jot them down on my pad. But then I notice the words a line above, scrawled in menacing letters, "death cult" and it all falls into place. Ignatieff's simple words—"I can think of no more noble a sacrifice than for U.S. soldiers to die defending an Iraqi polling station"—are a wonderful sentiment, on the surface. But that is just the point. It's only once the words are scraped with a blunter edge that their true significance can be uncovered. If al Qaeda represents a death cult for Islamicism, then highly influential and well-placed liberals like Ignatieff, many of whom originated in the New Left that emerged from the anti-Vietnam movement, have become part of a death cult for democracy. At first it sounds silly to say. Of course we are willing to sacrifice everything for our liberal system: soldiers have always died for democracy and freedom. It's what free persons are naturally drawn to fight for.

But then I look deeper. This has always been the rationale presented by politicians seeking public support for their military interventions. *We fight to protect the free world from fascism.* It was the same in 1961. But in those days, it was Berman and Ignatieff's generation that became famous for protesting a war their parents started, for exhibiting what became their defining trait, a critical skepticism of the state's motives to wage unilateral, unprovoked campaigns. But now, paralyzed by the mortal fear of annihilation, they have abandoned that questioning impulse to become highly influential supporters of a military enterprise that has cost thousands of innocent Iraqi lives. Not to mention the ever-increasing number of America soldiers wounded and injured in the guerrilla war. The same boys and girls Michael Ignatieff has just offered to the pyre as "noble sacrifices." Exactly whose child is

Ignatieff—a Canadian let's remember—offering up in the name of an Iraqi democracy? One that may inevitably provide institutional consensus for a society built on *sharia* law that contravenes the very core of his views as a social liberal.

These are the words I write, hunched over my knees, leaning on the far edge of my chair. I barely notice the talk has ended. I hear the audience asking questions, challenging the intellectuals' blanket support of the war. One man asks if they had ever considered that it was simply about oil. Berman answers that while it may be an element of the strategic value of Iraq, it was never a driving force when placed next to the very real threat of liberal extinction. I keep writing. Moments later, they are gone and the room erupts into an agitated chorus of murmurs.

I finish my notes and walk out into the blustery October night. Warm wind blows on my face and I feel energized; a target has been set before me. Berman and Ignatieff are a part of that generation of Baby Boomers who have dominated the political and social discourse in America since their voices began to change in the early 1960s. They have grown into the loosened skin and graying hair of middle age and begun to take on the same fearful, protective psychology as their parents. Naturally, there are many who still champion the virtues and values of their revolutionary youth. But for the most part, the generation who set the example for building mass movements and challenging entrenched, social, political and economic power have become part of that establishment themselves. After thirty years of accumulation, they now have something to lose. Even the liberals have become conservative.

In their prophetic book, *The Fourth Turning*, Neil Howe and Bill Strauss outline a system of 80–100-year cycles in which major, transformative crises, or turnings, occur every 20–25 years. Writing in 1997, Howe and Strauss predicted the fourth turning to come around 2005. It is one in which the Boomers will dominate the global political scene through a "Crisis" era that hits its climax in 2020. Though the authors do not attempt to foretell the nature of the calamity, they offer terrorist attacks, domestic economic collapse, and plague as likely scenarios. On how we will survive it, they are more specific. The responsibility for shepherding America through the crisis, Howe and Strauss write, will be in the hands of the Baby Boomers and their own children, Generation X, who will be responsible for reigning in the more destructive tendencies of the adults; arrogant selfishness and a propensity for despotism among them.[16]

As a member of that younger generation, the words I heard this evening have suddenly crystallized the source of this great threat to our future. It is not the ideological conservatives like Paul Wolfowitz and Bill Kristol—who have been so brazenly forthright about their global objectives—that worry me. It occurs to me that it is the quiet, respectful liberal academics like Michael Ignatieff and Paul Berman who present the most insidious danger. They come cloaked in the veil of humanitarian reformism and democratic activism, the proponents of a fair society, but underneath that flimsy fabric, they are just as much the members of an American elite as George Bush and Dick Cheney. And they have everything to lose when the United States finally begins the ugly tumble down from its imperial perch.

Yet, they will never admit this. In all the articles and debates featuring pro-war liberals, the proposition—from Sergeant Hollis and the anti-war crowd—that the invasion is a preemptive response to America's faltering hegemony is shouted down as conspiracy theory. But the reality is that since 9/11, the United States has been faced with a multi-front challenge to its status as the world's reigning superpower. As British political scientist John Gray writes, "The suicide warriors... did more than kill thousands of civilians and demolish the World Trade Centre, they destroyed the West's ruling myth."[17] But listening to Ignatieff and Berman speak tonight, and to the rest of the liberal hawks throughout the run-up to the war, one would think the only supremacy America was threatened with losing is that of a great liberal society. Economic power is not part of the equation. For it cannot be.

They are complicit and willing partners in the affair. Operating from their vaunted positions in the academies, they provide a containment policy for the elite, usurping the space in which authentic liberals would otherwise denounce the war and its illiberal objectives.* That it is not, in fact, a struggle to bring freedom and democracy to Iraqis, but, rather, to offer those alms in a sophisticated game of bait-and-switch that opens the economy to American commercial interests while simultaneously rendering the low-rent population, now dependent on them for work and survival, a compliant and malleable political society which will become America's base of operations in the Middle East.

These are my thoughts as I walk beside the broad dual carriageway on Park Avenue. The now clichéd quote from Louis D. Brandeis comes to mind: "The greatest dangers to liberty lurk in insidious encroachment by men of zeal, well-meaning but without understanding."[18] Is it possible, I wonder, that liberals like Berman and Ignatieff are simply unaware of the danger they present to the liberal system they so passionately want to protect? Passing a billboard for Jodie Foster's film *Flightplan*, I have one of those rare moments of synchronicity, when the external environment seems to collude with our inner thoughts. Beneath Foster's dazed robotic face, the tagline reads: "If someone took everything you live for,

---

* Soon after the Press Club event, Michael Ignatieff returned to Canada to run (and win) as a candidate for the Liberal Party. Musing on Ignatieff's support of the War on Terror—a position that put him at odds with the country's leftish electorate—*Globe and Mail* columnist Rick Salutin wrote, "Michael Ignatieff has often presented himself as a gadfly and a leftist (I do have trouble with leftists who need to keep reminding you how left they are). Yet here he's managed to emerge on the right of a party that is famously, cravenly centrist. A neat party trick, you could say."

how far would you go to get it back." It's a good question. Especially right now, when mainstream newspapers and financial journals are brimming with fear-inducing reports about the perilous state of the American economy. The nation's dependence on foreign oil is being exacerbated by historical highs in the price of crude, the huge trade deficit has dropped the value of the dollar below the euro, and signs of inflation threaten to pop the housing bubble which is the prime driver behind the current economic growth. Worse, there are real threats to America's global economic hegemony as China continues to expand its influence on the international market. Not to mention the ever-present threat of new attacks from al Qaeda.

So what do the leaders of a nation do when they are confronted by such vast threat to its power and prestige? Like any family, they close ranks and contain the debate. Most important, they ensure that the political situation is one that allows for maximum exploitation of the periphery. But they never admit there is a problem. They never tell the children.

IMMACULATE CONCEPTION

"Well, you're not an academic," said my publisher sympathetically, dropping his pen onto a clean white notepad. "You're one of the guys who started Guerrilla News Network. You direct videos for Eminem and 50 Cent. You go into war zones. That's how we are going to market the book and people aren't going to want to read some thickly packaged political theory."

It's been six months since the Berman/Ignatieff talk and I am here to pitch a book on the end of American liberalism to Gary Baddeley, head of the indie media label, Disinformation. Bolstered by months of researching the world's most influential political writers and high on unreasonably caffeinated coffee, my words have taken on the gravitas of an overwrought college professor aching to get back from a self-imposed sabbatical.

"The foundation of American political society is being irrevocably transformed," I begin. "Students of the game have long regarded the ebb and flow of conservative and liberal tides, and their associated administrations and policies, as the gravitational pull of historical cycles that ushered in new, regenerative phases; a dialectical engine capable of sustaining the kind of infinite ideological reinvention that made America into the unchallenged leader of the world's free societies. But today, that pendulum which once swung so dynamically between the political poles, has been reduced to a drastically narrower reach than in former times."

I can tell that Baddeley is taken by surprise.

"The liberal quotient of that scale has been reduced to a mere echo of what it once was," I declare, leaning my chair back from the table.

"You're probably going to have trouble convincing people that political discourse has been lessened. We're living under one of the most contentious and politically divisive administrations in modern history," Gary responds absently, looking past me at the bright, sunlit street bustling with the Friday afternoon rush of people and traffic.

"But that's just the point, I'm not arguing that it has lessened," I counter. "It's just been focused on debates that have no direct relationship to the true locus of power in the society. Stem cell research, *Roe v. Wade*, gay marriage, Supreme Court nominations, those are all just hot-button issues that the media and politicians push because they're easy and entertaining and they keep the public in perpetual state of ideological division."

"Right, between conservatives and liberals. So what's changed?"

"Everything. That's the whole point. Since the end of World

War II, the national debate embraced a wide spectrum of issues, but hinged on the role of the government in guaranteeing that each individual be given the chance to realize their maximum potential. This is what defined the modern liberal quality in American politics and created an authentic balance to the traditional view of limited government. Today that vision has been abandoned. America is broke and locked in a frantic struggle to sustain its global power. There is no true spectrum of opinion in Washington as far as economic and foreign policy initiatives are concerned. Those issues, which were once the substance of America's national discussion, have been replaced by cynical mud fights over public morality. What I am saying is that the traditional liberal foundation of American politics is being sucked out of the equation."

"Really."

"Yes. But you're not going to hear it from the top political commentators on either side of the fence. Nor from the leaders of American politics, because they're the most dependent on the old system. But what's actually happening is that American political identities are undergoing an evolutionary realignment. The core characteristics that define what we have generally known as "liberal" and "conservative" have lost all meaning in the trauma of our post 9/11 paradigm. So that the terms are merely used as semantic weaponry, to either categorize political allies or stigmatize their enemies. Other than that, they are completely useless."

"And exactly what is it that is causing this realignment? Do you have a theory for that?" Baddeley asks, sleepily.

"Uh-huh. It's a natural response by American leaders to the realization they are losing their place as the world's dominant economic and cultural superpower. Because once a nation is faced with the potential of its own decline, then its citizens make markedly different choices about the kind of political society they will tolerate. If you look at it through that prism, then you realize why conservatives are driving the zeitgeist. They've always been defending lost turf. Their entire worldview is shaped by the idea that traditional codes and power structures are under attack. So right now they're in their element and have even adapted to the challenges of the new era by shelving their isolationist foreign policy and appropriating the traditional liberal internationalism and neoliberal policies in a quest to maintain America's economic power in the world. In that sense, they can't even be considered conservative any more."

Baddeley nods, gently.

"But it's the liberals we need to worry about," I continue. "What we're looking at here is a phenomenon in which liberalism—the old humanistic, idealistic side of liberalism—has been traumatized; 9/11 made it irrelevant in the new millennial America. Liberalism is like a wounded animal, limping through the political forest, pretending to recover its strength. While, in fact, it's actually plunged headlong into a desperate search for its life force: a once universal and unthinking appeal. But that is gone. We can see it now, scrambling like a prey animal, unsure of how to resurrect its proprietary ideal of a socially tolerant, rights-based, welfare society. While that vision reigned during the Cold War, when America was literally competing against the communists to present the most favorable system for advancing individual and national welfare, it has no function now. So, in order to survive, liberals have been forced to change their values, to shift their ideological markers, not to the right, but away from the promise of modern liberalism."

"Okay," Baddeley says, rubbing his forehead, "so what is the book about?"

1

Birds of a Feather

"England and America are two countries
separated by a common language."
— George Bernard Shaw

Invariably, when one meets a member of the '60s era political rebels, they will explain that the etymological foundation of the word 'radical' means "going the root." The implication is that their generation's brand of radical social liberalism sought to overthrow the war-mongering bureaucracies by exposing the lies and corruption that lay at their core. It worked. The watershed moment for the anti-Vietnam movement was the leaking of the top-secret Pentagon Papers by State Department official Daniel Ellsberg which proved Lyndon Johnson had conspired to expand the war even while telling the U.S. public he was trying to end it. But what has happened to this powerhouse generation now that Baghdad is turning into a mini-Saigon (and fast becoming an Islamist Ho Chi Minh City) and the Bush administration has begun agitating for a confrontation with Iran? You'd think the neocons' well-branded War on Terror smells enough like domino theory to get a few million of them into the streets. But no. Instead, they have mostly receded into middle age, preferring to strike an absentee ballot than vote with their feet against what looks increasingly like a bad case of historical déjà-vu.

I wonder what force of nature transforms "radical" liberalism into something that looks more like State Department liberalism. Is it just a matter of growing older? Does the instinct and energy for political activism simply wither once we pass thirty? Or are there other factors involved? Looking back at the origins of the modern liberal philosophy, which had its birth in eighteenth century Britain in the writings of Jeremy Bentham and John Stuart Mill, it strikes me how much American liberals differ from their British counterparts, how far American liberalism has moved from its intellectual origins. This mutation is perfectly embodied in the path of Christopher Hitchens, who arrived in America with the immaculate pedigree of a brilliant leftist agitator and, twenty years later, morphed into the Iraq War's most eloquent protagonist. Who better to describe the inner process of abandoning those values that we once called "liberal"?

I would soon get to find out. A chance invitation to one of the world's most prestigious literary gatherings gives me the opportunity to take a page out of the radicals' book. I'll go back to the place where modern liberalism was born, hang out with a group of Britain's better-known liberal thinkers and find out just how everything has gone so horribly wrong.

THE KING AND HIS CASTLE

Richard George William Pitt Booth is sitting on a rickety wooden throne pointing a gnarled finger in my direction. His makeshift crown dips cartoonishly over his right eyebrow.

"*Corruptio optimi pessima*," he growls at me through the side of his mouth. "Don't you know what that means?"[1]

"*Corruptio*... ummm, *optimi*?" I stall, waiting for the imminent translation.

"The corruption of the best is the worst. It's a very well known

Latin tag." Satisfied, his majesty smiles benignly at me from the chair, positioned on a platform at the back of large room in his sixteenth century castle. Behind him, on an easel, is a portrait taken of Booth in this very position. I can't help thinking it's all getting a bit Monty Pythonesque.

Booth is the self-anointed King of Hay-on-Wye, a small shire-like village that lies on the eastern edge of Wales, just across the English border. As one of the world's best known purveyors of second hand books, Booth has made Hay his lifelong project and the foundation for a post-agrarian economic model he calls the Book Town concept. It originated in the early 1960s when Booth saw Hay being left behind by the new trends in globalization. In response, he sought to create a secondary industry that could attract tourists and help revitalize the local economy. Channeling his great love for used books into a business strategy, he initiated a plan to make Hay a primary destination for the global community of itinerant bibliophiles. The logic, as he explains it, "is quite simple: Ten thousand books at a pound each brings ten thousand tourists; which is how many hundreds of thousands in increased spending? The secondhand book economy transitions into a tourist economy."

Since he founded his first bookshop in 1961,* Hay has become the world's premiere Book Town with 39 stores, attracting a half million book-seeking tourists annually. With a population of just over 1,300, it's a good bet that Booth's plan more than paid off for the local merchants. Which is precisely why he is so annoyed.

"You know history is written by the winners. Nowhere in the Hay catalogue is it written that I was the founder of Hay."

* On April 1, 1977, Booth declared himself ruler of the Independent Kingdom of Hay. As he explained, "Marianne Faithful had just left Mick Jagger and about forty journalists were following her. One of them found me and asked, 'what's news in Hay?' I said, 'We're going independent of the British Isles.' Suddenly everyone took it seriously. So I held a press conference on April Fools' Day. The next week, somebody threw a brick through our window and said, 'What are we going to do about defense?' "

Booth has a tendency to shift, mid-sentence, between the two great passions of his life: his legacy as the savior of Hay and those who have come to rob him of it. In that struggle, he sees a vast conspiracy unfolding right outside the castle walls. This weekend alone, tens of thousands of people will walk past his door on their way to the site of the Hay Festival, which, in the two decades since its founding, has become the UK's premiere literary event. Each May, a roster of the English-speaking world's most prolific and celebrated authors descend from their lofty cerebrum to the lush Welsh countryside and engage the public in what can only be described as one of the few remaining intellectual events left on Earth. It is, to quote Bill Clinton, who spoke here in 2002, a veritable "Woodstock of the mind."

If nothing else, Hay is a place of prescient visionaries and eccentrics. Which is precisely why I am here. I'm on the hunt. There is perhaps no other time where I can be exposed to so many clever minds, many of whom are firmly rooted in the British literary and journalistic establishment, all in one place; like exotic birds that flock to one aquamarine pool of mirrored intellectualism. I feel like a game tracker on safari. Hunting for liberals; lovely, pleasant, smart British ones who will indoctrinate me in their mysterious ways. And I have chosen as my guide Peter Florence, the founder of the Hay Festival.

In setting himself the mission of establishing the new mecca for literature, Florence instinctually attached it to the great liberal project, which, from its inception, was a grand fusion of art and politics.[*] It's English roots date back to the early nineteenth century, when Romantic poets like Byron and Shelley rebelled

---

[*] "The point of Hay," Florence tells me, "is to redeem the idea of exchange, and infuse it with fun. We were all smarter when we sat up late at night at college arguing the world to rights without political or financial responsibility. If you can get those smart people, all grown-up, back round your kitchen table, then you have a chance of refreshing that idealism and energy. Imagine a young liberal heart firing a wise liberal mind again..."

against the political culture of conservatism that ultimately served to protect the elite from the common man. They sought a political expression that could channel the humanism of their day into the realm of governance. Over a century later, this brand of liberalism inspired the New Deal and Great Society platforms of American Democrats. As John F. Kennedy, reminded his liberal knights of Camelot, "When power corrupts, poetry cleanses, for art establishes the basic human truths which must serve as the touchstones of our judgment."[2]

At first, the Hay Festival was a small affair. Founded by Florence in 1988, the inaugural event attracted just over 1,000 people to hear 35 readings and performances by authors, poets and some local artists. When Florence invited Arthur Miller to be the toast of the festival's second year, the American playwright famously responded, "Hay-on-Wye? Is that some kind of a sandwich?"

Seventeen years later, Hay draws a paying audience of 120,000 and is considered one of the most important tour stops for both established and breakthrough authors. This year invitees include *New York Times* columnist Thomas Friedman, Gen X cult novelist David Eggers, Booker award-winner Kazuo Ishiguro, business guru Malcolm Gladwell, American icon Joan Didion, radical Russian journalist Anna Politkovska and Bob Geldof just as he is about to announce the Live 8 concerts… and that's just the opening weekend.

You can see why Richard Booth is a little discomposed. When his conversation shifts from second hand books to the Hay Festival, he goes from postindustrial innovator to Don Quixote in one fell swoop. And there is no end to the contempt he feels for the sole threat to his legacy as the great visionary who put Hay on the world map.

For Booth, who sells or gives away over one million used books a year, the festival represents a direct challenge to his project. Not only does it divert the spotlight from his efforts, but it also reasserts the dominance of new books, which he sees as a threat to the Book Town model of saving the developing world.

"The second hand book is an international economy, suitable for areas of poverty. I would say to Africa, I can bring ten thousand books to a town in Zimbabwe and they can set up a Book Town to get them out of poverty."

If Booth comes off as an idealistic crusader, that is his intention. He's not only the self-appointed King of Hay, he's also the defender of the worn volumes stacked from floor to ceiling in this old Welsh castle. Struggling to get up from his throne, he nearly whispers, "I want the second hand book to be seen as a great asset. Otherwise it will be destroyed."

One of the great traditions of the Hay Festival is that visiting artists are boarded in local houses, so they can get the full flavor of the Welsh experience. My luck of the draw brought me to Brynmelyn, Richard Booth's country estate, where I met the King early this morning and negotiated a guided tour of his castle.

As we walk out of rickety castle door, one of his booksellers steps up and grasps his arm, "Pace yourself your Majesty."

Strolling through the sloping, cobbled streets of the village we pass a dozen bookstores in less than 100 yards. As we pass by each shop, Booth describes its niche, "...that one specializes in English literature, modern first editions. This one's about travel and languages. If you want mystery and suspense, you can try there." Reaching the top of the road, Booth points down at the people streaming through the festival gates.

"They use as much electricity as the entire village of Hay."

I pat his arm and nod sympathetically. Promising we'll catch up again back at the house, I begin to walk down toward the teeming crowds, all moving like salmon toward the mouth of some great ocean.

THE GREEN ROOM

The Hay festival grounds are buzzing with excitement. Elevated above the verdant earth on wooden platforms, green-carpeted floors connect a network of pristine white tents and open-air restaurants. Sequestered in a remote corner, off the more traf-ficked gangways, is a quiet room with French doors that open to its own private garden. It is here, far from the madding crowd, in the exclusive Green Room, that small clusters of VIPs gather between events to drink tea, eat biscuits and swallow fresh strawberries.

During the rush and tumble of the festival, A-list authors and their well-groomed agents mix with politicians, actors and the children of British aristocracy. There is a Guinness and a Rothschild. Alexander Waugh, the grandson of Evelyn and son of Auberon, sits near Barney Broomfield, son of famed British docu-mentary filmmaker Nick, with his girlfriend Mary Nighy, who just stepped off the set of Sofia Coppola's latest film, *Marie Antoinette*. In the center of the room, a group of men are gathered around the beautiful violinist/actress/journalist Clemency Burton-Hill, whose concert performance the night before brought many in the audience to tears. There is one person conspicuously absent, all the more so because he has recently been the subject of yet another controversy. An irate Scottish politician has recently called him a "drink-sodden ex-Trostskyite popinjay," which makes him all the more central to the gossip of the day.

If Hay is to books what Glastonbury is to music, then Chris-topher Hitchens is the festival's resident Liam Gallagher. Like the lead singer of Oasis who lit up crowds with his zeitgeist lyrics, epic rudeness and raised middle fingers, Hitchens is the primary draw of Hay's opening weekend, pulling crowds of one and two thousand strong to see him chain-smoke his way through debates about religion, war or literature with some other chart-topping intellectual of the day. And if they're really lucky, they'll get to see him tell a member of the audience to fuck off.

However, with his sustained support for the ill-conceived and poorly executed military campaign in Iraq, his star has begun to sink with the fickle British literati. "Have you seen Hitchens recently?" one man asks rhetorically, "He's been a acting a little wired lately. He's just not himself."

Another opines, "Iraq, you know. It's taken its toll."

"Well, he's very good at deconstructing Michael Moore, but terrible at seeing the holes in his own argument. It's like, come on man, look in the mirror."

These petty attacks are nothing compared to the public denouncements he's received from his former comrades* on the left like Tariq Ali, who portrayed Hitchens's conversion to pro-Bush warmongering as a metaphorical casualty of the 9/11 attacks.

"He was never seen again," wrote Ali. "The vile replica currently on offer is a double." [3]

The common line is that Hitchens has succumbed to the rigors of drink and lost his moral compass in a sea of shifting allegiances, seduced by the attention of Paul Wolfowitz and his neocon fraternity. Still another rationale is that we are merely, at long last, seeing the true nature of his authoritarian impulses, historically believed to be a closeted evil of the far left ideologues. And while his critics have created new journalistic subgenre psychologizing Hitchens's motives, for me he serves as a vital case study in understanding the more far-reaching realignment of former institutional left and liberal thinkers with the State-authored war machine.

Hence the swirl of heads which turn to the door as Hitchens

---

* Other Hitchens apostates include Dennis Perrin, who published an "obituary" of his former mentor and George Scialabba, who claimed, in his essay titled "Farewell, Hitch," that Hitchens had made an "egregious ass of himself." Quote from George Scialabba, "Farewell, Hitch," originally published in *n+1*, Spring 2005.

finally makes his entrance. He walks in without any affectation and makes his way to a corner table. Wearing a blue collared shirt, tan brown suede jacket and blue jeans, his wolfish beard, whisked with grey, brown and white hair sits like a pedestal under tired sunken eyes. As he scans the room for one of the pretty girls who ferry drinks in from the makeshift bar, he catches my eye and I nod respectfully. Seeing that he is now being swarmed by well-wishers and old friends, I save myself for another encounter when he is less harried.

I turn to find Florence, the omnipresent director, standing behind me. "You want to meet someone absolutely marvelous? She'd be perfect for what you are writing about."

THE CRUMPET

Joan Bakewell looks past me, scanning the faces of the gathered literary elite. Now older than seventy, the British radio and television celebrity has maintained that rare quality of beauty which expresses itself in both physical and intellectual elegance. It must the reward for living such a controversial public life, and serving as a reluctant sex symbol during the last stand of the BBC's patriarchal establishment.[*]

As one of the most known faces at Hay, she's not easy to isolate for an interview, but I'm close. So I drink tea and stand awkwardly beside her. She glances at me and asks, distractedly, "What are you writing about?"[4]

"Liberalism," I say. "Liberals in America."

---

[*] As a testament to the power now held by women in British broadcasting, veteran BBC newsreader Michael Buerk told the *Independent* that "almost all the big jobs in broadcasting [are] held by women," and that men have been reduced to "sperm donors." In the August 2005 interview, he said that typically male characteristics have been sidelined. "The traits that have traditionally been associated with men—reticence, stoicism, single-mindedness—have been marginalised," he said. Buerk quoted in "Buerk Attacks Women Broadcasters," August 16. 2005.

"Well, I thought they all lived in Manhattan."

Cambridge-educated and a champion of '60s era sexual liberation, Bakewell has endured the unique brand of British chauvinism that alternately labeled her the "thinking man's crumpet," and the "arts tart." But what she's most known for, outside her work as a broadcaster and author, is the seven-year extramarital affair she had with celebrated British playwright Harold Pinter. Dramatized in his moving, emotionally charged 1978 play, *Betrayal*, the affair was made all the more fascinating and publicly scrutinized by Pinter's friendship[*] with Michael Bakewell, Joan's husband at the time.

More recently, she caused a minor stir in England by reading James Kirkup's sexually explicit poem "The Love That Dares to Speak its Name" on her BBC show, *Taboo*. In broadcasting the poem, which is written from the perspective of a gay Roman centurion who has sex with Jesus's corpse after the crucifixion, Bakewell directly challenged Britain's archaic blasphemy laws. One can only imagine the scene at Buckingham Palace as she recited the words, "The shaft, still throbbed, anointed with death's final ejaculation." [5]

In defense of the act, Bakewell explained that she was making a point. "You need to show people how sensibilities are offended. It was the very fact that it was to do with Jesus and the disciples that shocked religious people."

Provoking society in the name of individual expression is obviously something that Bakewell finds comfort in. But the idea of freedom means different things to different people. Leaning across her folded legs, she explains, "I use 'liberalism' in the Enlightenment sense. It's the legacy of enlightened ideas about free expression and individual liberty."

---

[*] Pinter would later acknowledge that for him, the ultimate moment of betrayal was in discovering that Joan had told her husband of the affair two years before it ended.

Referring to the evolutionary set of social and economic values that emerged from the Enlightenment period of the seventeenth and eighteenth centuries, Bakewell triggers memories of anesthetizing poli-sci classes at university. Names like Spinoza, Locke, and Rousseau, forgotten within days of my final exams, suddenly reemerge like lotus flowers on the dark surface of my mind. These were the philosophers who sculpted the intellectual foundation of modern Western society. They straddled the historical divide between darkness and light, presiding over the pinnacle years of what became known as the Age of Reason: an epoch that saw the great unwashed mob of European civilianry collectively lurch past what Immanuel Kant described as a state of "self-imposed incompetence," coming to understand themselves as individuals with the potential for rational thought and individual religious and economic freedom. No longer could the monarchy and their adjunct class of feudal lords suppress the majority through the claim of some divine right, allocated by the Unseen. Now, it was determined, all men were equal and free, with natural human rights of life, liberty and property to boot.

But, we were taught, these gains had to be fought for and won. A series of revolutions in Europe soaked the Earth with the blood of rebellious hearts so that future generations could live in their Utopia. This radical Enlightenment concept of individualism is the essence of what later became known as liberal philosophy. It is the guiding principle that drove future American revolutionaries Jefferson, Franklin and Thomas Paine like spermatozoa toward the ideological womb of an independent American state. To free themselves from the shackles of imperial England and its system of, as my eighth grade teacher iterated with mind-numbing repetition, "taxation without representation."

So, the rebel leaders gathered men and weapons and beat off the British occupiers, creating what is still, for many in the world, a lasting symbol of political freedom and liberal society; the United States of America.*

Joan Bakewell sips her tea and looks past me again, into the crowd.

"America has the most fabulous record of liberal thinking. Its Constitution and the lawyers who forged the American way of life were exemplary and honorable men—I'm sorry they were all *men* but that's how it was in those days."

Bakewell continues, "But their thinking was very clear. Ideas like tolerance and brotherhood, you know, Philadelphia, the brotherhood of man."

Bakewell invokes the great aspiration of the classical liberal philosophy, that all of humanity can exist as one family, where none is more equal than another, where each is the master of their own destiny. The values enshrined in the Declaration could only guide future governments, not be protected by them. It was understood that the American people would be the ultimate guardians of their own freedom, and the destiny of the nation they had ripped from England's grasp. This emphasis on popular sovereignty and the repudiation of government as an all-powerful force is the legacy of classical liberal thought. Made sacrosanct by Thomas Jefferson in the Declaration of Independence, it authorizes the people to "alter or abolish" any government that becomes despotic. In this sense, the American revolutionaries had successfully migrated the values and ideals born of the Enlightenment era and integrated them into their vision of a free nation.

Meanwhile, the new economic order had inspired a radical strain of thinking that sought to liberate the realm of trade from the restrictive harness of government power. In the same year that

---

* Acknowledging the applied legacy of Enlightenment values in America's founding, historian Henry Steele Commager dubbed the self-governing republic "the Empire of Reason."

Thomas Jefferson completed the Declaration of Independence, Adam Smith published his own radical manifesto, *The Wealth of Nations*, which heralded the birth of free market economics and laissez-faire* capitalism. What made Smith's ideas so revolutionary at the time was their direct attack on what he called the mercantile system which, over the sixteenth and seventeenth centuries, had become the dominant trade policy of the major imperial powers. It was based on the idea that nations had to compete for the world's resources, which naturally pitted empires against each other. It also placed trade restrictions on goods from competitive powers, forcing colonists, like the Americans, to buy from England at rates higher than those of a free and open market with other national producers.

So, just as the liberal social theorists had championed a cause of individualism and freedom from authoritarianism, Smith's economic philosophy argued that by freeing the market from government control, it would be guided by an 'invisible hand' that was essentially self-regulating, creating a natural harmony between supply and demand. More, it would empower individual merchants to pursue profits on their own terms, as free agents. In his view, economic, just as much as social life, was regulated by the market and not the state; hence, the "free" market. [6]

"Laissez-faire was the great development of the Victorian era, which was then exported to America and became the great liberal agenda," Joan Bakewell explains, placing her teacup on the table. "Free trade for all and free trade to negotiate your way into the world. That's the essence of liberalism."

It's no wonder, then, that for many people, capitalism and free society are linked. They are both products of that paradigm shift which gave birth to the liberal project. Ironically, the evolution of

---

* Laissez-faire is a French term that literally means "leave things alone, let them pass."

liberal thought ultimately brought modern liberals to turn their backs on the laissez-faire philosophy. As the process of industrialization further entrenched the populations of Europe and America into defined economic classes, a new brand of liberalism emerged, challenging the "tyranny of laissez-faire" and pushing for government intervention to protect those who had become the victims of unrestrained capitalism.

Pointing across the room at a spectacled man holding a flower, Bakewell concludes, "But that's the liberal intelligentsia agenda epitomized by the *Guardian* and such newspapers in this country."

THE GUARDIAN

Alan Rusbridger stands in the Green Room clinging to the stem of a white rose, looking a bit lost. As chief editor of the *Guardian*, the primary corporate sponsor of the festival, he is a prominent fixture during the opening weekend, chairing debates and conducting interviews on Hay's main stage. Hence the pristine flower, which is a parting gift for festival 'performers.' Unassuming and boyishly cerebral in his manner, Rusbridger projects the remarkable apparition of a grown up Harry Potter.[7]

Sitting with Rusbridger in a quiet corner out of earshot from the Green Room, he recounts his trajectory toward becoming one of the most powerful progressive liberals in Britain.

"I went to the local paper in Cambridge and did all those things that you do as a reporter. Suddenly you become aware of a completely different town—of poverty and deprivation within this rather rich East England town. And I think if you're any good as a reporter, you'll constantly be forced into situations like that, which do then wash back into your politics. That's what happened to me."

It's also what happened to nineteenth century British liberals who could not deny the miserable poverty in the back alleys of their industrial theme park of a nation. As a response, the new liberal agenda imposed human dignity as a requisite for individual freedom. It called for minimum wages and safety standards for workers, laws against child labor, improved education for the poor, health care, welfare, and old age pensions. Positioning itself as a beacon for this new, modern liberalism, the *Guardian* used its platform to launch investigations into social problems that would bolster the liberal cause. Eventually, it paid off. From the end of World War II to the beginning of the 1980s, liberalism's crusade for broader distribution of wealth and extension of the welfare state became the conventional wisdom of Britain's political class, dominating the domestic agenda of every government that came to power.

When Alan Rusbridger joined the *Guardian* as a reporter in 1979, Margaret Thatcher had just come to power and the paper was the only non-conservative daily in Britain. Today, it beats out the *Independent* for socially progressive readers, but is third in circulation behind the two most powerful conservative papers, the *Daily Telegraph* and Rupert Murdoch's *Times*, which, respectively, triple and double the *Guardian*'s daily print run.

I ask Rusbridger how he would describe the editorial character of his paper. Twirling the rose in between his fingers, he replies thoughtfully.

"A liberal, progressive, intelligent paper. Operating in that kind of zone of debate. I mean, if we had a long time, I would talk about how you identify that. Is it through your news reporting? Is it through your comment? And I increasingly think that you have to find a message in news reporting which people trust—i.e. where the politics doesn't drive the presentation of facts. But I think the reason the American press is in such trouble is that it is hung up on this notion of objectivity, which I don't think exists. I'm very struck, in the pages of the *New York Times*, which was otherwise a great newspaper but—the range of debate on its Comment page, is tiny. I mean try to find Muslim or Arab columnists there on a regular basis. [They're] not there."

The *Guardian*'s incremental penetration of the U.S. media market is testament to that lack. With the rise of the internet* as a source of news, Rusbridger's paper has developed an international audience that seeks more robust debate of the issues confronting global society. Beyond its coverage of daily news events, the *Guardian* features a roster of columnists who represent a wide spectrum of political thought, from George Monbiot, the pacifist-humanist critic of globalization, to David Aaronovitch, the pugilistic former Communist and now pro-war agitant.

Maintaining an openly critical stance on the Afghanistan and Iraq wars, the *Guardian* became the dominant paper for anti-war Brits as well as Americans who sought a balance to the overtly pro-war U.S. newspapers. When I ask Rusbridger how he would describe the state of American liberalism, he shrugs and permits himself a short laugh.

"A bit lost."

I push him to elaborate.

"I mean, I have a vision of American liberalism that is enshrined in the Democratic Party from about 1925 to the 1970s, and since then it seems to have…"

He stops and mulls it over for a moment and then offers, reluctantly, "Well, I suppose there were some aspects of Clinton that you could describe as liberal, but it seems a bit dead now."

Of course, the period to which Rusbridger refers is that of

* On the web, the *Guardian* consistently dominates all other UK papers, as well as the top U.S. dailies. For the past six years, it has won the British Newspaper Awards for Best Daily Newspaper on the net. In 2005, the *Guardian Unlimited* website beat the *New York Times*, the *Washington Post*, the *Wall Street Journal*, winning the Best Newspaper category in the 2005 Webby Awards.

the great American experiment in social democracy, embodied in economic interventionist strategies that spanned Franklin Roosevelt's "New Deal" to Lyndon Johnson's "Great Society." While their British counterparts had laid the foundations of their welfare state before the First World War, American economists and politicians did not react to the excesses and deprivations of the capitalist system until the Great Depression of the 1930s, when most of the industrial world was crippled by huge unemployment and the loss of economic prosperity. Ironically, it was the work of another British economist, John Maynard Keynes, that challenged Adam Smith's theory of an invisibly guided, self-regulating market and inspired the American shift into a welfare state. For Keynes, Smith's theory was a dangerous ideal that ignored the most basic values of the capitalist system which, he wrote, "is the astounding belief that the most wickedest of men will do the most wickedest of things for the greatest good of everyone." [8]

Keynes's theory was that government should strategically inject money or withdraw money from the economy to manipulate the demand for national products and services. By providing financing for new schools, hospitals, or roads, demand for workers and supplies would increase and the economy would be reinvigorated with the enhanced buying power of workers and corporations. Roosevelt incorporated Keynes's theory into his post-Depression New Deal and then took the next step of implementing a state-run welfare system. New Deal-inspired legislation* like the Social Security Act of 1935, for example, empowered government with the responsibility of providing financial assistance and relief to the unemployed, elderly and handicapped.

Over the next thirty years, this interventionist approach to

---

* Other New Deal legislation included Fair Labor Standards Act, establishing the 40-hour work week and minimum wage, and the National Labor Relations Act, granting the workers rights to form unions.

monetary policy paralleled the growth of a burgeoning civil rights movement, ultimately consolidating the American liberal philosophies of social justice and economic welfare. By the time John F. Kennedy was assassinated in 1963, the Democratic Party had re-engineered the liberal interpretation of government, making it more than just a neutral organ, existing solely to mediate between competing interests. For modern American liberals, government was the ultimate guardian and benefactor of the citizenry.

But for British liberals like Alan Rusbridger, this was the limit of America's flirtation with the modern concept of 'positive' liberty. By the end of the 1970s, the crime rate had risen dramatically and the inner cities of America were symbols of racial unrest and class division. As Ronald Reagan put it, the liberals "fought a war on poverty, and poverty won."

So the pendulum swung again, shifting the American political balance to the right. This would have a pivotal effect on the future of modern liberal thinking. Emboldened by the radical 'neoliberal' writings of Milton Friedman,* Ronald Reagan became the figurehead of the New Right movement: a modern hybrid of social conservatism and classical economic liberalism. Reviving authoritarian qualities like patriotism and order, Reagan simultaneously rejected the Keynesian system and immediately sought to reduce the role of government, shackle organized labor and introduce tax cuts for the wealthy. Soon America was booming again and the legacy of the Great Society drifted down the churning sinkhole of the nation's short-span historical memory.

The success of "Reaganomics" eventually pushed modern American liberals to abandon the pursuit of authentic social

---

* Friedman, who also advocated the legalization of drugs and marijuana, rejected the Keynesian approach to fiscal policy in favor of laissez-faire capitalism. "A major source of objection to a free economy is precisely that," he wrote in *Capitalism and Freedom*, "it gives people what they want instead of what a particular group thinks they ought to want. Underlying most arguments against the free market is a lack of belief in freedom itself."

welfare. 'Liberal' became a bad word—the L-word—one that George Bush Sr. used to stigmatize and ultimately defeat his 1988 Democratic presidential rival, the prototypical "Harvard liberal," Michael Dukakis. One cannot underestimate the impact this had on the political culture of American liberalism. The three successive Republican administrations of Reagan and then Bush Sr. shaped the platform for Bill Clinton, a liberal in every sense except in his legislation. In fact, Clinton, whose major achievements—welfare reform, trimming the federal payroll and a balanced budget—would be the cornerstone of any Republican administration, did little to slow the attack on the legacy of his professed Democratic heroes, FDR and LBJ.

"After the fall of the Berlin Wall, the Left just rolled over. We can't think of an economic model that is better than capitalism, so we argue about the limits of regulation within it, which is a weak position to be in." Alan Rusbridger pulls one of the petals off his white rose. "It's a rather insipid position to be in."

It's the first time someone has come close to admitting that free market capitalism has finally won over the liberal project. I look up at him to see the expression on his face. He still wears the smile of an optimist, but his fixed eyes betray the durable intensity of a realist. Nodding to someone across the floor, Rusbridger excuses himself and heads back into the crowded room.

THE ECONOMIST

The Green Room is suddenly brimming with the chattering classes. It looks like everyone who's anyone has come in for a last minute drink before the main event of the opening weekend, the *Economist* Debate. A testament to the Hay festival's commitment to the full spectrum of liberal thought, two major sponsored debates are programmed on the opening weekend; one from the *Guardian*, and another from its ideological antipode, the *Economist.*

Established in 1843, the *Economist* has no rival in world media as the most authentic servant of classical nineteenth-century liberal ideas. On its website, the editors profess an undying dedication to the principles of its founder, a Scottish hat maker named James Wilson, who believed in "free trade, internationalism and minimum interference by government, especially in the affairs of the market." [9]

This internationalist, free market idealism remains at the core of the *Economist*'s editorial mission. Written with its unique brand of pithy and, at times, cheeky analysis, each weekly issue covers the planet's financial and political issues through an unapologetically pro-business lens.[*]

"At the *Economist*, we always claim that we're nineteenth century liberals, which basically means that we don't like the State and that we want to give people on the whole as much freedom as possible," explains the *Economist*'s John Micklethwait, "In America, 'liberal' has become synonymous with, at least to a lot of people, the idea of big government. And from that perspective, we earnestly write we would like to reclaim the word liberal, or what was originally liberal thought." [10]

Gracious and articulate, Micklethwait has a disarming quality that masks the true nature of his power. As U.S. editor for the *Economist*, he influences and shapes the way his elite readers perceive America's economic and political agenda. He is rumored to be one of the few journalists permitted access to the super-secret Bilderberg meetings, held annually for the world's most powerful corporate and governmental leaders. The only catch: he is not

---

[*] Now over a century and a half old, the *Economist* has a circulation of 1 million. With 80 percent of its readers residing beyond Britain's border, no one can say they aren't walking their talk. With a tip of the hat to its demographic, the *Economist* defines its audience as those with "higher than average incomes, better than average minds but with less than average time…" Quote and other information from "About our History" www.economist.com.

allowed to report on the proceedings. Micklethwait is at Hay for what is one of the most highly anticipated events of the opening weekend, the *Economist* Debate, which pairs him with Christopher Hitchens to argue that history will be kinder to the pro-war duo of Bush and Blair than their adversaries, French president Jacques Chirac and German chancellor Gerhard Schröder. Debating for the opposition will be former Labour politician Roy Hattersley and foreign policy analyst Mark Leonard, both of whom write for Alan Rusbridger's *Guardian*.

But even if the *Guardian* is the *Economist*'s liberal alter-ego, Micklethwait and Rusbridger agree on one thing.

"Liberals in America have all sorts of problems at the moment," Micklethwait smiles apologetically, "because firstly, what amounted to a liberal ideology back in the 1960s has slightly fallen to bits."

Micklethwait is the author—with his *Economist* colleague Adrian Wooldridge—of *The Right Nation* which argues that the Republican Party is now set to become America's "natural party of government," a consensual perception controlled by the Democrats since the end of the Depression. Perhaps more disappointing to hopeful American liberals, Micklethwait believes even a Kerry victory would have done little to change the country's conservative predisposition. Faced with a nascent Republican dynasty, the Democrats have had to radically right-click their political message.

"You're dealing, in the Democratic Party, with a party which is further to the right than the British Conservative Party. And that is amazing."

But, Micklethwait explains, this is not surprising for anyone who has an informed perspective of world politics. On issues that spark the most fervent debate across the globe, the United States consistently falls on the conservative side of the spectrum.

"In America, there is obviously a greater carrot and a greater stick than there is in most other developed countries. There is a greater carrot because it is possible to make gigantically huge sums of money. Far more, on the whole, than you can make in Europe. But secondly, there is a greater stick because if life doesn't work out for you in America, there is far less of a welfare state to support you than there is [in] Europe, which spends roughly ten points more of its GDP on the State, and a lot of that is provision of services to people."

Micklethwait pauses for a moment, as if to confirm that I understand these are not solely hard facts to him. That they also have a very real human downside.

"Looking at it from the outside, there's no doubt that you see some poverty in America that's just shocking to European eyes. And it could be a very, very harsh life in America if things don't work out for you."

For the most part, Americans are willing to live with the risks of this extremely individualistic system. Implicit within it is the potential of realizing great personal wealth. But the melting pot has its own set of rules: if you want to get along, you go along. No one likes a loser. Stand up on your own two feet. These are the mantras of a 'frontier ideology' that place a premium on ingenuity and individualism and became the ideological meta-narrative for the Reagan administration, just as it had been for the original liberal revolutionaries who founded America two hundred years before him.

I ask Micklethwait if he isn't concerned that the true casualty of this rightward shift in American opinion will be its legacy of modern liberalism and social justice, of helping those who can't support themselves. Aren't those integral values that make up a part of the whole of American national identity, the other pole of the pendulum swing?

Micklethwait shrugs his shoulders and leans toward me, "Are those integral American values? You talk about helping people—I mean, this would be a conservative's answer. They would say, look, two things: One, America has not risen to the country it is by being a sort of welfare state-style country... And secondly, there is this huge tradition in America, unlike in Europe, of massive private philanthropy. So in other words, although the welfare state is weaker, it's saved by a much bigger voluntary 'state' sector. So at least, in principle, they would query the idea that it was necessarily all hard-hearted and that people weren't getting help. They would argue that the people who are getting helped are the ones who want to help themselves."

Unsatisfied, I push in a little deeper, citing a major critique of the *Economist*, which on the one hand advocates free trade and the opening of markets, but on the other does little to report on the negative impact its policies are having on the very people it is supposed to liberate.

"We address that frequently. [Recently], we looked at South Carolina textile workers. Exactly the sort of people who have been hammered by free trade, who free trade has done nothing but harm to. And we feel a responsibility, in a weird way, to record some of the people who suffer because of the creed which we essentially support. And particularly on trade, because on trade we feel most vulnerable. Because, as people who have campaigned religiously for free trade—and we do it knowing that free trade is, for some people, a deeply discomforting experience—we argue repeatedly that government should intervene to help people in that way."

"But you never propose an alternative."

"To free trade? No." Micklethwait laughs, "After one hundred and fifty years I think it would come as some shock to our readers."

It does seem ironic for a laissez-faire capitalist like Micklethwait to suggest government intervention as a source of relief for the perils of the free market. But, at the same time, this is the same phenomenon that Alan Rusbridger remarked on. America has now been reduced to a set of political adversaries who have lost the creativity and courage to offer new solutions to old problems. They simply argue about the best way to operate within the system that has become the status quo. While it is still possible to turn on the BBC and see an articulate debate between, say, a socialist and a capitalist, the most radically left-leaning Democratic politician who gets any airtime is Howard Dean. "Doesn't that cripple the dynamic of liberal democracy," I ask, "if there is never an authentic representation of the political poles? We never get to see that in our mainstream media."

"Oh but you did." Micklethwait interjects, laughing. "America briefly had one experience of [British far left]-like behavior which was George Galloway appearing in the Senate."

"Gorgeous" George Galloway, as he is better known in the UK media, is a former Labour Party MP who was expelled in October 2003 after a series of controversial statements about the Iraq war. Among them, he advised British troops to "refuse to obey illegal orders" and then called for a 'jihad' against them; the former nearly earned him a charge of treason.

Earlier that year, Galloway had come under intense public scrutiny after a series of documents were found in Iraq linking him to payments made through the UN's scandal-ridden Oil for Food program. The documents were later determined to be forgeries. However, in May 2005, a U.S. Senate report accused Galloway of receiving oil allocations worth 20 million barrels under the program. The implication was that the allocations were a reward for his outspoken opposition to the UN sanctions against Iraq in the 1990s. Arriving in Washington to testify before the Senate committee, Galloway told Reuters, "I have no expectation of justice from a group of Christian fundamentalist and Zionist activists under the chairmanship of a neocon George Bush who is pro-war." [11]

Sitting in front of Senator Norm Coleman, the Republican head of the Senate committee, Galloway used the spotlight to ridicule the charges against him and deliver what, even his critics admit, was one of the most articulate and impassioned public denunciations of America's legacy in Iraq. Responding to the committee's allegations that he had benefited under the Oil for Food program, Galloway stated, "Senator, I am not now, nor have I ever been, an oil trader and neither has anyone on my behalf. I have never seen a barrel of oil, owned one, bought one, sold one—and neither has anyone on my behalf. Now I know that standards have slipped in the last few years in Washington, but for a lawyer you are remarkably cavalier with any idea of justice. I am here today but last week you already found me guilty. You traduced my name around the world without ever having asked me a single question, without ever having contacted me, without ever written to me or telephoned me, without any attempt to contact me whatsoever. And you call that justice."

"Now, Senator, I gave my heart and soul to oppose the policy that you promoted. I gave my political life's blood to try to stop the mass killing of Iraqis by the sanctions on Iraq which killed one million Iraqis, most of them children, most of them died before they even knew that they were Iraqis, but they died for no other reason other than that they were Iraqis with the misfortune to born at that time. I gave my heart and soul to stop you committing the disaster that you did commit in invading Iraq. And I told the world that your case for the war was a pack of lies." [12]

Even John Micklethwait—who immediately qualifies that he doesn't agree with Galloway on many issues—admits the hearings were a spectacle, regardless of one's political sympathies. "He was magnificent to watch because he did articulate a point of view which, perhaps, does not get as much air. He represented the sort of left-wing view of the world which really has no voice in America.

That's short of Barbara Boxer and maybe one or two congressmen, but there isn't enough of a view of that. And when I say enough, I'm not making any judgments about whether that's a good or bad idea, I'm just saying it simply isn't there. And that does affect American discourse."

American discourse. It almost has the feel of an oxymoron. When was the last time Republicans and Democrats engaged in anything remotely like rational, outcome-driven conversation? Micklethwait's reference to George Galloway brings me back to Hitchens, who is probably downing a last glass of scotch in advance of the imminent *Economist* debate.

Back in Washington, DC, as Galloway walked into the Senate hearing, Hitchens joined a gaggle of journalists who had gathered around him. When Hitchens asked about Galloway's tacit, if unspoken, support of Saddam's financial backing for Palestinian suicide bombers, Galloway, refusing to answer the question, called Hitchens "a drink-soaked former-Trotskyist popinjay."* When Hitchens attempted to interrupt him, Galloway sealed the exchange with a shot at his physical integrity, "Your hands are shaking. You badly need another drink."

Rarely one to find himself on the wrong end of a verbal stick, Hitchens shot back, weakly, "And you're a drink-soaked..." before giving up. "You're a real thug, aren't you?" he muttered, and walked away.

Writing in the *Weekly Standard*, Hitchens recounted the confrontation, casting Galloway as an opportunistic phony who "had had to resign as the head of a charity called 'War on Want,' after repaying some disputed expenses for living the high life in dirt-poor countries... Prolier than thou, and ostentatiously radical,

---

* A popinjay is "a vain and talkative person." Ernest Hemingway defined it thusly: "A writer who appreciates the seriousness of writing so little that he is anxious to make people see he is formally educated, cultured or well-bred is merely a popinjay."

but a bit too fond of the cigars and limos and always looking a bit odd in a suit that was slightly too expensive." [13]

With the groundwork laid for an all-out public brawl, the UK website Labour Friends of Iraq issued a challenge for the two to engage in a formal debate with rules and a proper Chair. Now at Hay and back on Galloway's turf, Hitchens used an earlier appearance to take the offensive, proclaiming his eagerness to get it on.

"I know I'll see him because I will go on telling the truth about him and if he thinks he can sue me, I'll sue him. And the last person who sued me had to sell their house, just to pay the lawyer's bills. Don't fuck with the Hitch."

The polite British crowd tittered in their seats.

While more caustic and personal, Hitchens's feud with Galloway is part of a wider conflict with his former comrades, now generally associated with the anti-war left. While some critics locate the origin of this split in Hitchens's vocal support for the post-9/11 invasions of Afghanistan and Iraq, the truth is it began during NATO bombing of Serbia under Clinton's administration, which splintered the liberal and left wing of Western countries. At that time Hitchens was less destructive with his attacks, perhaps because it was beyond the geopolitical perimeter for most Americans. But Iraq, as we know, was far more contentious. It was the watershed moment that drew out the militant side of the '60s era Boomer liberals, many of whom were quick to shelve their celebrated questioning of unilateral attacks on sovereign nations. Though he stood apart from the rest of his generation in the amount of scorn he has taken for his position, Hitchens is perhaps the most emblematic of their shift away from rebellion and towards what some have labeled "state department liberalism." Perhaps conscious of how close he has come to the platform of the pro-Vietnam administrations of Johnson and Nixon, Hitchens has aggressively taken all comers.

Which is exactly why 2,000 people have crammed into the large central marquis at Hay to watch him do battle against Roy Hattersley, the seventy-year-old socialist and old school Labour politician.

The debate begins with the moderator, Channel 4 news presenter Jon Snow, taking a quick vote from the audience to see where they stood on the resolution, "History will be kinder to Bush and Blair than to Chirac and Schroeder." It is noted that an overwhelming majority of hands shoot up against it.

In his opening volley, Hitchens steps into his well-traveled defense of the invasion, linking to it the broader transformation occurring in the Middle East and Arab countries, including the recent concessions of Libya's Muammar Qaddafi.

"Did Qaddafi capitulate to Kofi Annan? No. Did he capitulate to Chirac or the EU or Herr Schroeder? Not at all. He came to Blair and Bush and said, 'I give up on the hunt for WMD.' And Libya had much more material than we thought."

Farther into his monologue, Hitchens switches gears, criticizing Bush and Blair for not intervening against the genocide in Darfur, Sudan and effectively playing the anti-war side's complaint about the Allies non-compliance with the United Nations against itself.

"This is the final shame and I'll close on it. On the matter of Darfur we're following UN rules, EU rules, international diplomacy rules. We are giving the aggressor government every bit of time to negotiate that he needs to complete the [ethnic] cleansing, as in Bosnia. And then negotiate on and from the stolen territory. Well that's what happens when you try it their way. I criticize Blair and Bush for playing along with that..."

In closing, Hitchens offers a plea to all those "with a sense of history or ethics" that they realize the value of the proposition so that they had not "totally wasted" their time with the debate. The audience rewards him with a rousing applause.

Before introducing Roy Hattersley, whom, he says, "needs no introduction," Jon Snow announces that the debaters will get a minute of rebuttals before going to the audience for questions. Hitchens leans over and kindly offers to cede his minute to the audience.

Hattersley then opens with a shot directly at Hitchens by way of his American president, declaring, "First of all I want to give George Bush credit to one cheek. I think he's the only man in history who could have created circumstances which enabled George Galloway to look like a hero."

The crowd's immediate response is to break up into laughter and applause. Hitchens looks down at them incredulously, "What are you laughing at?"

Hattersley then continues with a stock defense of international law, asking the audience to ignore what Hitchens has been arguing, which is, "really the Clint Eastwood theory on how to clean up the town. That it doesn't matter the message you use, as long as you get the object that you set out to achieve in the first place. I want my politicians to behave in a better way than that."

Responding directly to Hitchens's argument that Iraq has "a sort of domino theory, in which the Middle East suddenly falls in line between competitive economy and genuine democracy," Hattersley claims it "is one more last refuge for people to justify the war."

Finally, turning to Hitchens like an old schoolmaster scolding his former socialist student, Hattersley corrects him on Libya, which he explains, "didn't respond to the attack on Iraq. Libya responded to the hard need of economic necessity to buy and sell from the West."

Hitchens does not react, looking on stoically as the crowd applauds Hattersley's argument. But if he gives the impression that the points have not registered, Snow gives away the bluff, telling Hattersley, "you scored one, because three minutes into your contribution, Christopher leaned into my ear and said 'Could I have my minute back?'"

And once his turn comes after the other panelists take their minutes of rebuttal, Hitchens immediately addresses Hattersley's invocation of his nemesis, George Galloway, saying:

"Beware my lord what you joke about. Beware ladies and gentleman, comrades, brothers and sisters, what you laugh at. If Bush has made Galloway look like a hero, as was alleged, and you applauded, it must mean that to some people here he is one. Could I have a show of hands of who that would be?"

Despite the laugh given to Roy Hattersley's joke, very few hands are raised. Hitchens looks pleased. But when Jon Snow pushes him to comment on Galloway's "performance," Hitchens is forced to admit that he might be "partial because he called me a drunken ex-Trostkyist popinjay."

With the audience now giggling nervously and hanging on every word, Hitchens has them right where he wants. And he uses the platform to further his revenge on the absent Lord Galloway.

"Now do I give him grand rhetorician status for that, perhaps not. This is in the course of refusing to answer a direct question... What I always said about Mr. Galloway is that he is a pimp for fascism overseas, and an exploiter of religious sectarianism at home, and a guttersnipe and a liar."

Hitchens ends his flurry of insults by restating his challenge to Galloway to engage in a proper debate. The crowd applauds his bravado. But with the floor now open to audience questions, he immediately becomes the target of a disillusioned ex-fan, who obviously sees him as a traitor.

"Christopher, what happened to you? You've fallen so far... you started brilliantly attacking Henry Kissinger, years ago, and you wrote a brilliant book, and now you've ended up as an apologist for a bunch of murderers!"

Hitchens takes a drag from his cigarette.

"To give you a short answer, I much prefer the new friends I've made on the Iraqi and Kurdish and Arab Left than the false creepy friends that I've said good bye to on the Anglo-American Left, who joined the side of inaction and have stayed there and are proud of it."

Looking down at the man, Hitchens suddenly recognizes him.

"And a Galloway fan, you put up your hand as a Galloway fan. Didn't you? I saw you. Yes…"

The crowd begins to laugh and clap spontaneously, enjoying the altercation. But Hitchens isn't finished with him. Glaring down at the man, he shouts over the noise, "Well, fuck you! okay? You have no right to ask me this question." The room explodes. The otherwise mannerly main stage at Hay has now taken on the atmosphere of a pub in which a brawl could break out at any minute.

With a final swipe at the questioner's reference to his *Trial of Henry Kissinger*, which was used as a blunt weapon against him—as if being against Kissinger implied a direct opposition to all militarized foreign policy initiatives—Hitchens dismisses the man.

"And Henry Kissinger, and Lawrence Eagleburger, and Brent Scowcroft, every member of Kissinger Associates was opposed to this war… and the facts, which were give here, and which you haven't even bothered to read. So enough of you!"

After Jon Snow regains control of the room, and Hitchens's fury at Galloway has dissipated, he is allowed to make one final statement that exemplifies the position of the new wolves who have surfaced at the edge of the international perimeter; that of liberal interventionism.

"[America] is a hegemonic superpower. It may well serve its

own interest, and the interest of it's own people."

Pausing for a moment, he draws the crowd into careful consideration of his conclusion which like so many in these times, comes in the form of a question.

"But why can it not be a good thing that there's one super-power in the world that is occasionally, I would like to say, willing to consistently intervene on the side of democracy and against dictatorship?"

Why not, indeed. Later on, in the Green Room, I sit with a group of longtime Hay attendees. The subject, of course, is the debate. One of the men, who has been involved with the festival from the early days confides, "That is the first debate Christopher has lost on a Hay stage."

THE ROMANTIC

A girl in a nurse outfit with white garters and red stockings is screaming at me. I think she's talking about Michael Moore, but I can't risk coming too close or I will have to wade through the mist of beer and saliva that punctuates every word.

"So I'm at this show he's doing. At a theatre. And what he's basically saying is what the Bush administration is doing to American democracy is like being on an airplane where three guys are holding up 200 passengers with plastic knife. And I was like, you're one fat man is holding up 300 people with a microphone. What's the fucking difference? It's irritating."

I nod at her. "Irritating, yes."

It's late evening and Hay has dispersed its revelers to a constellation of private parties. Somehow I've ended up at a themed event called the Naughty Party being held in an old Victorian estate somewhere in the Welsh hills. The house is packed with what Evelyn Waugh would have called bright young things: vibrant, educated members of the higher social class. As far as Ben Ramm's concerned, they might just as well be vile bodies.

"It's your sort of Bacchanalian Oxford experience. Having just graduated from Cambridge, I can tell you there is very little beauty left there. And even in Oxford, which is slightly more romantic... it's unfortunately not like that. And nor was it really ever," says Ramm.

"Oh really," I ask, happy to have finally found someone who can speak drily. I'm surprised, because this is precisely what I imagined when reading Waugh's accounts of the roaring British 1920s. Only, instead of gangster suits and flapper dresses, these half-naked hotties cover the spectrum from drag to bondage gear, swirling to electronic music high on Class A drugs and cheap wine.

"Yes, it's a myth. I've been to a couple of parties like that and let me tell you I would have preferred to rip out my pancreas than speak to some of those people, not because they were odious or politically oppositional to what I believe, but because they are so inanely boring. I mean, the only people who do those things any more are the dead upper classes."

If Ramm sounds embittered, he's probably still a little raw from the recent coverage he received in the *Friday Thing*, an irreverent "weekly email comment sheet" that described him as a "hunched smarmy figure with little presence... oozing charmlessness and viscous nasality" that "sounds like some kind of goblin, hepped up on goofballs and liberalism." This from a report of a public debate in which Ramm was one of the featured speakers.

As editor of the newly resurrected nineteenth century magazine,* the *Liberal*, Ben Ramm has been busy. Fresh out of college,

---

* In 1822, Romantic poets Lord Byron and Percy Shelley conspired to produce a magazine that would challenge the day's conservative publications with a selection of original poetry, prose fiction and reviews. They called it the *Liberal* and brought together some of the foremost influences of the Romantic movement for its inaugural release. But before the magazine would formally launch, Shelley died and the project ultimately dissolved after the fourth issue.

he has single-handledly dedicated himself to "rehabilitating" the term liberal and, sorry, liberating it from those, like John Micklethwait's staff at the *Economist,* who have used it to justify rampant and selfish capitalism. So far, he's off to a good start; the *Independent* newspaper distributed 380,000 copies of his fourth issue just before the 2005 British general election.[14]

So while young college grads in America are joining conservative think tanks and studying the works of Leo Strauss, in Britain, the *haut monde* of Oxford and Cambridge are struggling to redefine liberalism.

"The liberalism I'm interested in is a specifically Romantic liberalism. It's speaking about major redistribution of wealth but it's not identified with a centralized, authoritarian, Socialist tendency. [Rather] it's the radical progressive politics of Shelley and his contemporaries that spoke of government in an almost Marxian image, dissolving away once it's provided everybody the tools with which to live."

By Romantic, Ramm is referring to the late eighteenth century movement of artists and intellectuals which sought to emphasize the aesthetic and heroic value of Nature and the individual's role within it. Ramm starts to list British artists and poets like Blake, Coleridge, and Wordsworth who, he claims, were "bearing down on a radical liberalism." But if this all sounds like a bunch of elitist mumbo-jumbo, Ramm quickly checks himself, "But I'm rambling on," and comes to the point:

"For me, and for Romantics the barometer is whether government can *allow* the individual, *enable* the individual. Ultimately it's about the individual imagination. As Leigh Hunt says, 'to realize the political equality of man and the individual imagination.' And so politics is only of the means by which to provide the individual with the tools with which he or she can realize the brilliance of his or her imagination."

Ramm thrusts a *Liberal* magazine into my hands and we walk out into a large room where a crowd has gathered to watch a beautiful Indian woman dance with unseen spirits. Ramm winces and keeps walking. Now upstairs and a safe distance from the sound system, we walk down a long inspiral carpeted hallway. In front of us two girls in plastic dresses are running from door to door, peaking inside each one until they find an empty one and duck in.

We get to the end of the hall and walk into a large salon and install ourselves at the back of the room. Ramm slouches into a chair and launches immediately into another monologue. He's easily one of the best-read and articulate 22-year-olds I have ever met. But he also has a point. For him, liberalism in the political sense does not have to be compartmentalized from liberalism in the artistic sense. We all speak of attending college for liberal arts degrees, and yet the virtues and principles of those *arts* never make it past the ivy-covered gate.

"Blake wouldn't have accepted the late twentieth century division between politics and art. Bearing in mind the use of the word *sublime* was very important in the eighteenth century, Blake says 'the most sublime act is to set another before you.' And that is, in a nutshell, the Romantic project. The idea that a redistribution of wealth is not only a political act, it's an aesthetic act. It's a metaphysical act, it's an act of truth. To raise someone out of poverty, to make sure someone isn't starving, to intervene where there is genocide, is not merely an act that one should do by international law or because it's politically expedient. It's an act of truth. And people need to start acknowledging that art is not for the gallery alone, but that there needs to be a public art, there needs to be an understanding that politics and aesthetics are not two separate things."

I can't help thinking that Ramm is just a more impassioned—

and perhaps idealistic and naïve—proponent of the arguments offered by Paul Berman and Christopher Hitchens. "But," I ask, "isn't that just the same language that imperialists once used to justify their own conquests?"

Ramm smiles. "Yes, but there's a more polite term for it now. They call it liberal interventionism."

So he supports the invasion of Iraq?

"No. Let me say that my position against the war is not that I disagree with liberal interventionism, per se, or even in Iraq. I believe in liberal interventionism, I'm a hawk on War on Terror. But if you genuinely believe in liberal interventionism, a child starves to death every five seconds and it's disingenuous to argue that the interventionism in Iraq is more acute and more pressing and more in need of action than the liberal interventionism that is needed in Darfur, that is needed in Latin America and that is needed in the areas where poverty not only breeds rebellion but is simply unacceptable. And for that reason alone, there has got to be a critique of liberal interventionism."

Watching the naughty partiers stream into the room looking for drugs and free sex, I suddenly feel the dark pall of inevitable doom that is carried in the war chant of the new liberal visionaries. Sitting in front of me is a man barely past 20 years, with the vocabulary and intellectual vernacular of a forty-year-old, who speaks of 'war' as a cure for all of the world's ills. His rationale for resisting the invasion of Iraq is that the nations who endorsed it have not done enough to fight world poverty and starvation. I shudder to think about the power of a leader who does make the minor economic concessions to alleviate that suffering and then wages war on all nations that do not comply with the dominant moral universe. Who would be left to resist the use of violence as a first resort?

Clearly, Ben Ramm is not a warmonger. Given a choice between invading Iraq or feeding Niger, he will choose the latter. But in this new era of ever-present danger, people will necessarily start looking for consensus, they will be more willing to trade on their shared interests than what ultimately separates them. Divide and be conquered.

"That is why liberalism will be the philosophy of the twenty-first century," Ramm declares with finality.

"A radical liberalism that can content people on the right by speaking about individual rights and self-determination and... can appeal to those traditionally on the left by saying 'Look, we are here to fight great poverty. We are here to speak about equality and community and solidarity.' And only a philosophy that will do that will ever attract the Right and the Left enough to be politically viable."

And where does this radical liberalism find it's ideological foundation? Ben Ramm locates it in the birth of the American nation, where the seeds of liberal interventionism were first planted. Proving he knows more U.S. history than most Americans his age, he recites a conversation between Benjamin Franklin and Thomas Paine at the end of the American Revolution.

"Franklin said to Paine, 'Where liberty is, there is my country,' saying he wasn't tied to any one nation. And Tom Paine said, 'Yes, and where liberty is not, there is mine.' As in, where liberty is not, I will call that my country and I will fight for the liberal right of freedom and democracy."

And they've been doing it ever since.

A CONSERVATIVE GESTURE

I wake early from jet-lag and stare up at hieroglyphic caricatures of Egyptian kings being carried by their soldiers, followed by a train of ornamental half-human figures. For a moment I can't remember exactly what country I am in, let alone what house. But just beyond my door I can hear a small voice uttering my name.

"Stephen, your tea is ready. You don't want to be late."

It all comes back to me now. The voice belongs to Hope Booth, wife to King Richard, and the room—appropriately named the Egyptian—is housed in Brynmelyn, the Booth's Welsh estate where I have been quartered for my sojourn at Hay.

If Richard Booth has a penchant for the dramatic and self-aggrandizing, Hope is his conjugal antithesis.[*] Patient, receptive, she is the yin to his yang. A quiet and unselfish intelligence exerts itself from behind her pale eyes, which have the quality of straddling two realms, the ephemeral world and this one. I open the door to see her standing at the end of a short hallway, smoke rising from her right hand. She seems to smoke ceaselessly, even at this early part of the day.

In the kitchen, Hope pours tea into a mug emblazoned on one side with the portrait of a Nicaraguan farmer. Sitting in silence, I sip the warm liquid and watch as she takes another long drag from her cigarette.

"How is your book going?" she asks, "What's the subject of it?"

"The end of American liberalism," I reply, realizing for the first time that I give each person a different answer depending on where I imagine their political sympathies lie.

Hope doesn't look up. "Oh, and the end of democracy."

I smile and turn the warm mug in my hands. Opposite the farmer is the iconic image of Che Guevara. Beneath him, in black text superimposed on a red strip, is a quote from the Brazilian Paulo Freire:

---

[*] If I knew them better, I would insert the word long-suffering. The village history has no shortage of legendary nights at the local pub in which Richard was the star performer. And now, with his health on the decline and his erratic passion focused on his various quixotic battles, it seems that much of the responsibility for maintaining the sanity of the household sits firmly with Hope. As one person told me, "She's the saint of the family."

Washing one's hands of the conflict between the powerful and
the powerless means to side with the powerful.

I down my tea as Hope explains how to cross the farmer's
fields to reach the festival site. I thank her, grab my notebook and
head off down the hill from the King's manor. I feel a sense of
optimism rising within me. Unsure if it is just the stunning blue
sky or the potential that I will finally crack Hitchens, I keep my
eyes on the road and head toward the village.

The path takes me past a small stream, through a quiet wood
and then up onto the wide open fields. I reach the top of the path
and look up at the clouds which extend into the horizon like a
dragon's spine, strafing shadows across the rolling hills and forest
clusters below. It's Hobbit territory, I think to myself, jumping
over a fence and onto the road that leads to Hay.

Back inside the Green Room, I distractedly pick at a bowl of
strawberries and try to get a better look at the three people seated
across from me. A young boy sits between two men, one of whom
I recognize and the other who has his back directly toward me.
I get a little shock when I realize it's Christopher Hitchens. The
shock comes not because of the early hour but that the person
he is seated with is none other than his younger brother Peter,
with whom he has been engaged in a nasty public feud for over
four years.

Suddenly Peter Florence walks into the room. The group rises
and begins to walk toward one of the tents. I snatch a handful
of strawberries and follow them to the Guardian tent where a
small chalkboard announces the next event, *Hitchens vs. Hitchens*.
Walking in, I grab a seat in the middle row as the *Guardian*'s Ian
Katz, takes his seat between Christopher and Peter and introduces
the surprise event of the festival, a debate between the warring
brothers. Using all the vernacular of high level diplomat, Katz

explains that the *Guardian* has arranged for the reunion, which is the product of last minute negotiations between the two sides.

The Hitchens brothers had not spoken since Peter wrote an article containing the implication that Christopher was once a militant pro-Communist. Published in the UK *Spectator* in the wake of 9/11, just as Christopher was making the argument for regime change in Afghanistan and Iraq, Peter expressed surprise at Christopher's pro-Americanism considering his one-time claim that he "would not mind seeing the Red Army watering its horses in the [Thames];" in other words, a Communist invasion of the United Kingdom.

Peter's story had the immediate effect of pitting the far right, isolationist anti-war American conservatives against Christopher at the same time that he was fending off his old friends on the left. Christopher's reaction was outrage and harsh words, delivered in a published letter to *Commentary* magazine, in which he denied the remark, demanded a retraction and called Peter "a fanatic and a fool." [15]

But for Peter the point was not that Christopher had once been a Communist. Rather, for him the issue was his brother's sudden conversion from a leading socialist polemecist to a leading neoconservative hawk, a transference which, in some ways, followed the transformation of the United States from what Peter calls "an arsenal of reaction—which is why I liked it—[to] a sort of multicultural, liberal global force which [Christopher] rather more approved of."

The feud lasted four years until Christopher chose to breach the topic in a *Vanity Fair* article on the subject of sibling rivalry. After a brief history of the phenomenon spanning from Cain and Abel to the De Havilland sisters, Hitchens turned to that of his own estrangement from his younger brother.

"The last thing that Peter and I agreed on was the impeachment of President Clinton."

But it had not always been this way. Both he and Peter had once belonged to the International Socialists. Somewhere along the way, Peter—who had once told a University tutor "I am sorry I am late. I was trying to start the revolution,"—had gone astray:

"He is a staunch Christian and an abstainer from alcohol and tobacco." Christopher wrote in *Vanity Fair*, "He lacks also, I sometimes think, my strange, hypnotic power over women. Moreover, he is a man for whom the word 'reactionary' might have been invented. In his many columns for the British and American press (he is a contributing editor for Pat Buchanan's rancid *American Conservative*), he defends capital punishment, denounces the liberations of Iraq and Afghanistan, upholds religion, and manages to be both anti-European and anti-American." [16]

When Peter and I speak later, he explains that his shift away from the far left socialist ideology did not come as the product of some a-ha moment. Rather, he explains, "It's a long journey. And the idea that it is some kind of Damascene* conversion, or epiphany, is a mistake. A mistake." [17]

He pauses and reflects for a moment, "You change your mind piece by piece, or what happens is that you find something you used to believe no longer holds up. And this may not suit you, because a lot of your friendships and a lot of your attitudes towards life may be based upon that, so you'll hesitate for a long time over actually admitting to yourself that it *has* changed. That *you* have changed. But when you do, there's then a kind of slow, progressive collapse which affects all kinds of other things that you used to believe, which, to some extent, is involuntary."

Peter, who is just as quick-minded as his brother—and just

---

* The term "Damascene" refers to the Biblical story of Paul, who initially persecuted Christians until he had a vision of Jesus on the road to Damascus, which led him to become a disciple. Hence, a "Damascene conversion."

dismissive when I ask what he believes to be an inane question—suddenly tires of the subject.

"I don't actually find this very interesting, because it's a perfectly normal classic development in the lives of people. It was, at least, up until recently. I forget who said this, the old cliché was that if you weren't on the left when you were young, there was something wrong with your heart, and if you weren't on the right when you were older there was something wrong with your head. There's nothing unusual about it at all, and as I say, I find it quite dull discussing it."

Unsure of what to say next, and yet fascinated by his candid exposition of evolutionary conservativism, I just laugh nervously and wait for him to continue. After an awkward moment, he does.

"Why would anyone do anything else? All the answers to the question are clichés: you gain experience, you get older, you earn a living, you pay taxes, you own your own property, you travel, you have children, and so you learn. What astonishes me is that so many people of my generation have been through all those processes and remain as radical as they were when they were teenagers. Is there something wrong with me? Or is there something wrong with them?"

Clearly he believes there is something wrong with them. Writing in the *Spectator* just a few weeks before the fall of Baghdad, Peter chastised the American-led war effort and took another shot at Christopher and his tribe of liberal interventionists.

"The idea that naked force can create human freedom is itself a left-wing idea. Even more socialist are the war faction's contempt for the sovereignty of nations and their unashamed belief that ends justify means. No wonder that the war's hottest-eyed supporters on both sides of the Atlantic are ex-Marxists who have lost their faith but have yet to lose their Leninist tendency to worship worldly power." [18]

For Christopher, his brother's unabashed anti-war conservatism only fortifies his position that those who oppose the liberation of Iraq are inherently conservative. While those who are for regime change represent the true essence of liberalism, which is the natural opponent to authoritarianism, wherever it exists in the world. Glancing quickly across the stage towards—but not at—his brother, he admits, "Peter's position is fantastically helpful to me, as I hope mine might be to him, because… it's perfectly right that those who are extremely conservative should be the main opponents of it, as they are and always have been in the United States. […] I think it's very clarifying to find that I'm doing what I'm supposed to do, which is saying, 'Yes, I'm for change and the reactionaries are against.'"

Speaking privately after the debate, Peter isolates another aspect of George Bush's not so conservative neoconservatism, specifically what he describes as "idealistic rhetoric" that has transformed the idea of patriotism from "a love of and loyalty to, a country; the place where you live… into an idealistic nationalism which celebrates the essence, supposedly, of the country. And believes that you're not so much defending and extending the power and survival of America—the place and country—as Americanism, the principles of democracy and liberty."

For Peter Hitchens, the conservative, this patriotism has its roots in one of the most radically liberal movements of the Enlightenment period. "In fact, there's an argument that this kind of nationalism was actually invented by the French revolutionaries, and is wholly different from the conservative nationalism of more old-fashioned states, and is, in itself, a radical, political idea. So there is a way in which American patriotism has been turned into an ideology—which, of course, it could well be a vehicle for neoliberalism and globalism, and I must confess I have been very unsure about whether I'm all that keen on that…"

But if the Hitchens are at odds about the rationale for war, they acknowledge a surprising consensus about its impact on the domestic political society. Writing in Ben Ramm's *Liberal* magazine, Peter railed against the "opportunism of authority" which uses war as a way of ratcheting its levers of control over the populace. "The state's answer to the terrorism of a tiny, foreign few," he wrote, "is—literally—to disarm its own people whom it seems to distrust and dislike." Picking up on the theme during the debate, he professed an allegiance to the core values of his conservatism, those of the classical liberal.

"What I have come to value above all things is liberty and liberty of conscience, without which we don't seem to me to be able to survive. The assault on the liberty of the subject and the citizen under the guise of this war against terror seems to me to be deeply shocking."

To which Christopher rejoined, "War can be a great force for progress, and often has been and always will be. Also, as Randolph Bourne said, 'war is the health of the state.' The great downside of the revolutionary and progressive impact of warfare is the attempt by the state to make the citizen into state property. It has to be very, very, very sternly resisted, and I couldn't agree with him more about that." [19]

And so it was the two brothers ended up conducting their reconciliation in public. One that Peter only agreed to on a lark, believing that Christopher would decline. But if he thought the discussion was going to remain fixed within the boundaries of the political, he was wrong. The *Guardian*'s Ian Katz, seemingly unable repress the more tabloid-esque curiosity that this kind of event inspires, pushed past the perimeter of good taste and asked one last personal question:

"One thing that you, Christopher, have talked about in the past, is your mother's suicide when you were, I think, a student.

Can I ask how formative an experience was that, and how did it change the dynamics of your family?"

Christopher sits still for a moment, his head hanging over his chest, and then replies, "Yes, you can, though I sort of wish you wouldn't have."

I'm not sure what kind of impact this has on the rest of the audience, but for me, at this moment, the spectacle of the reunion loses all sense of time and space. It would be impossible to not feel the intensely awkward nature of the intrusion, and the way that it takes effect on the discussion. For a moment I wonder what all of Christopher's enemies would feel, sitting in front of him, as he breaches what has to be one of the most tragic and defining events of his life. He begins with a clarification.

"Concerning Mama, the reason I'm reluctant to speak now is that I wish I'd never said anything earlier. When I'm interviewed for a profile or about a book I've written or whatever, I tend to think I owe an answer to every question the interviewer has. I feel, as a journalist, a fool if I say, 'well can't we go off the record.' It's what I don't like in public figures. So I say, all right, since you ask, I'll tell you. I've often for that reason said more than I should have or more than I wished to, and I should sometimes have said nothing at all. But since I have, I suppose I have to answer your question."

In 1973 Christopher had just landed a job at the *New Statesman* when he woke to find news of his mother Yvonne's death in an apartment in Greece. The initial reports described it as a murder, but once Christopher arrived in Athens to identify the body, he learned that she had committed suicide with her lover. Of being the sole representative of the family to make the trip, Christopher explains,

"I was quite happy to do it, but it was a wretched time. It also coincided with a military-backed coup in Athens. There were tanks in the streets. When I first saw the Acropolis it was from my dead mother's hotel window."

Christopher found a suicide note addressed to him. It said, in effect, 'You will understand one day.'

Of that note, he once told *New York* magazine, "Knowing and believing you're your mother's favorite is a great thing for a guy, Freud says, but it's another thing to have it in writing."

With the audience now sitting silently and in rapt attention, Christopher lets down his guard, allowing a glimpse at the emotional impact the adverse public opinion has had on him. "If I was the kind of person you might think I am, I would have written a piece about that, but I haven't."

Ian Katz asks Peter if he has anything to say about his mother's death, to which he replies icily, "No, no."

Given the chance to ask questions, a young woman in the audience remarks that the two brothers have not made eye contact throughout the entire debate.

"And I just wondered whether, for this final moment, whether there was a chance you could just look at each other?"

Peter pushes himself up in his chair, "You have no idea what we've just been through."

Christopher offers, "I don't mind giving the odd squint."

Unsatisfied, she persists, "So will you do it?"

Peter is the first to look over at Christopher, who brings his head up in a long arc. Their eyes lock for a moment and the crowd emits a collective sigh of relief and begins to applaud.

Peter smirks at the reaction. "They want everything to be all right."

Christopher crushes his cigarette into the table, "They want a happy ending—that's their problem."

HITCHENS-ON-WYE

It is late in the day and the crowds have started to thin on the Hay festival grounds. Stopping by the Green Room for a last drink of tea, I see Hitchens standing with a few people who are preparing to leave. Sensing my last chance, I step in and ask for an interview. Looking at me, he hardens his lips and shrugs his shoulders. "Why not?" I am catching him at the end of a full day. He still has a dinner party to attend, and I promise his chaperone he will be down the road with good time to catch the first course.

A few moments later, Hitchens is seated again, looking at me through brown-tinted aviators. I ask him what it's like, the world seen through a brandy bottle. "Sherry," he corrects me and lights a Rothman cigarette. Sitting next to me on a floral patterned wicker chair, he looks tired. I ask him if perhaps we should postpone the interview to another time.[20]

"No, I find this topic rather energizing."

In the next hour Hitchens will smoke seven cigarettes and beckon twice for the girls in the Green Room to bring him more "apple juice" and fizzy water while I struggle to avoid asking a stupid question. It begins with a simple one: "Do you call yourself a liberal?"

"A few people have introduced me as or referred to me as a 'former' liberal and I've never been one, and in fact, I've hung on calling myself a socialist probably a little longer than I should have. Partly because it was a way of stating one wasn't merely a liberal. And that's because I was brought up, politically, at least, a lot in England where liberal suggested simply middle-class compromising."

Hitchens's major inspiration to become a writer came while sitting in a public library in Devonshire, reading an essay[*] by

---

[*] Hitchens called the essay by Connor Cruise O'Brien, which appeared as the Introduction to *Writers and Politics* (1965), "the best essay on the subject [of liberalism as a middle class compromise] ever written..."

Connor Cruise O'Brien, the Irish diplomat and historian. In it, O'Brien refers to liberalism as "the word that makes the rich world yawn and the poor world sick." Being labeled a liberal was a charge considered "damaging" in Africa, Asia and Latin America where, O'Brien explains, "the American and European liberal has too often been—and is perhaps increasingly—a false friend." Casting the Kennedy-era American UN ambassador Adlai Stevenson as the liberal voice *par excellence*, O'Brien describes how the liberal state's benevolence looked to its recipients:

"From this viewpoint, Mr. Stevenson's face, with its shiftily earnest advocate's expression, is the ingratiating moral mask which a toughly acquisitive society wears before the world it robs: 'liberalism' is the ideology of the rich, the elevation into universal values of the codes which favoured the emergence, and favour the continuance, of the capitalist society." [21]

It was an indictment that resonated with Hitchens, then a budding eighteen-year-old socialist.

"Actually, if you read that essay," he explains, "it was exactly what I felt for us on the left in Britain: The word liberal was a very rude thing to call somebody. Liberalism was an attempt to drape capitalism with some kind of pious social conscience... It used to be preceded almost always with the term 'wishy-washy.' "

Hitchens takes a long drag on his cigarette, adding, "In America now, liberal is the word that the right uses to defame secularism, welfarism, anti-militarism and so on. I think because it's no longer plausible to attack communism. There used to be two ways of attacking liberalism. One was to say 'limousine liberal'—it's very much what one would call myself—and the other was as 'soft on' communism."

In fact, these were both identifiers that could have been pinned on the pre-9/11 Hitchens. As far back as his student years at Oxford, he was adept at playing both sides of the class line, between revolutionary socialists and high class fashionistas. As Martin Walker, one of his classmates, recalls, "He was criticized for being a 'champagne socialist' or a 'country-house revolutionary.' "[22] And this flirtation with elite groups wasn't lessened by his status as a Washington journalist, even when he was still writing for the *Nation.* As early as 1999, the *Washington Post* described Hitchens as belonging to "a rarefied world where the top pols and bureaucrats sup with the media and literary elite at exclusive dinner parties. It's a cozy little club of confidential sources and off-the-record confidences..."[23]

For many of his critics, the most damning evidence of his duplicitous turncoatism hinges on the articulate case he made for the indictment of authoritarian statesmanship in *The Trial of Henry Kissinger* (2001). For younger readers, myself included, this was our introduction to Hitchens the polemicist. And the understanding, though simplistic, was that he was against government agents who used their power selectively, justifying any use of covert or widescale military force as necessary for the preservation of the American interests.[24] But for Hitchens, his contempt for Kissinger not only made sense in terms of his socialist politics, but also as a foundation for his support of the invasion of Iraq.

"When I wrote the Kissinger book, where would I have been then? If someone would've said 'are you a socialist' I would have been reluctant to deny it. And I certainly wrote it from—it's the outcome of years and years of struggling against Kissinger, trying to expose him from the left. As for me being in support for regime change in Iraq, that to me is a direct extension of the critique of Kissingerian realism. Or neo-realism."

In fact, this was the very point on which he found consensus with the neoconservatives, who were newly installed in Washington just as *Trial* was being released. Hitchens recalls his first meeting with Paul Wolfowitz—"I was very flattered, I suppose, some might say I had been unduly impressed"—in which the deputy secretary of defense was "at pains to make it clear to me that he regarded himself he as the opposition to, the opposite of Kissinger."

Clearly, for the neocons, whom we later learned had their eyes set on Iraq long before they took power in the Bush administration, Hitchens was a perfect ally. As one of the highest profile leftist writers in America, and a sympathetic comrade of Ahmad Chalabi, the former head of the Iraqi National Congress who once bragged of feeding the U.S. intelligence false information about WMD in order to bolster the case for invasion, he would prove to be one of their greatest assets in prosecuting the war.

But while the case can be made that Hitchens, like *New York Times* martyr Judith Miller, became an unwitting channel for the Pentagon's pre-war propaganda, he sees it differently. Writing in the preface to *Regime Change*, his 2003 collection of essays on Iraq, he argued his position for U.S. military intervention from the "viewpoint of one who took the side of the Iraqi and Kurdish opposition to Saddam Hussein, who hoped for their victory, and who then had come to believe that the chiefest and gravest mistake of Western and especially American statecraft had been to reconfirm Saddam Hussein in power in 1991." [25]

So for him, the issue* was always one of liberation for the Kurds and Shia first, the rest of the country second. The ends would justify the means, even if that meant racking up a hundred thousand Iraqi casualties in the military action and subsequent occupation. It almost sounds… *Kissingerian.*

I wonder if the neoconservatives have the same compassionate register for the victims of Saddam's brutal regime of which, even Hitchens admits "the worst atrocities, mass murder with genocidal

---

* On the way that Bush and Blair argued their case for pre-emptive war based on the threat of WMDs, Hitchens told the Hoover Institution's Peter Robinson, "Mr. Bush and Mr. Blair, I'm sorry to say, both decided that it was a little easier to frighten people than to persuade them. This is a common political temptation."

intent, torture, aggression, and so forth were committed when Saddam Hussein was the recipient of Western favor and protection." Or if that even matters.

For Hitchens the war in Iraq represents a kind of dual regime change for both Iraq and the United States. In the past, they were linked by a status quo policy that protected men like Saddam. It was in American interests to have strong leaders who were allied to them. But with the neocons all that has changed.

"I think it's a good thing that American national interests are present in, and can apparently be made congruent to, the spread of democracy. It doesn't happen without people fighting for it. It's not just objectively true. You have to fight to make it true, so that it becomes so. It comes to a very interesting point that a lot of people don't recognize, where the U.S. realized that, especially in the Middle East, it couldn't go on wanting this political slum, where they're using proxy leaders and client regimes, or movements, and picking up and dropping different clients according to shifting allegiances. Investing themselves in the survivors, they would have to take the risk that even though more democracy might not make people act in pro-American ways, it's much better than status quo."

But as Sergeant Hollis told me in Iraq, the risk was not entirely uncalculated. And the status quo was something Saddam Hussein's Iraq represented the most Westernized of the Persian Gulf states. This was a by-product of American patronage and his iron-fisted clampdown on the kind of Islamism that could threaten his power. And it offered the best chance for an American-style democracy to take hold. "So," Hollis explained, "the administration believes that we start with Iraq to make a change in the world."[26]

Hitchens sips quickly from his glass and lights another cigarette. "We went to war on the status quo in the Middle East. Which is a pretty amazing thing for an isolationist republic. It was mainly because a couple of people, Wolfowitz among them, won that argument in the White House, and in the Republican Party. They converted Cheney. Which is very important."

Important because for corporatist political leaders like Cheney, the only use for Iraq was under the sand.

"Cheney wanted to lift the sanctions." Hitchens leans forward and affects a sterner expression, channeling the ogreish VP: "Fuck this, this is liberal humanitarianism. Let's get back to doing business. Buying and selling a bit of oil, that's what we do. The rest of it can go fuck itself. They can't drink the oil. In the end, they'll come around to see things our way."

So the neocons converted him. Shook out the selfish short-sightedness and got him on board for the bigger vision thing. But I'm curious about something. In all of the reading I have done on Hitchens's advocacy of the regime change, he never intimates that there is any economic benefit in the occupation. I take a broad swipe at it.

"The word neoliberal is often used to describe the way America asserts itself economically in the world."

"Yeah."

"Do you feel that is a relevant term and how would you describe its nature and relationship to U.S. world power?"

"The U.S. needs access to everyone else's markets. And that world order is often described as neoliberal, yeah."

I look over at Hitchens and I see him speaking out his thoughts. He is now engaging in a confession of his own loss of faith in the great socialist dream, the one that once offered a glimmer of hope in the face of capitalism's all out assault on the virtues of a communitarian society.

"There's obviously been a great trial that could've been about social democracy... And you see, that's what people don't believe anymore. That's what made me give up. There is no other plausible internationalist movement with a socialist agenda, nor is there a plausible theory of power; that capitalism could be challenged. There isn't. For the first time in its history, capitalism doesn't have an ideological enemy.

"So in effect, capitalism is having another revolution. So you have to go back to the original Marxism and look at the Manifesto and remind yourself, 'That is what the old boy said.' This is the greatest revolution in human history, all we need is to have it run by workers, not by the owners. We need to have those who produce, making the production decisions. Extremely powerful and attractive ideology."

"It is," I submit.

Hitchens pauses and drinks. The Green Room has suddenly gotten very quiet. The most quiet since I arrived. Looking around, I realize that we are among the last people remaining.

I wonder if he is finished with his thoughts, since he has almost ceased to look at me, it is as if he is talking to himself. Taking out another cigarette, he continues.

"I think the verdict of history is in, one may feel a little wistful about it, but wistfulness is no good as a dialectical method. At all. So, in fact, capitalism is reasserting itself as the only revolution. And it takes a Marxist to see it, sometimes."

"Asserting itself as what kind of revolution?" I ask.

"As the only dynamic revolutionary force in the world, reasserting itself after having gone through terrible decay; after all capitalism led to imperialism, to fascism, to war. Led to the great crisis in the 1920s and 1930s. It's true, don't let's forget. And not just morally true, it's politically true. It looked as if it were dead-ended. It really did. And to most of its supporters it did too. And that's why they went Keynesian. They thought, we can only save it this way. You had to buy [the workers] off. That's what's happened since: you've got to give these guys a health service, protection of work, and this and that. And also give them some money so they can go on buying things."

In his essay that so inspired the young socialist Hitchens, Connor Cruise O'Brien* chronicles a conversation between himself and Kwame Nkrumah, the pan-Africanist leader who became the first Prime Minister of Ghana. Nkrumah was then involved in trying to make Ghana into a socialist society. Of this effort, O'Brien writes, he believed "this government had been right to reject the façade of liberalism," and that he saw in it a "greater sense of responsibility to the people—not in a formal sense but in a profound one—than [in] neighbouring states with more apparently liberal constitutions."

When Nkrumah asked O'Brien, who was there to work with the government, if he was a socialist, the Irishman replied that he was, understanding that to be a liberal in Africa was a to be a "false friend." But driving home after the interview, Connor explains, he realized that a liberal was in fact what he was.[27]

"Whatever I might argue, I was more profoundly attached to liberal concepts of freedom... than I was to the idea of a disciplined party mobilizing all the forces of society for the creation of a social order guaranteeing more real freedom for all instead of just for a few."

I wonder if Hitchens is aware at just how much he echoes the reluctant admission of his literary polestar in his own acquiescence to the fatality of the socialist ideal. As one of the highest paid writers in the United States, what else can he do but accept his own latent capitalism.

"It means we've conceded," he says, "that capitalism has embarked on another revolution. It's not only survived the battle

---

* It's also worth mentioning, in lieu of the ongoing situation in Iraq, that O'Brien also had this to say: "The Western liberal, of the kind most often and most widely heard from, uniformly displays acute myopia in the face of various forms of Western puppet governments which cover so large a part of Africa, Asia, and Latin America."

with socialism but it's replenishing and extending and strength-ening itself, without a viable or plausible alternative."

With the daylight now flirting with the crimson hues of sunset, Hitchens rises from his chair. Bidding me goodbye, he wishes me luck in discovering my own path, away from the left he now sees as reactionary defenders of the status quo.

"There's no longer any Left and I can't be any part of it. It took a lot for me to get to the realization that it was," he pauses for effect, "conservative. I wasted so much time... you could save yourself the trouble. You'll feel better."

I watch as he makes his way out of the building and into a waiting car. Standing alone in the Green Room, I bend to collect my things. It is beginning to get dark and I'll have to hurry if I want to eat my last dinner in Hay with its King.

2

Imaginary Forces

I don't approve of the global village.
I say we live in it.
— Marshall McLuhan

ACTUALLY, IT'S ROUND

Sitting in the departure lounge at Heathrow, I sift through the notes from my various conversations over the past few days. Naturally, there is a spectrum of opinions about the virtues and authenticity of new millennial liberalism. But one consistent theme that threaded all of my interviews at Hay is that whatever the state of the liberal project, the capitalist one is doing just fine. Indeed, without any viable ideological competitor, as Christopher Hitchens declared, it has "embarked on another revolution."

Now every true revolution has a scribe, someone who is able to channel the zeitgeist into a passionate, living chronicle that fuels the insurgency and propels it to its ultimate historical destiny. The French Revolution had Voltaire, the American had Thomas Paine. For the new capitalist revolution, there is *New York Times* columnist Thomas Friedman. I know this because as I walk through the business class cabin of my United Airlines flight, passing all the young legionnaires of the jet-set globalist contingent, I count four copies of his bestselling book, *The World Is Flat,* and that's just in the first three rows.[1] Seeing the books reminds me that Friedman was the only major figure to refuse my interview request. It's a drag, because there is probably no other liberal who fits the description of a wolf in sheep's clothing than America's preeminent globalization advocate.

Friedman was one of the first A-list liberals to peddle the idea that Iraqis would treat American soldiers as liberators. He believed the overthrow of Saddam Hussein represented the very best aspects of American liberalism. Six months after the invasion—the same week I was interviewing Sergeant Hollis in Samarra—Friedman declared "this is the most radical-liberal revolutionary war the U.S. has ever launched—a war of choice to install some democracy in the heart of the Arab-Muslim world." Like so many of his other liberal peers, Friedman denied there was economic dimension to the conflict. This war was different from past wars that their generation had protested. "U.S. power is not being used in Iraq for oil, or imperialism, or to shore up a corrupt status quo, as it was in Vietnam and elsewhere in the Arab world during the cold war," wrote Friedman in his column.[2]

And yet, as many Iraqis told me during my time in-country, the imposition of democracy from a foreign power seemed to contradict the very essence of political freedom. Especially when the Americans were doing everything in their power to control the new system. Overwhelmingly, Iraqis seemed to believe that the creation of an authentic democratic structure would mean adoption of Islamic (*sharia*) law, which a great majority of them want. But for American liberals like Thomas Friedman, *sharia* represents a major failure; it would mean having spent billions to liberate a society only to see it retreat from the secular freedoms imposed by its former dictator.

To protect itself from this outcome, the U.S. stacked the newly liberated nation's political deck with as many pro-Western Iraqis as possible. But this only strengthened the convictions of many who saw the invasion and its promise of delivering true freedom as a wedge to open Iraq for U.S. corporate and military goals. A few days before leaving Baghdad, I listened to Rana al Aiouby, a young Iraqi translator, argue over tea with Hesham Barbary, an Egyptian businessman who had come to cash in on the new reconstruction contracts.

"So the Americans came here to save the Iraqi people?" al Aiouby asked incredulously.

"Partially," Barbary replied.

"They didn't come here to help the Iraqis. Everyone knows why the American came here... because their economic system just collapsed. So they have to help themselves, and even if they'll make a disaster for the others, just, they want to survive. That's it."

Voices like Rana al Aiouby's are not present in Thomas Friedman's real time history of globalization. They can't be. Pro-war liberals like Friedman, architects of the new millennial liberal project, cannot afford to second-guess the motives driving America's War on Terror. From the outset, Friedman believed implicitly that Bush's Iraq War plan was a high stakes gamble based on ideological motives, "the greatest shake of the dice any president has voluntarily engaged in since Harry Truman dropped the bomb on Japan." Others echoed the sentiment—"this is Texas Poker," as arch-conservative Robert Novak put it—pushing the idea that Bush had risked billions of dollars and thousands of lives like some Vegas roller.[3] The analogy is instructive. Who bets the house on an abstraction? No one. So we're to believe that Bush and Cheney went for broke to bring democracy to Iraq? That's insanity. This is an administration so mired in cronyism and conflicts of interest that to believe they would take such a huge bet on a political ideal is delusional. And yet that is exactly what the pro-war liberals have done. The question is: why?

In Friedman's case, I believe it is because he implicitly understands that America is facing an insurmountable challenge to its global economic hegemony. His research for *The World Is Flat* brought him around the world to investigate the new paradigm emerging in transnational business. What he finds is that the old vertical ("command and control") systems are being replaced by horizontal ("connect and collaborate") ones and, in the process, blowing away walls and ceilings that were once integral to the rigid hierarchical structure of global commerce. He first made this discovery in Bangalore, India where menial data entry and phone operator jobs in the accounting and banking fields are now being performed by English-speaking workers. This has been going on for years but, as Friedman explains, he was too busy covering the War on Terror to notice. It's not until Nandan Nilekani, the CEO of Infosys—India's equivalent to Microsoft—tells him "the playing field is being leveled," that Friedman realizes what he has stumbled upon.[4]

Over and over again he exclaims: the world is flat, the world is flat, the world is flat! Capitalism *is* undergoing its new revolution, one that will be as transformative as "Gutenberg's invention of the printing press, the rise of the nation-state, or the Industrial Revolution."[5]

But, like all revolutions, this one will have its winners and losers. Of the former, most obvious are corporate CEOs who will fatten their bottom line by tapping into the vast reservoir of cheap foreign labor. On the other side is Joe Six Pack, who will suffer from a net loss in American jobs. Much of the success of Friedman's book lies in his dire warnings to Americans that they are on the verge of a major crisis. Not only are hard-working, low-wage Indian workers stealing their jobs, but hard-working, tech-savvy Chinese students are increasingly taking seats in top undergrad and graduate college programs. And, Friedman frets, if America doesn't wake up, it will face a potentially disastrous decline.* Or, as Infosys's CEO Nilekani later explains, the American middle class "has not yet grasped the competitive intensity of the future. Unless they [do], they will not make the investments in reskilling themselves and you will end up with a lot of people stranded on an island."[6]

So what does his support of the invasion of Iraq have to do with his *The World Is Flat* thesis? Everything. Like any good writer, Friedman understands that America loves a disaster movie, but only if it has a happy ending. So while the outlook may be grim for average workers, he is careful to paint a picture that is ultimately reassuring. The coming storm, he explains, will catalyze the transformation of America. "Each of us as an individual, will have to work a little harder and run a little faster to keep our standard of living rising."[7] But this is never applied to the realm of U.S. foreign policy and how it might be shaped by these new threats to U.S. supremacy. Instead, a sort of delusional picture of globalization is presented, one in which the government plays no role whatsoever. And in this omission, in his obscuring of such an obvious force in world finance, we are given a hint at the lengths to which Friedman will go to deny the truth. Placing his Iraq coverage side-by-side with *The World Is Flat*, the message is that government is driven by a mission to liberate and democratize the world, the vast majority of whom will, like the post-Saddam Iraqis, joyfully embrace American-style capitalism. Not only is this a verifiably distorted vision of reality, it is a dangerous one. Because it keeps the millions of readers who bought Friedman's book from understanding why so much of the world has turned against America. And how dire the consequences of this ignorance will prove to be.

---

* "The truth is," Friedman warns, "we're in a crisis now, but it is a crisis that is unfolding very quietly. We're a bit like a person who is sleeping on an air mattress, and the air is slowly coming out—so slowly you can barely feel it, until your head hits the cement." Thomas L. Friedman, *The World Is Flat: A Brief History of the Twenty-First Century* (New York: Farrar, Straus & Giroux, 2006), p. 326.

POX AMERICANA

Slipping into my window seat, I smile to myself. There, in the adjacent seat pocket, with a gold sticker shouting its status as "the bestselling nonfiction book in the world today," is another copy of *The World Is Flat*. I nod hello to the young female executive sitting next to me and pull out the book I have brought along. It's a thin essay by the 75-year-old Marxist intellectual Samir Amin that issues its own grim warnings about the future of our globalized world. Titled *The Liberal Virus: Permanent War and the Americanization of the World*, the cover photo shows a Chinese kid dressed in army fatigues, standing on the Wall of China holding a Coke can.[8]

If Thomas Friedman is the prophet of twenty-first century capitalism, then Samir Amin is his anti-Christ. But to hear Amin tell it, Friedman is the only one leading humankind into the depths of Hell. Writing from Dakar, Senegal where he runs the Third World Forum, Amin's thesis is essentially that liberalism, if allowed to continue on its path of creative destruction, will lead to an apocalyptic end. He likens the globalizing force of liberalism to a virus that has destroyed all ideological competitors and which is now making its final assault on its host species. According to Amin, the ethic of liberalism—"long live competition, may the strong win"—is now ravaging societies of the Third World, causing further "social alienation and pauperization of urban classes."[9]

It's nothing new from the far, far left. There are shelves full of books by anti-globalization writers from the developing world. What made me pick up Samir Amin's essay, though, was the striking specificity of his warning. In *Liberal Virus*, he argues that liberalism's most decisive effect will be to divide the world into an apartheid system that sees three billion peasant farmers pushed from their land and forced into the cities where they will die. This, he explains, will result from the implementation of a 2001 World

Trade Organization (WTO) mandate that all agricultural markets be opened to the expansion of commercial agribusiness producers. Without the ability to make a subsistence living from their own land, half the world's population will have to migrate to the urban centers where there is no work for them. And thus, he concludes, they will be trapped in an "organized system of apartheid" on a global scale.[10]

"What is going to become of these billions of human beings, already for the most part, the poor among the poor?" Amin asks. You don't have to be a red-blooded socialist to intuit his answer. "Capitalism," he concludes, "has become barbaric, directly calling for genocide." In this drive to satisfy the insatiable hunger for new markets of its Western clients, the WTO is sanctioning a process that will "destroy—in human terms—entire societies." Writing in a style that starkly contradicts Friedman's cheery cartoon of the flat world, Amin paints an ominous image of capitalism as a force that is in constant need to consume itself and the communities that lie in its path. Through his eyes, the agents of globalization bear an eerie resemblance to the Borg that battle *Star Trek*'s Jean Luc Picard and his Enterprise crew. American liberalism echoes the Borg with the claim that it only seeks to "improve the quality of life for all species" through the spread of democracy while simultaneously warning the world that "resistance is futile—you will be assimilated." But that is not to say Amin views liberalism as the victor. Rather, he describes it as a "senile system" that ultimately cannot stop the horror of its destiny.* [11]

---

* Perhaps it's fitting that Friedman places his journey in the tradition of the great "explorers." He begins his book by citing a passage from the diary of Christopher Columbus which states: "Your Highnesses, as Catholic Christians, and princes who love and promote the holy Christian faith, and are enemies of the doctrine of Mahomet, and of all idolatry and heresy, determined to send me, Christopher Columbus, to the above-mentioned countries of India, to see the said princes, people, and territories, and to learn their disposition and the proper method of converting them to our holy faith..." Friedman, *The World Is Flat*, p. 3.

Again, it isn't hard to find doomsday prophecies about the evils of capitalism. But what is interesting about Amin's book is that he offers an explanation for the phenomenal success of Friedman's ideas. Expanding his metaphor, Amin describes the liberal virus as one which "pollutes contemporary social thought and eliminates the capacity to understand the world, let alone transform it." So there is a kind of delusional episode occurring within the mass American psyche, one that has obscured what Amin terms "really-existing capitalism" and replaced it with a fictitious model based on an "imaginary capitalism." According to Amin, liberals like Thomas Friedman conjure the illusion of a system that is inherently just and self-regulating while, in reality, it only creates permanent instability and requires constant intervention and protection by the armored shield of the state. "The globalized 'liberal' economic order," he writes, "requires permanent war—military interventions endlessly succeeding one another—as the only means to submit the peoples of the periphery to its demands." [12]

I started reading Amin's book a few weeks after finishing *The World Is Flat.* And what struck me was that his description of the forces driving globalization was far closer to that of Sergeant Hollis, the tank commander I met in Iraq, than to Thomas Friedman's. What's more, his theory about the impact of the liberal virus on our ability to interpret the world drove me back into Friedman's book, where I found a quote that basically mirrors Amin's. Just before the halfway mark, Friedman writes: "The perspective and predispositions that you carry around in your head are very important in shaping what you see and what you don't see." [13] Of course, he's not applying this to himself. Rather, it's a blunt critique of the fearful, knee-jerk reactions that American politicians and union leaders have thrown up to "protect" the U.S. economy from a genuinely "open" market. But the point is that, as we well know, everyone is the captive of their perspective. It frames and defines our world-

view. Hence, for Friedman, the liberal business columnist, globalization = good, while for Amin, the African Marxist intellectual,
globalization = bad. And for millions of readers who aspire to be a
part of the new capitalist revolution, Friedman's vision is far more
appealing than Amin's. Who can blame them?

But what if he's wrong? What if Friedman is as short-sighted
and ill-informed as the military and government leaders who
claimed to have had no forewarning of the September 11 attacks?
Beyond the sheer tactical breakdown of that day, much of the blame
for the failure rests in a kind of voluntary blindness assumed by
a great majority of Americans. It was that myopia that prevented
so many brilliant and influential foreign policy analysts, defense
experts and journalists from foreseeing the coming threat. And
they continued to ignore the messages being sent from the developing world, collectively evading the difficult work of questioning
what aspects of American foreign policy might have brought
on such an attack, even after thousands of Mexican soccer fans
chanted "Osama" at a post-9/11 match against the United States.
Proving how little he has learned from his worldly travels, Friedman
repeats the hollow mantra in his book, describing the terrorists
as "angry, frustrated, and humiliated men and women."[14] And
not far behind them, in his estimation, are the anti-globalization
protesters—comprised mostly of Trotskyites, anarchists and old
hippies—who are influenced by a heavy dose of anti-Americanism
and defined by their denial of the inevitable triumph of flatness,
arguing over the moot point of *"whether we globalize."* Naturally,
Samir Amin is one of these people.

And herein lies the most troubling aspect of Friedman's
popularity. He, and his readers, assume that anyone who opposes
globalization from the side of the developing world—either
violently or ideologically—is driven by a deep sense of shame
at their poverty and inability to keep up with the West. But, at

least as it applies to Samir Amin, nothing could be further from the truth. What Amin is articulating is a detailed warning about the same globalized world for which Friedman is such a wide-eyed proponent. But Friedman, and the millions who buy his books, is immune to it, because from his perspective, the forces of liberalism have only left enriched and industrialized societies in their wake. And this is precisely the kind of shortsightedness that crippled the West's ability to understand, or indeed prevent, the 9/11 attacks. In the somber days after al Qaeda hit New York and Washington, DC, Americans like Friedman were unwilling to identify the causal forces that had inspired the terrorists. "Why do they hate us?" Friedman rhetorically asked in his column. Because of our freedom, he answered. Because, the liberal answered, we are liberals.[15]

It would be easy to attribute Friedman's blockbuster sales to his orgiastic, gee-whiz, look-ma-no-hands celebration of all things corporate—he never fails to name-drop his favorite brand names, from eating a Cinnabon while waiting to board a Southwest Airlines flight on the way to see his daughter at Yale to the 3M logo'd cap being worn by the caddy of an Indian executive who uses a distant HP skyscraper as a tee-off marker. Or to the fact that it is easy and very profitable to scare the shit out of an entire generation of Baby Boomers by essentially telling them their kids are in a neck-and-neck race to the top of the global food chain and, guess what, they're losing. In those respects, the book is a brilliant and well-conceived product. But I believe there is a much deeper significance to Friedman's success. And it has to do with the fact that America has reached a stage in its quest for global dominance in which it has no choice but to aggressively and openly tap these impoverished countries for cheap labor. And Thomas Friedman has come to put a lipstick smile on that old, twisted visage.

Scribbling notes on a drink coaster as the plane climbs past 10,000 feet, I think of Thomas Friedman writing his book in his own spacious business class seat on Lufthansa. Looking out of my window, I suddenly realize how he came so easily to his revelation. There, below me, the dark blue Atlantic Ocean stretches west for 1,000 miles and darned if it doesn't look flat. I wonder how much of Friedman's worldview has been shaped by the rarefied company of billionaire CEOs he keeps. Perhaps he has fooled himself into thinking that the invisible hand of liberal economics still softens to caress the weary shoulders of the poor, offering the opportunity for all people to reach the heights of corporate domination. We'll never know. What we do know is that it's been a long time since the champions of free market capitalism pretended to have any priority other than their quarterly profits and year-end bonuses. Of course, many of them have started making noises about the environment and poverty, but never in a way that will actually bring them to analyze root causes of these global ills. Until that happens, we can assume that it's mostly PR. And in this regard, Friedman plays a very important role as a kind of useful idiot. If capitalism is the sport of wolves, then the kind of happy-go-lucky globalization heralded by Thomas Friedman is the sheep's clothing. It's a sheath to cover the glint of their blade.

But what is the harm in a fictional version of capitalism? I have no reason to believe that Samir Amin's scary hypothesis has any more validity than Friedman's. But in a truly flat world, the kind of urban catastrophe that Amin is predicting would have more severe repercussions for all of us than 9/11. So it's worth visiting some aspects of globalization that Friedman omitted from his book. It's worth asking the kind of tough questions that have the most to do with the collective safety of the United States, primarily: What if the truth is that American capitalism is in decline and that globalization is just another facet of U.S. foreign policy, one that has become so welded to corporate interests that the War on Terror, as Sergeant Hollis implied, is just a means of extending the reach of American capital into crucial new markets? And what if it isn't shame and humiliation that is behind the developing world's increasingly stubborn resistance to American advances, but instead, a deep-seated fear at the sight of a remorseless, ravenous pack of wolves which will seemingly stop at nothing to get what it needs? Because it is one thing to be in the eye of the storm and quite another to be in its path, and desperate people will resort to desperate measures. The only question that remains is, who's more desperate: us or them?

MILITANT GLOBALIZATION

A few days after my return from London, I am on the phone with political scientist and Chancellor Professor (Emeritus) at the University of Massachusetts, Naseer Aruri. As a renowned commentator on human rights—appearing on television and radio networks across the spectrum, from CNN and NPR to PBS and al Jazeera—and a past board member of both Human Rights Watch and Amnesty International, Aruri is uniquely qualified to speak on the disconnect between Thomas Friedman and Samir Amin. In his first sentence, he is quick to warn me that focusing too much on the present course of the neoconservatives will give the impression that militarized globalization is a product of the recent Bush administration.[16]

"In undergraduate American foreign policy courses," he tells me, "the first thing you teach the students is about the bipartisan element in American foreign policy."

"But," I ask, "liberals and conservatives have always had very different views on how to exert American power in the world."

"Right," he answers patiently, "but, you know actually America has never ceased to be capitalist, right? It's been capitalist from day one, and, at least since let us say in the post-1945 period, it's been the business model that has guided American foreign policy in the world."

Clearly, capitalism is not the exclusive property of liberals or conservatives. In fact, it may be the one ideology that they both unequivocally champion. But that isn't to say there haven't been strong debates within the circles of American political power about the doctrine that would frame its exploits in the world. Aruri explains that back in 1956, when he took his first course in international relations, the argument was not between liberals and conservatives, but instead, realists and idealists.

In the pre-World War II era, foreign policy was defined by the idealism of Woodrow Wilson. Elected president in 1912, Wilson preached a humanist code, crafting an American mission to provide the world with a model of individual liberty, societal morality, and a democratic political structure. In his first inaugural, Wilson declared, "Men's hearts wait upon us; men's lives hang in the balance; men's hopes call upon us to say what we will do. Who shall live up to the great trust? Who dares fail to try? I summon all honest men, all patriotic, all forward-looking men, to my side." [17]

For many Americans, especially the soldiers who fought in First and Second World Wars, these were principles that warranted their sacrifice. But after World War II, the theme shifted away from the moralistic Wilsonian Idealism to a more practical vision. The most influential thinker of this period was Hans Morgenthau, a German political theorist who came to the University of Chicago in 1937 and forged a new school of thought based on his concept of Realism. The philosophy framed international relations as a struggle for power in which the determining factor was "national interest." In Morgenthau's words, it was an amoral vision that stressed "the rational, objective and unemotional." In this sense, Realism articulated the fundamental attributes of capitalism, integrating a corporatist philosophy within American foreign policy. [18]

But, Aruri tells me, even when the Wilsonian Idealism was guiding U.S. foreign policy, it was still driven by a single objective: expansion of its economic and military hegemony. Regardless of the dominant ideological force of the day, he continues, "the outcome was the same—the pursuit of what Hans Morgenthau and many other realists referred to as the 'national interest.' Wilsonian idealism, on the other hand, like today's neocons, rationalized military intervention in highly moralistic terms (eliminating terrorism) also in pursuit of the 'national interest.' " *

Of course, since the nation's founding, American foreign policy has also been the subject of a more polarized debate between "internationalists"—of which both the realists and idealists are part—and "isolationists." And Aruri does not diminish it. But the fact is that the isolationists, while vocal and, at times, newsworthy, have never had much impact on American policy nor the mass consciousness. As *Newsweek*'s Michael Hirsh wrote in the run-up to Iraq:

"In the end the internationalists have always dominated national policy. Even so, they haven't bragged about their globe-building for fear of reawakening the other half of the American psyche, our berserker [isolationism]. And so they have always done it in the most out-of-the-way places and with little ado." [19]

Hirsh is euphemistically referring to the many covert CIA operations in the '50s, '60s and '70s which were waged against nationalist leaders in the developing world who dared to challenge

---

* The ideological continuum that Aruri sees is corroborated by a remark made by retired U.S. General Jay Garner, who compared the seizing of Iraq to that of the Philippines in 1899. That earlier war, which was fought over three years and which is still considered one of the most violent in American history, was driven by an ideological belief in what Rudyard Kipling termed the "White Man's Burden," namely bringing modernity to less civilized nations. But what the Philippine-American war actually delivered were U.S. naval bases that it maintained through 1992. Of Iraq, Garner remarked, "Look back on the Philippines around the turn of the twentieth century: they were a coaling station for the navy, and that allowed us to keep a great presence in the Pacific. That's what Iraq is for the next few decades: our coaling station that gives us great presence in the Middle East."

American interests. While the justification for those murders and coups was always that of eliminating the potential spread of Communism, Aruri sees that as a cover.

"That was the post-1945 business model," he laughs. "Here we are talking about the Soviet threat, but in fact what was going on here is economic penetration in the Third World—trying to find resources in the Third World and get access to these resources."

Aruri pauses for a moment and then cites a laundry list of countries that were targets for intervention during the Cold War period: Allende in Chile, Arbenz in Guatamela, Mossadeq in Iran, Lumumba in Congo, Ortega in Nicaragua.

"You know, this kind of attack on nationalist leaders, the fact is that it was all really bipartisan. It would be difficult to say that the liberals (or the neoliberals) were more guilty of attacking nationalists under the guise of combating communism or containing communism than conservatives. It was pursued no matter who was in power."

In his 2003 book *Dishonest Broker*, Aruri traces what he calls an "amazing consistency" in U.S. policy toward the Middle East from 1945 to 2003. What began as a stated effort to fight off Communism lead to the bolstering of corrupt, murderous leaders like the Shah of Iran, Saddam Hussein in Iraq and the Saudi royal family who were allied with the U.S. against the rising tide of Arab nationalism that sought to reclaim their vast natural resources. The anti-communist rhetoric of that era, argues Aruri, "was really an attempt to camouflage the real goal, and that is the petroleum."[20]

But today the goal is more than just oil and natural gas. To sustain its economic growth, the U.S. must look past its own borders for new consumer markets and cheaper labor supplies. And the modern term for this quest is what Aruri calls "the non-threatening and rather benign 'globalization.'"

I ask what he thinks of Thomas Friedman's globalization

timeline which asserts that we are now in a 3.0 phase, in which individuals, not nations (1.0) or corporations (2.0), are driving transnational business.[21] I can almost hear Naseer Aruri shaking his head through the phone. "I disagree with Friedman on this issue. I think that the role of the state has become really to serve the corporations."

Aruri credits Bill Clinton with developing a philosophy that perfectly merged the dual interests of U.S. foreign policy and business interests. It was called "market democracy."

When "market democracy" is applied to U.S. foreign policy, it directly, overtly implies what Naseer Aruri terms "the economic rationale for the possible use of force." Where once democracy was something that Americans fought to make the world safe for—as in World War I—now it was something that was imposed to make nations safe for free market capitalism. The primacy of human rights remained, but it was no longer an emphasis on the rights of those in the target nation. Rather, as Aruri wrote near the end of Clinton's second term, "the humans whose rights are really being promoted and protected are executives of large corporations slated to reap the main benefit of trade legislation and the new foreign policy emphasis on the market, as well as the rights of their wealthy overseas partners who facilitate the marketing of their products." *[22]

These were the embryonic days of what would later come to be known as globalization. Of course, the term had been used long before that, but what Clinton's fusion of economic and political

---

* Speaking to the Council on Foreign Relations in 1996, Clinton's National Security Advisor Anthony Lake summed up the new philosophy in a way that almost directly responded to Samuel Huntington's challenge to find a new rationale for American power. "Halfway between the end of the Cold War and the dawn of a new century, our nation is at peace. Our economy is strong. The tide of market democracy is rising around the world, bringing freedom and prosperity to more people than ever before and new opportunities for us." Quote from Anthony Lake, "Remarks to the Fletcher School of Law and Diplomacy," April 25, 1996.

liberalism offered was a vision that could enfranchise a wider network of global institutions, including GATT, the World Trade Organization, the World Bank, the IMF, NATO, the EU and the Security Council. Now the post-Cold War era and its political generation had been given a *raison d'etre*. They became united around the goal of "integrating" nations within the global order through a highly developed basket of economic and political devices. Those leaders who opposed or, through their actions or policies, made the climate unsafe for the implementation of market democracy—like nationalists, Islamic fundamentalists, or ethnic combatants—were considered "fragmentary." Thus, integration and fragmentation became the new duality, replacing the Cold War dichotomy of capitalism and communism.

And while much of the work done under the banner of that early phase of globalization was done by bankers and trade analysts who developed economic models designed to open these national markets to American capital, the reality was that lurking behind it all was the military component.

"In those cases," Aruri says, "where the environment was not calm to the extent that was commensurate with the requirements of American business, then we would 'kick butt' as they say." *

"And it's justified—"

"Because," he interrupts, "we, with integration, are the good forces. I suspect that the unwillingness (or inability) of Friedman and like-minded liberals to make a connection between globalization and the War on Terror, avoiding any reference to economic motivations for the war, is due to a real feeling that the U.S. has a

* So when reports and images of Serbian troops ethnically cleansing Kosovar Albanians emerged, Clinton led the charge to overthrow Yugoslav leader Slobodan Milosevic. And while the issue of whether the bombing of Belgrade was motivated by humanitarianism or the cause of market democracy has been hotly debated, as I discuss later in the book, the one major outcome of that campaign was the integration of free market liberalism within a society and economy that was still gripped by its socialist legacy.

God-given right to much of Third World resources."

In this way, Friedman and the pro-war liberals have fallen back into the Wilsonian idealism of U.S. foreign policy. "Thus," Aruri continues, "when we invade Iraq, the coalition, which is presumed to be endowed with a superior mission, is pitted against backward and envious terrorists who resist change, democracy and modern values."

If this view of new millennial globalization seems to exist in an alternate universe from the one presented in Thomas Friedman's book, it does. While Friedman communicates to a daily readership of millions, the proponents of the war-as-globalization thesis rarely make it into the mainstream North American papers. Instead they are relegated to left-wing journals like the *Nation* and British papers like Alan Rusbridger's *Guardian*. And while the stars of this universe may not be able to draw the kind of audience that flock to Friedman's *The World Is Flat* hypothesis, they present a very persuasive case that he is the one living in a dream world.

NUTS AND BOLTS

Two months after the 9/11 terrorist attacks, I sat in a dark Manhattan theater listening to a woman sob quietly in the seat next to mine. She wasn't crying over the rubbled skyscrapers that used to stand just 20 blocks from here. Instead, it was the words of a Jamaican dairy farmer that had so deeply affected her. On the screen in front of us, Stephanie Black's documentary *Life and Debt* told the story of Jamaica's economic devastation under the policies of the World Bank and International Monetary Fund (IMF). The film is a powerful and eloquently-made exposition of the kind of globalization that is excluded from Thomas Friedman's Flat World thesis. In *Life and Debt*, we see the inner workings of a supposedly independent system of advisory and banking bodies that preys on weak developing nations in order to further the goals of its First World backers.

Perhaps the most strikingly unfair and tragic part of the film comes during an explanation of trade liberalization rules imposed on Jamaican dairy farmers during the Clinton era. While farmers in the U.S., Australia, New Zealand, and the European Union were allowed to continue heavily subsidizing their milk industry, the Jamaicans were forced to eliminate their own subsidies and reduce tariffs on foreign milk products. The result was that imports of powdered milk cost less than the Jamaican fresh milk supply. In a poor country where people can barely afford to feed their families, the powdered milk captured the market, forcing the Jamaican farmers to slaughter their cows and dump millions of dollars of unpasteurized milk.

When *Life and Debt* shows Stanley Fischer, deputy director of the IMF, being asked why Jamaica was forced to abandon its own trade barriers, he replies: "The reason is that Jamaica is a very small country. It's not a country that could thrive by producing only for itself. We believe very firmly that countries are going to grow better if they're integrated into the world economy and that means reducing tariffs. It needed to allow its importers and its people, access to goods from around the world rather than have them rely on this little," Fischer holds back a laugh, "little economy."

A farmer brings it all down to the bottom line. "The end of day result will be that we will have no national food security and that when milk powder finds its real cost, where there are no subsidies in Europe and North America, it will be more expensive than the milk we currently produce. What do we do in the meanwhile? We go out of business."[23]

Of course it wasn't just the milk industry that was targeted. The same fate has come to local potato, onion, ginger, and carrot farmers, many of whom, after generations of working their land, have had to find new jobs. Suddenly, Samir Amin's radical hypothesis of 3 billion subsistence farmers being forced to abandon their crops and head to the cities for work doesn't sound so hypothetical. The only thing standing between these forces of globalization— which are not part of the Flat World—and small developing nations are the leaders who govern them. And even when they are not the corrupt, larcenous types that the World Bank has historically been happy to deal with, so often there is simply no other choice for a government that sees its economy failing.

Michael Manley, the former Prime Minister of Jamaica, was faced with exactly this situation when the 1973 world oil crisis nearly crashed his national economy. Despite having campaigned on an anti-IMF platform in 1976, one year later he was forced to sign an IMF deal, an act he describes as "one of the bitter, traumatic experiences of my public life."* Today, Jamaica is still saddled with debt, one half of every tax dollar goes to pay off the interest on their loans. The cities are plagued with crime and the security industry is one of its fastest growing sectors. Near the end of the film, a confidential World Bank memorandum evaluating the success of the reforms confirms that after twenty-five years, "these loans achieved neither growth nor poverty reduction." [24]

Walking out of the theater I heard one man say to his female companion, "if it doesn't break your heart, then you don't have one." But all I could think about was that if some of those Jamaicans had access to the kind of money that Islamic militants do,

---

* At one point, Manley remembers, he attempted to bolster his failing agricultural sector by giving farmers loans at 10 percent interest. But the IMF would not allow it. Manley traveled twice to Washington to protest the policy, saying "it is wrong economic policy, it is wrong socially! It is wrong to say that we must force the farmers to pay that rate of interest or you won't lend us the money. And I remember saying, 'which of you will face an American farmer and tell him that to borrow something for his farm, he'd have to pay 23 percent? I said they'd run you out of the White House and out of Congress.' Oh, they said, 'that's their business, we're dealing with your business.'" *Life and Debt*, directed by Stephanie Black (Tuff Gong Pictures, 2001).

they would have been just as driven to fly 747s into any building called the World Trade Center. It is precisely this side of "world trade"—which remains beyond the understanding of average Americans—that provides the foundation for the alternate vision of globalization presented by Samir Amin and Naseer Aruri. It is precisely these austere programs of "structural adjustment" imposed on nations like Jamaica that not only pushed them further from financial autonomy by crippling them with unmanageable debt, but also placed them in a new kind of dependence that reeked of the same kind of racism as that which dominated the colonial era.

As Charles Lewis of the Center for Public Integrity remarked in Eugene Jarecki's award-winning film *Why We Fight*, "It's basically economic colonialism. No one uses the colonialism word, but instead of just taking over the countries, we have a better way. We just go in and have free markets. Whether we are trying to sell our products to their citizens or mine their resources, we need to be in that country for some reason and therefore we're going to talk about free markets and free trade. But what's really going on is we want our countries to get rich in your country."[*][25]

My conversation with Naseer Aruri provided a good foundation for understanding the broad strokes of the militant globalization thesis. But to get a sense of the mechanics, I turn to Naomi Klein, author of Generation X's most successful political softcover, *No Logo*. In a short conversation, Klein explains that it was precisely because these IMF and World Bank-authored free trade policies—otherwise known as the Washington consensus— have been so disastrously wrong that the U.S. is now forced to use

---

* Another quote from Charles Lewis in *Why We Fight*: "We have a process that has a seamlessness, where the corporate interests that stand to benefit are so intertwined and interwoven with the political forces that the financial elites and the political elites have become the same people." *Why We Fight*, directed by Eugene Jarecki (Charlotte Street Film, 2006).

military force in order to open new markets.[26]

"The market," she smiles, "finds itself in a situation where its usual suppliers, its usual dealers, are cutting it off. That's what is happening in Latin America. When attempts to privatize energy and water in Bolivia are resisted, when huge popular movements are saying 'we don't want the free trade area of the Americas,' when poor countries banded together and said 'we'd rather have no deal than a bad deal.' That means that they're getting cut off."

According to Klein, the old system of using the WTO or IMF to coerce trade agreements from desperate leaders was "free trade lite." But the new framework is entirely different. It has been upgraded to one she refers to as "free trade at a barrel of a gun, or free trade supercharge."

"I believe that the goal of this war was to bomb, into being, a new free trade zone," Klein tells me. "Precisely because of the enormous backlash against these economic policies by countries that have already adopted them. Capitalism functions like a drug addict. The drug is growth. It needs growth to survive. It needs growth to expand."

So, forcing regime change in Iraq was conceived as a means to open a new market that could produce income for American companies. "Not just oil," Klein says, "but water, roads, schools, hospitals, private jails, anything that can be turned into a commodity and sold."

Moreover, with the supercharge model, American free traders were able to achieve in Iraq what took them three decades to engineer in Latin America: the wholesale privatization of the national economy.

"In a single day," Klein explains, "[Director of Reconstruction] Paul Bremer passed a set of policies that literally usually take three decades to get passed. Iraq's economy was protected, somewhat. In Iraq's constitution it very clearly says that there are sectors of the economy which are considered essential services and not open to privatization. Not just oil, but water and so on. And it also says that Iraqi businesses cannot be foreign-owned—very clear rules embedded in Iraq's constitution."

"On September 19, 2003 Bremer introduced Order 39, which overturned Iraq's constitution. It allowed 100 percent foreign ownership of Iraqi businesses and it put 200 Iraqi state companies up for privatization, up for sale. And it also said that companies coming into Iraq can take 100 percent of their profits out of the country. It also gave them a massive tax break. Bigger than anything Bush has been able to achieve. The top tax bracket in Iraq before Order 39 was 45 percent, which is what it is in Canada. It's now a 15 percent flat tax. So this is an economic overhaul. It is shock therapy. It has already led to 70 percent unemployment. And we're not hearing about it."

Klein points to the constant and extensive media coverage of the military aspect of the occupation, which generally paints the situation in a negative light. But seen in the context of the liberal economic model that has been implemented, this is a smokescreen to cover up the fact that it has been a complete success. She quotes Republican Senator John McCain who described Iraq as a "pot of honey that's attracting a lot of flies," adding, "and we know what the honey is. And we know who the flies are: Bechtel, Halliburton and MCI. And they're having a field day."

I ask her if this new free trade supercharge is the new template for globalization.

She nods and says something that is truly radical. "But that doesn't render the old model obsolete. Because the other countries see this, see what happens when you don't cooperate and that makes their trade negotiations a little bit easier. So I think that the free trade lite and this free trade supercharge work hand-in-hand."

I'd love to hear Thomas Friedman's response to that. Unfortunately we won't be treated to a debate between Friedman and Naomi Klein anytime soon. Friedman seems to ignore the young upstart, but maybe that's because she refers to him as "the White House's unofficial brand manager." So we, the ones out here in the peanut gallery, are stuck between two extremes, two mutually exclusive narratives. The problem is that, in a world that has become polarized between good and evil, Islam and Christianity, globalization and anti-globalization, most people seem to be satisfied to live with their own familiar version of the truth. This is a phenomenon that the great American economic theorist John Kenneth Galbraith elaborated in *The Affluent Society*.

"Because economic and social phenomena are so forbidding," he writes, "or at least so seem, and because they yield so few hard tests of what exists and what does not, they afford to the individual a luxury not given by physical phenomena. Within a considerable range, he is permitted to believe what he pleases."

This resignation, as Galbraith put it, to "associate truth with convenience," is a trait that isn't relegated to liberals or conservatives, layman or academics. We all have a yearning to see our view of the world corroborated in the ideas of others, especially those more famous than ourselves. To describe these widely acceptable and predictable ideas, Galbraith coined the term "conventional wisdom." He likened the act of listening to conventional wisdom to a religious experience, one that grants its audience a form of "affirmation like reading aloud from the Scriptures or going to church."[27]

So now we have been inside both temples. At least two very well constructed structures that frame two very specific, if not antagonistic, views of American-led corporate globalization. But have they brought us any closer to knowing whether Thomas Friedman's benign vision is more valid than Samir Amin's, or Naseer

Aruri's or Sergeant Hollis's vision of militant globalization? No. All we have are two competing conventional wisdoms. And, if we are to believe John Kenneth Galbraith, they should make us equally wary. So, in the effort not to drown in the electric Kool Aid of the anti-Friedman camp, I decided the next part of my journey would focus on finding someone who could tear down that wall and bring me closer to understanding "true" globalization.

ROUND PEG, SQUARE HOLE

"Well, on the left it's an article of faith that corporate globalization and the war are connected," Mark Engler tells me during a phone conversation from his Brooklyn office. "In that sense, it's just in the water, okay? Everyone feels it. And it's not unfounded because, I think, in a deep way they're definitely connected but the way we try to talk about those connections is way too shallow and, in a lot of ways, is wrong."[28]

Engler is a widely published journalist and policy analyst who made waves within the anti-globalization camp with his 2004 article titled "The War and Globalization: Are They Really Connected?" While he clearly admires writers like Naomi Klein and Arundhati Roy, he takes them to task in the article for simplifying the complex relationships between members of the business class and George Bush's neoconservative advisors in order to fit the war-is-globalization thesis. "These activists risk reading causality into tangential relationships," says Engler, arguing that conservative groups are not monolithic co-conspirators and the war in Iraq has been as unpopular with many top global business leaders as it has with the Cindy Sheehan gang.[29] In fact, aside from a few billion dollar contracts awarded to companies with close ties to the Bush administration, the adversarial, unilateral approach taken by the neoconservative authors of the conflict has deeply rattled the multinational consensus that is the framework and foundation for the globalization effort.

Ironically, Engler believes it is the Left's own disorganization and disunity that distorts its view of the divisions within the world's financial and political elite. The activists believe that since the corporate globalizers are winning, they must have their house in order. But, Engler tells me, that is simply not an accurate perception.

"We assume that capital is a monolith, it's always united, it's always a fist. The fact of the matter is that's not true. There's always competing interests among the global elite, there's always fractures within capitalism, especially at this moment, where you have that Clinton model of corporate globalization that was working very well for everyone, it was a very profitable period for everyone. And that's being trashed by these neocons in the Bush administration." *

Engler insists that it's flawed logic that frames the Iraq war as something designed primarily to create a free trade bonanza to benefit Western corporations. "And this goes against what Naomi Klein is arguing when she talks about military intervention as the next stage of neoliberalism," Engler explains in a confident tone. "And I'm going to say it's not a next stage of neoliberalism."

Pushing back with the thrust of Naomi Klein's argument, I ask about the wholescale neoliberal upgrade of Iraq's economy. Citing Paul Bremer's introduction of Article 39 into the interim Iraqi constitution, Engler admits that Klein has a valid point.

"It definitely is the case that they've implemented neoliberalism through this military arm," he says, "Now, the problem with this argument, where it runs into problems, is when we get back to

---

* While Anthony Lake was busy constructing Clinton's vision for "market democracy" from his office in the West Wing, Larry Summers had left his post as chief economist at the World Bank to join the Treasury Department. According to Engler, Summers was instrumental in framing the "rules-based global order" that would act as a united front for capital under the vision of corporate globalization.

the fundamental question: Did they invade Iraq in order to implement neoliberalism? And again, I would say the answer is no."

"But of all the plans we had for Iraq and reconstruction," I interject, "the new economic system seems like the one thing that they actually followed through on."

"Look," Engler answers, "once they've taken over the country, they're going to bring in a capitalist economy. And, of course, because the people involved are total ideologues, they're going to put in a very extreme neoliberal economy. To me that was more opportunistic than anything else. But they didn't invade Iraq in order to do that. And, you see, the logical extension of [Naomi's] argument is that neoliberalism, through the IMF and World Bank, has reached its limits, and therefore you need to have direct military intervention. That is the next stage of neoliberalism. So basically any recalcitrant country that will not implement neoliberalism will be invaded and will have neoliberalism forced upon them. I don't buy it."

"Why not?" I ask.

"Three reasons," he answers. "First, if you talk about the real cause of war, I think you have to take the neocons at face value."

Engler argues that instead of trying to divine some corporate-driven motive behind Bush's Iraq adventure, we should take the neoconservatives at their word. Their stated goal is to gain a foothold in a strategically important region of the Middle East. While open access to Iraqi oil is a benefit of the invasion and certainly achieves the objective of becoming less reliant on Saudi Arabian or Iranian oil, the larger vision is based on a quest to secure American economic hegemony for the next half century and beyond.

"I think that's a perfectly sensible reason for war from their perspective," Engler explains, "and it's a much deeper type of argument than just to say 'well, we did it for oil.' So in this context, that argument about war profiteering becomes a footnote. It's not the cause of war and the Left's argument really falls flat."

The second reason he rejects the idea that the invasion of Iraq represents a new phase in neoliberalism is that global capital is against the war. It wasn't just European banks and traders—whose CEO's loudly voiced their objections to Bush's Iraq strategy at the 2003 World Economic Forum in Davos a few months before the war—that stood to lose, but also companies like Disney and Coca-Cola, which depend heavily on the quotient of goodwill that America secures from the rest of the world. Most modern corporate CEOs prefer what Bill Gates has called "frictionless capitalism," one that, in effect, says, 'let's shred hierarchies, love the environment and just all get along.' And this goes for a majority of the companies in the financial and services sectors that trade on Wall Street. As Engler explains, "these people may be very Republican in certain ways; they like Bush's tax cuts obviously. But in terms of this aggressive militarist foreign policy, do they think that's going to be good for the markets? No. Wall Street was very skeptical of Bush."

Engler asserts the occupation has had a negative effect on the globalization project. He describes the neoconservatives as a political aberration that have divided the global business community and created the potential for trade wars that could further cripple the U.S. economy. "Actually," Engler writes in his article, "much of the business elite would prefer Clinton's multilateralist globalization to Bush's imperial version."

I cite Naseer Aruri's contention that, while there may be disagreements between the neoliberals and the neoconservatives, in the end U.S. foreign policy is part of a long-term bipartisan drive to satisfy the national interest. I ask him if it mightn't just be a case of Bush sacrificing international harmony to promote and protect the interests of American corporations.

"Look, Bush is a sectoral president. He's good for Big Arms, he's good for Big Oil, he's good for the Halliburtons. But was the

Iraq war a war for Disney? Was the Iraq war a war for Coca-Cola? You've got to ask yourself these questions. Look at the markets they're going after and ask yourself what they had to gain by that.

"This is where Bill Clinton is a much better capitalist than George Bush," Engler says, reminding me that Clinton presided over "one of the longest upswings of a business cycle in the last hundred years." That was a period when the world was generally at peace with America and no one was burning down KFC and Taco Bell.

"But now, the whole world has turned from an attitude of goodwill toward the United States to an attitude of anger and revulsion. That's very bad for the Coca-Colas and the Disneys of the world. That's why I think you'll find a schism in capital here. Especially in terms of how to manage our foreign policy." *

"But," I ask, "obviously corporate America benefits from the neocons' long term plan for America."

"Maybe. But corporate America doesn't look at the 50-year picture. Corporate America looks at their next quarter profits. If you're telling me that your strategy for Disney is for the United States to enter into a trade war with Europe or to antagonize huge portions of the Muslim world—which are both things the Bush administration at various times has been willing to do—it's in direct contradiction to their corporate strategy, which is to increase market share, to create better access to those external markets, which are massive. And those can, oftentimes, conflict with the neocons' goal."

The third argument Engler makes against the Naomi Klein's war-is-globalization thesis is complicated, but significant in its

* Indeed, the *Washington Post* reported on March 23, 2003, that: "Discord over the Iraq War is putting uncomfortable strains on economic links between the United States and Europe, a relationship that many view as a cornerstone of global prosperity. Guardians of transatlantic harmony are scrambling to keep the diplomatic rift from poisoning economic ties." Quote from "Anxiety Over Trade Rift Grows," *Washington Post*, March 23, 2003, A12.

verdict for the anti-globalization movement. According to Engler, even if Klein is right and the goal of invading Iraq was to institute a so-called capitalist paradise, the unilateral invasion and subsequent quagmire and global divide it has created is simply "bad capitalism" and there is little support for doing it again. Hence it cannot be the new phase of anything. Instead, as he says, it is a throwback to an older version of imperial globalization, the kind that Thomas Friedman refers to as Globalization 1.0.

More important, however, is Engler's contention that while the Bush administration has been treating the multilateral institutions like they have exhausted their value, they are, in fact, still viable means of accomplishing neoliberal goals. As he wrote in his "War and Globalization" article, "the more subtle mechanisms of corporate globalization—i.e., conditions imposed by the International Monetary Fund (IMF) and World Bank—are still functioning quietly and effectively, constraining the potentially autonomous economic policy of countries like Brazil, for example."[30] So the danger lies in falling into the trap of the duality, of reacting so negatively to the Bush agenda that the Left allows the pendulum to swing back to the old Clinton globalization model, which has never gone away.

Engler believes this is exactly what will happen and admits that, after years of campaigning against the World Bank, IMF and WTO, suddenly the Left has entered a kind of *Twilight Zone* in which their strongest allies are the neoconservatives.

"Now we have these strange bedfellows on the right who also don't believe in having these institutions make policy for us. And then we have some influential voices in the anti-globalization movement changing their position on these institutions. They're saying, 'I was wrong to be saying that we should get rid of these institutions altogether.'"

I get the sense he is implying that Bush's policies have indirectly fortified the credibility of the neoliberal institutions. By creating a false dichotomy, a good cop and bad cop as it were, people who are seeking a more just form of globalization will be tricked into believing they must choose between the two. He points to liberal strongholds like Air America Radio and MoveOn.org, which are so anti-Bush that they have started to embrace Clinton-era globalization and foreign policy architects as the only viable alternative. In his article, Engler warns that "because there are many who will oppose George Bush while eagerly anticipating a return to the high times of an earlier neoliberalism, the struggle to build an alternative globalization will continue..."

In other words, we have to be careful not to get caught in a game of lesser evils that will make the benign globalization thesis of Thomas Friedman and Bill Gates—the "frictionless" globalization—seem like the most attractive model. By focusing too closely on the teeth-baring wolves who have driven America into the Middle East, we are in danger of losing sight of those who have the same ferocious imperial drive, but who come in a more deceptive package. For within the grey, shadowy realm that sits between the two visions of globalization, there exists a cadre of analysts and bankers who work to further the mission of U.S. hegemony but are not subject to the laws or scrutiny of the American government or its people. These men and women have created systems that have the appearance of altruism and relief, but which in fact are only designed to further entrap and enslave the nations of the developing world. It is to these economic hit men that I turned my focus next.

BITTERSWEET SYMPHONY

On July 2, 2005, ten simultaneous Live 8 concerts were held across the world to raise awareness of African poverty. Timed to coincide with the twentieth anniversary of his original Live Aid concert, Bob Geldof hoped the event would pressure leaders of the G8 countries (UK, France, Germany, Italy, Japan, U.S., Canada and Russia) into canceling the debt of the world's most impoverished nations. Though it has never been easy to get politicians to do anything for the poor, Geldof felt his chances were good since he had the ear of the G8's new president, UK prime minister Tony Blair.

Back in 1985, when he was still an aspiring socialist and junior member of the British Labour party, Tony Blair attended Live Aid.* Years later, he told Bob Geldof that the experience had shaped his vision of African policy and so, in 2004, Geldof persuaded Blair to head an examination of African poverty and the role the international community has played in its tragic history. The study was titled the Blair Commission for Africa and focused on debt relief and increased aid as the most direct means of alleviating the "living wound" of Africa's plight.[31] The next step, Blair and Geldof decided, would be to convince the leaders of the world's richest nations to commit to the Blair Commission program. And what better way to force these politicians into a deal than to get a billion people involved in the process. So, as Blair got set to host the G8 summit at a golf course in Scotland, Geldof called Bono, Madonna and Pink Floyd, set up his speakers in London's Hyde Park and invited the world to the show.

I sat among "thousands of millions," as Bob Geldof put it, watching the concerts from their homes. Switching between MTV and AOL's live-to-net broadcast of the concerts in London, Paris, Berlin, Toronto, Philly, Rome, I hummed along with a roster of

---

* "I am a socialist not through reading a textbook that has caught my intellectual fancy, nor through unthinking tradition, but because I believe that, at its best, socialism corresponds most closely to an existence that is both rational and moral. It stands for cooperation, not confrontation; for fellowship, not fear. It stands for equality." Quote from Tony Blair, British House of Commons, July 6, 1983.

stars that, as much as they tried, just couldn't muster the earnest save-the-world insurgent spirit that had made Live Aid such a global phenomenon. Watching Kate Moss's then-boyfriend Pete Doherty wander deliriously onto the stage and then barely get through a shrill rendition of T-Rex's classic "Children of the Revolution" seemed like the symbolic moment. For a generation that has the world at its fingertips, which truly lives in a virtual global village, they have less sensitivity and connection to the plight of starving Africans than the kids did 20 years ago.

Sure, everyone wore their white wristbands, cosmetic evidence of their unity with the campaign to Make Poverty History. But in a development that was representative of the disconnect between the glossy, star-driven first world campaign and the soul-draining struggle of the global poor, it was later reported that millions of the bands were produced in Chinese sweatshops where workers are paid 25 cents an hour.[32] As usual, the intentions were good, but you know what they say about the road to hell. And the irony wasn't lost on many in the Western media. When Geldof announced the concerts on CNN, declaring they were "dealing with the roots of that poverty," critics assailed him for assembling a "hideously white" roster that only included two African-born performers. Many saw it as a ploy to raise the sagging profile of old, unfashionable rock stars like The Who, Paul McCartney and Duran Duran, while others charged that it was the rock stars who were being used by the G8 politicians.

Bono brushed off the latter criticism, saying "Is there some degree of being used here? Yes. But I am not a cheap date, and neither is Bob Geldof."[33] Which may well be true. As a result of the Live 8 and Make Poverty History campaigns, the G8 agreed to cancel the debt of the world's eighteen poorest nations and double 2004 levels of aid to Africa from U.S. $25 to U.S. $50 billion by the year 2010.[34] But when this failed to impress the very people Live 8 was created to benefit, neither Bono nor Geldof had any snappy comebacks.

"One should not be surprised," wrote the African scholar Samir Amin in his *Liberal Virus*, "that at the very moment when capitalism appears to be completely victorious, 'the fight against poverty' has become an unavoidable obligation of the rhetoric of the dominant groups." [35]

It's something that the Western media missed entirely. Here we were, fifteen years after end of the Cold War, long after capitalism has been declared the world's ideological victor, still focused on world poverty. And, with a situation in Africa no better than twenty years ago when the last world aid music event was held. Now, of course, many would say that it is not the fault of liberalism that African countries have not been able to institute sustainable fiscal policies. And that would be true if there wasn't a long legacy of liberal economic intervention on the continent of Africa, much of it designed around the goal of relieving poverty. So what's wrong with this picture?

Samir Amin claims that for representatives of the World Bank, IMF and rock stars like Bono and Bob Geldof, poverty is only ever seen as an empirical measurement, one that can be conquered through mathematical reasoning. Increase aid, remove the debt... problem solved.[36] But this is just rock star economics. The reason nothing has changed for Africans since the last time Geldof and Bono beamed their message into hundreds of millions of homes worldwide is that they have been sucked into playing the game of the G8 leaders. They discuss poverty without challenging the methods and mechanisms that generate it.

Now, for Amin the Marxist, the foundations of African poverty are a deep and winding road, produced mostly from the evils of capitalism. But it wasn't just the far left that was questioning Live 8. Two weeks after the concerts, the *New York Times* published an op-ed by Cameroonian journalist Jean-Claude Shanda Tonme which essentially built on Amin's criticism, but from a different perspective.

"Our anger is all the greater because," Tonme wrote, "we didn't hear anyone at Live 8 raise a cry for democracy in Africa. Africa's real problem is the lack of freedom of expression, the usurpation of power, the brutal oppression... Don't they understand that fighting poverty is fruitless if dictatorships remain in place?"[37]

At a time when the armies of America and Britain are supposedly fighting anti-democratic insurgents in Iraq and Afghanistan, these words should have stung the eyes of pro-war liberals who applauded the debt relief program as a crucial step toward ending poverty.

"Neither debt relief nor huge amounts of food aid nor an invasion of experts will change anything," wrote Tonme in the *Times*. "Those will merely prop up the continent's dictators... We would have preferred for the musicians in Philadelphia and London to have marched and sung for political revolution."[38]

But revolution is hardly the kind of thing that Geldof's government-friendly spectacle was designed to inspire. The closest anyone got was a Versace-clad Madonna singing "Music makes the people come together. Music makes the bourgeoisie and the rebels come together." And there's good reason for that. Because revolution in countries like Cameroon, Chad and Togo would demand overthrowing leaders who have a long relationship with the IMF and World Bank. Leaders who, according to former contractor who worked in the developing world, are given huge sums of money that are never expected to be repaid "because the nonpayment is what gives us our leverage, our pound of flesh."[39]

GANGSTER ECONOMICS

John Perkins was recruited by the National Security Administration (NSA) and then put to work as an analyst for the international consulting firm of Chas T. Main. It was there, as he describes in his bestselling book, *Confessions of an Economic Hit Man*, that he became one of the titular assassins, or EHMs as they were known in the industry. His job was to create optimistic financial projections for developing countries that would justify huge IMF and World Bank loans. Though the money was supposedly lent to recipient nations for infrastructural development, much of it never left the United States since it went directly to Main or other U.S. construction and engineering companies like Bechtel or Halliburton which were contracted to do the work. More importantly, Perkins writes in *Confessions*, he would bring in such high loans that it would drive the countries bankrupt and they would be "forever beholden to their creditors, and... would present easy targets when they needed favors, including military bases, UN votes, or access to oil and other natural resources." [40]

From 1971–80, Perkins worked in key, mineral-rich nations like Indonesia, Iran, Saudi Arabia, Colombia, and Ecuador. His conscience-free manipulation of statistics and long-term financial projections brought huge contracts to his firm and he was quickly promoted to partner, the youngest in the company's hundred-year history. But his motivation was not solely financial. He was trained to see the work as critical to the fight against Communism; by channeling American dollars into these poor nations, they would not fall into the trappings of Marxism. [41]

But soon cracks began to form in the veneer. In 1977, while working in Tehran under the U.S.-supported Shah, he was brought to a clandestine meeting at the edge of the desert. There he met a man who had been tortured by the Iranian security service, SAVAK. The man told Perkins that the Shah was as fascistic and bloodthirsty as Hitler, responsible for the death of thousands and, he explained, "with the full knowledge and support of your government." He warned Perkins that the Shah would be overthrown by a fundamentalist coup and that contractors like Chas T. Main would not be paid. At first Perkins did not believe him. He, and all the Americans working in Iran, were convinced that the shah was loved by his people. But two days after he left Iran—when he was ushered out of the country by an old friend—the Shah fell and the Islamist Revolution of Ayatollah Khomeini swept through the country in the fall of 1979. In a fury of anti-Americanism, Muslim students stormed the U.S. Embassy in Tehran taking seventy hostages and beginning the fourteen month standoff that helped usher in the Reagan administration.

Of the experience, Perkins wrote, "Iran illustrated beyond any doubt that the United States was a nation laboring to deny the truth of our role in the world. It seemed incomprehensible that we could have been so misinformed about the Shah and the tide of hatred that had surged against him." [42] But they were. Just as so many Americans, influenced by Thomas Friedman's happy-go-lucky vision of globalization, were shocked by the sense of relief that rippled through much of the developing world after 9/11.

Speaking to Perkins on a quiet Sunday, he explains that this collective naivety about America's legacy in the third world isn't solely the fault of the people. [43]

"It is amazing," he sighs, "I want to use the word 'conspiracy,' but it isn't a conspiracy because it's not illegal. But there is an incredible array of tools and institutions set up in this country to keep us from understanding what's really going on in the world. It starts in our education system, in the first grade or before that, where we are told about the ideals of this country and how we support them everywhere we go. We are taught to perceive all of our actions as altruistic."

And even when the darker truth is allowed to filter into our minds, that no man, no country does anything for entirely charitable reasons, then there is the second layer of the brainwash: that what we do in the world will always be of benefit to the other party. But as Perkins ascended to the higher realms of power, becoming one of the most powerful economic hit men in the world, he realized that his work was only enriching corrupt leaders who then scattered the crumbs of their graft into the public coffers. Worse, the industrial parks and power plants his firm built only further entrenched these men in power by creating the illusion of great political and economic leadership.

"It's a sham, it's a subterfuge," he says solemnly.

Perkins views the recent pledges by the G8 to Make Poverty History as the latest chapter in this legacy of economic entrapment.

"This program to forgive debt in eighteen nations, with another twenty-two on the back burner, that's an amazing tool of economic hit men. I believe totally in debt forgiveness, but this is not about debt forgiveness. Every one of those countries is being asked to allow American corporations or international corporations to privatize their electric and water systems and many of their other resources. They are asked to accept the trade barriers we have in the United States and the other G8 countries and yet not keep their own trade barriers to protect their markets from our products. So we are using this debt forgiveness ploy as a way to get them more entrenched in the empire. It's a very, very subtle and effective economic hit man tool and yet, most people don't seem to realize that."

Just one month after the G8 leaders made their highly publicized vow to cancel debt for the poorest eighteen countries, a document leaked from the World Bank severely undermined the credibility of their promise.* Penned by Geoff Lamb, the bank's vice president for concessional finance, the document explained that "most countries receiving 100 percent debt cancellation would be classified as 'green light' and therefore become eligible for new borrowing." Even more damning is Lamb's reference to a G8 document instructing that those nations receiving debt relief should be "eased into new borrowing." [44] According to Perkins, this borrowing will then funnel right back into projects earmarked for Western companies.

Commenting on the leak, Dave Timms of the World Development Movement (WDM) said the World Bank was essentially "asking the executive directors how quickly they can get the countries that receive debt relief back into patterns of borrowing and back into debt." A World Bank spokesman dismissed the controversy, describing the document as "an informal and preliminary presentation." [45]

So much for debt relief. As former Jamaican prime minister Michael Manley explained in *Life and Debt*, most poor countries cannot get loans from private banks, so they are forced to deal with the IMF and World Bank. And the cycle begins again.

But what about Perkins's assertion that, as a condition of the debt relief, these countries would be forced into privatizing their resources and lowering trade barriers? A quick glance at the Blair Commission report, the UK government's analysis of African poverty that formed the basis for Bob Geldof's partnership with Tony Blair in Live 8, is telling. Its opening line states that, "for its part, Africa must accelerate reform." Reform, of course, is a code

---

* The World Bank document was circulated by The Jubilee Debt Campaign and the World Development Movement (WDM), two non-governmental organizations dedicated to poverty relief. In a joint statement, they warned "the Bank's analysis shows that it is exploring the conditions under which debt repayments would be re-imposed on those countries." Quote from "G8 Debt Relief Could Lead to New Borrowing" US Network for Global Economic Justice, August 2, 2005.

word for privatization. Clearly, despite all the nice talk, this is still the modus operandi for the neoliberal forces of globalization. In September 2005, a report published by WDM showed that of the IMF and World Bank's official poverty reduction strategy papers (PRSPs), which enforce conditions for debt relief, loans and aid on a country-to-country basis, "90 per cent contain privatisation measures... and over 70 per cent include trade liberalisation." Trade liberalization is another euphemism for lowering of trade barriers.[* 46]

Finally, I decided to do a random check on one African country that was scheduled for debt relief—the *New York Times* op-ed writer Jean-Claude Shanda Tonme's beloved Cameroon. In October 2005, just four months after Live 8, Cameroon announced that it "plans to privatise its state airline, water utility and telecommunications company as part of an IMF-backed economic reform programme aimed at obtaining debt relief."[47]

It took me less than half an hour to Google all of the above data and double check it for verification. How can a massively influential icon like Bono not spend the time to understand the deceptive game of debt relief before lending his name to the effort? How will history judge him when people find out the proposed charity is a ruse to further entrench the poor countries while simultaneously rehabilitating the reputations of the G8 and the multilateral institutions?

Perkins suggests that one of the reasons people cannot identify the system's exploitive design—even when it seems to be proposing solutions—is that they are directly benefiting from it.

---

* A report from Council on Hemispheric Affairs explained the G8 "debt relief" scheme this way: "Candidates seeking debt relief are caught in a classic Catch-22 dilemma: in order to relieve poverty they must institutionalize the circumstances that created it in the first place. This compromise does not end when external debts are finally relieved. Rather, countries must continue to conform to IMF/World Bank expectations in order to win the good credit ratings that are the password for attracting foreign investments." Quote from "Latin American Debt Relief, Less Than Meets the Eye," September 18, 2005.

"You know, it's also true that most of us lead very good lives because of this system. In fact, five percent of the world population, us, is consuming over 25 percent of the world's resources. And even our poorest people, for the most part, live pretty good lives compared to millions of other people around the planet, who live much worse lives."

When you are the prime beneficiary of that system of exploitation, it is easy to fall into the trap of justifying it. One part of Mark Achbar's acclaimed documentary, *The Corporation*, deals with the issue of sweatshop labor. One activist group rummaged through the garbage bins of some Indonesian factories and discovered Nike documents showing the workers were getting an average of three tenths of one percent of the retail price of the goods. Activists called this "the science of exploitation."[48] But Michael Walker, an economist and corporate consultant at the Fraser Institute, had another perspective.

"Let's look at it from a different point of view. Let's look at it from the point of view of the people in Bangladesh, who are starving to death, the people in China, who are starving to death, and the only thing they have to offer to anybody that is worth anything is their low-cost labor. And, in effect, what they are saying to the world is," Walker starts waving his arms as if holding a large flag, 'Come over and hire us, we will work for ten cents an hour, because ten cents an hour will buy us the rice we need not to starve and come and rescue us from our circumstance.' And so when Nike comes in they are regarded by everyone in the community as an enormous godsend."[49]

Thomas Friedman once bragged that the conditions were so good at a Sri Lankan Victoria's Secret factory that he'd let his daughters work there. He was joking of course, but the implication is, like that of the Michael Walker, by bringing low-cost work to impoverished nations, we are doing them a favor. But for the people who live in those countries, who have no choice but to toil as seamstresses under strict production quotas making two dollars a day, it feels like slavery. John Perkins says it's worse.

"In fact, those corporations are paying that person less than what slaves in pre-Civil War plantations made, in real terms. If those slaves were given room and board for themselves and their families, they were, for the most part, kept fairly healthy. It was the plantations' benefit to keep them healthy. In third world sweatshops, where they make two dollars a day, people cannot feed and house their families on those incomes. And they don't get healthcare. If they get sick or die, they are just replaced by another worker. So in many respects, what our corporations are doing today around the world is much worse than what our plantations were doing in this country before the Civil War."

But while the Civil War was fought, to some extent, over ending slavery, in our modern political society the exploitation of developing nations is a bipartisan enterprise. Politicians in both the Republican and Democratic parties are funded and controlled by large corporations that will go anywhere in the world to extract mineral resources or find cheap sources of labor. And, as John Perkins explains in *Confessions*, it is the job of economic hit men to use multilateral institutions like the World Bank and IMF to pry their way in.

According to Perkins, this nexus between corporations, the U.S. government and the EHMs was embodied in Robert McNamara, the World Bank president from 1968–1981. McNamara had already been the CEO of Ford Motor Company before serving as secretary of defense under Presidents Kennedy and Johnson. In the latter role, he is blamed for igniting the Cold War nuclear arms race with Russia and reviled as the architect of the disastrous military strategy for Vietnam. As the head of the World Bank, McNamara was instrumental in Americanizing the institution. Where its officers had previously regarded the Bank as an independent organ, functioning within the framework of the United Nations, under McNamara it became an instrument of U.S. foreign policy. Loans, which had historically been awarded cautiously on the basis of rigid economic projections, were now being funneled into regimes that represented barriers to the expansion of Communism. In a rare glimpse at the inner workings of the Bank, leaked internal memos show McNamara rewarding Philippine dictator Ferdinand Marcos after he declared martial law in 1972: "A rather surprising meeting! No more of the criticism of early years (politics, corruption, income inequality), but a rather general feeling that we should increase our lending program. ...We should aim to lend on average $120 million a year in FY74-78, 50 percent more than proposed," wrote one World Bank worker after a meeting with McNamara.[50] In his thirteen-year tenure, *Le Monde* reports, "the volume of loans rose from $1bn to $13bn a year, its staff increased fourfold and administrative costs tripled." * [51]

To finance this huge increase in loans, McNamara raised money on the national money markets. Undoubtedly, these investors saw a great value in supporting the World Bank's front line economic war against Communism, even if it meant supporting dictators that were blatantly anti-democratic. Under McNamara, the Bank compiled a client list that would have made Mata Hari blush: Chile's Pinochet, Indonesia's Suharto, and Romania's

* The fact that McNamara's leadership of the World Bank was never mentioned in Errol Morris's Academy Award-winning documentary, *The Fog of War*, says a lot about this hidden realm of globalization. Of his legacy there, Jerry Mander wrote, "Countries that did not sign on to the globalization programme would be left behind. McNamara pushed hard, and most countries felt they had little choice but to sign on. No longer destroying villages to save them, he was destroying whole economies. Today the countries that went along with him are saddled with silted-up mega-dams, crumbling roads to nowhere, empty high-rise office buildings, ravaged forests and fields, and the overwhelming, unpayable debt. Whatever harm this man caused in Vietnam, he did more during his tenure at the World Bank." Jerry Mander and Edward Goldsmith, ed., *The Case Against the Global Economy*, (San Francisco: Sierra Club Books, 1996).

murderous tyrant Ceausescu, who received $2.36 billion between 1974–1982, making him the eighth highest borrower by the time McNamara left the bank.[52]

While John Perkins owed much of his success to McNamara's new policies at the World Bank, by the end of the 1970s the spell began to wear off. He began to equate his actions as an economic hit man with the broader goals of America foreign policy. He realized that even while he had permitted himself to become a rapacious "slave trader," he had always held a vision of his country as a virtuous republic; one that was founded on the great moral vision of justice, equality and human liberty. But now, instead of a light that offered hope to the world, he saw America as "the republic's nemesis... self-centered, self-serving, greedy, and materialistic." He and the nation were one and the same. But most alarming to him was his realization that institutions originally established to bring financial independence to the world's impoverished nations had also been corrupted and conscripted to serve the same imperial force.[53] As he writes in *Confessions*, "I see now that Robert McNamara's greatest and most sinister contribution to history was to jockey the World Bank into becoming an agent of global empire on a scale never before witnessed."[54]

I ask him if the appointment of Paul Wolfowitz—former Defense Department official and one of the chief architects of the Iraq war—to the presidency of the World Bank is proof that legacy is still in tact.

"I think, more than anything else, it symbolizes the fact that it's not a 'world bank,' it's a U.S. bank," he answers sternly. "We determine policy, regardless of what anybody else thinks or cares. If we were a 'world bank,' then we'd be concerned with who the Thais want as president, and the Ethiopians, and the Ecuadorians. And, as I understand, most of the rest of the world didn't really want him in that position."

In 1980, Perkins quit Main and became a private consultant, traveling to many of the same countries he had once been responsible for sabotaging. Through new eyes he saw the devastation and poverty that had been left in his wake. He saw communities of people unable to overcome the corrupt governments that had been empowered and enriched through the very schemes that he had devised. Driven by his guilt and the desire to atone for his crimes, he began to write his *Confessions*.

Combining his insider accounts with an unfading passion for statistics, *Confessions of an Economic Hit Man* is a powerful indictment of the liberal legacy in the developing world. The picture we get is of a system that is flawed in its very foundation. How else can we explain the fact that, from 1960 to 1995 the income ratio of the world's top fifth countries to the poorest fifth increased from 30–1 to 74–1?[55] Despite this reality, Perkins writes, "the World Bank, the U.S. Agency for International Development, the IMF, and the rest of the banks, corporations and governments involved in international 'aid' continue to tell us they are doing their jobs, that progress has been made." And because no one is challenging the system itself, we have now seen an entire generation of young, concerned adults hoodwinked into believing that debt relief and increased aid will solve the problem.[56]

Perkins dedicates his book to two Latin American leaders who were assassinated for standing up against this system—Jaime Roldos, president of Ecuador, and Omar Torrijos, president of Panama. In 1981, one year after Perkins left Main, both men died in plane crashes a few months apart from each other. In the Preface to *Confessions*, Perkins writes, "we EHMs failed to bring Roldos and Torrijos around, and the other type of hit men, the CIA-sanctioned jackals who were always right behind us, stepped in." While these murders were initially strong deterrents for other like-minded nationalist leaders, by the mid-1990s a new wave of populism began to sweep across the southern hemisphere.[57]

Perhaps no single leader personifies that spirit more than Hugo Chávez, the somewhat erratic, showboating president of Venezuela. In 1992, while he was still a colonel in the army, Chávez led a failed coup attempt against then-President Carlos Andres Perez. After spending two years in prison, Chávez moved into open politics, declaring himself the leader of a movement named after Simón Bolívar, the Venezuela-born general who lead South America's nineteenth century battle for independence from Spain. Campaigning on a Bolivarian program to aid the poor by liberating Venezuela's massive oil revenues—it is the fifth largest oil exporter in the world—from the control of a corrupt elite, Chávez won a landslide victory in Venezuela's 1998 presidential election. Suffice it to say, this was not good news for America.

From the presidential palace, Chávez launched his Bolivarian revolution. He moved the economy away from neoliberal policies, instituting programs of income and land redistribution, and social welfare, including a free healthcare system. Next, he fired the president of the state oil company, Petroleos de Venezuela and appointed five political allies to the board. In retaliation, hundreds of thousands of protestors took to the streets and surrounded the presidential palace where they clashed with his supporters. On April 9, Chávez was taken from the palace and flown to a nearby military base. Next, Venezuela's top military commander announced that Chávez had resigned from the presidency and installed an interim leader who immediately revoked all of Chávez's Bolivarian policies and returned the fired oil executives to their posts.

In the Unites States, the mood was triumphant. A *New York Times* editorial declared, "With yesterday's resignation of President Hugo Chávez, Venezuelan democracy is no longer threatened by a would-be dictator. Mr. Chávez, a ruinous demagogue, stepped down after the military intervened and handed power to a respected business leader."[58] The State Department declared its "solidarity with the Venezuelan people and [we] look forward to working with all democratic forces in Venezuela to ensure the full exercise of democratic rights."[59] But in Caracas, where Chávez had been democratically elected, twice, his supporters rioted and looted. Four days after the coup, loyal members of the army reinstalled him to power.

John Perkins makes an interesting connection between the post-9/11 situations in Iraq and Venezuela. By December 2002, both countries were controlled by leaders who were vocally anti-American. And, Perkins contends, Chávez would have come under far heavier pressure had the Bush administration not been so focused on Saddam and the War on Terror.* But that doesn't mean they didn't have a hand in his temporary overthrow.[60]

Indeed, in the aftermath of the coup attempt, the Bush administration came under intense scrutiny. Even the generally conservative *LA Times* reported that "Bush administration officials acknowledged Tuesday that they had discussed the removal of Venezuelan President Hugo Chávez for months with military and civilian leaders from Venezuela."[61] But the tone of the mainstream media was generally one of disappointment and derision for his Marxist rhetoric.

For Perkins, this goes back to his original point of the brainwashing of the American public. Leaders like Chávez and Evo Morales, the president of Bolivia, are uniformly denounced in the press and by the government.

"They call these people 'socialists' and 'communists' as if that's always a very, very bad thing. While, in fact, they are simply fighting

---

* In 2002 George Friedman, chair of the intelligence organization Stratfor, suggested that Chávez was a primary military target for George Bush. "You've got a team in the White House that is unafraid of world public opinion because they know it is unreliable, self-serving and hypocritical," he declared. "Oil War: 23 Years in the Making," *Toronto Star*, March 9, 2003.

for their countries' independence. They're fighting to stop being exploited by U.S. corporations, and they've been terribly exploited. The truth is not being told about these people, including Hugo Chávez. So from the very beginning we hear things that make it very difficult for us to get to the truth behind the facts." *

Like Thomas Friedman, for example. Here he is on January 27, 2006, warning that his "call for spreading democracy will never be achieved if some of the worst regimes on the planet—Iran, Sudan, Venezuela—have so much oil money they can misbehave and ignore the world, and if the rest of us—Europe, America, China and India—are forever coddling them to get access to their crude."

How can Friedman honestly class the democratically elected leader of Venezuela with those of theocratic Iran and genocidal Sudan? Easy. Because for Friedman, and the great majority of liberals in America, democracy and capitalism are inextricably linked. There can be no authentic political freedom without a free market. So Venezuela, with its socialist Bolivarian revolution, is not a democracy. Even if a majority of the people who participated in an uncontested election voted for Hugo Chávez. According to Friedman, that collective act contravenes his "call for spreading democracy." Well, then we have to wonder what kind of democracy he is after. Because what I have learned from my interviews with

---

* One of the most oft repeated charges is that poverty has increased under Chávez. In May 2006, the Washington-based Center for Economic and Policy Research (CEPR) published a study of major U.S. media reports on the Venezuelan economy. Across the board, the journalists got it wrong. For example, the most consistent claim is reflected in the May/June 2006 issue of *Foreign Affairs*, where Jorge Casteñeda wrote "Venezuela's poverty figures and human development indices have deteriorated since 1999, when Chávez took office." But the CEPR report clearly shows that this is based on selective readings of economic data. They list the bi-annual figures from 1999–2005, clearly showing "the household poverty rate was reduced by 12.9 percent." Moreover, with the implementation of free healthcare and the large investment in a national literacy program, there are inherent benefits that cannot be reflected in the pure statistical analysis. See Mark Weisbrot, et al., "Poverty Rates in Venezuela: Getting the Numbers Right," May 2006.

Naseer Aruri, Mark Engler and John Perkins is that the single most tangible legacy of the neoliberal policies championed by people like Friedman has been the loss of human freedom and political liberty for those in the developing world.

So we're back to the start. Clearly there are two independent versions of globalization. And I can only assume that if Thomas Friedman's version excludes and invalidates the political will of an entire hemisphere of the planet, then his is the imaginary one. But it is more than that. Because by allowing the illusion to be perpetuated, he stands in the way of the realization of economic justice for these people. He has placed the political ideology and material needs of America above those who are weaker than us, and thus, has become an enemy of the very liberal revolution that America was born from.

3

Once Were Radicals

I am ashes where once I was fire.
— Lord Byron

GENERATION GAP

J.Z. threads his thick fingers through the handle of a coffee mug and lifts it to his mouth. I watch his jaw tense, as if he is drinking in anger. He glares at me.*

"I think you've been hanging around the ivory towers too long, the lack of oxygen is starting to go to your brain."

Sitting in a small, mildewy basement of an Anglican Church, which serves as the ad hoc headquarters for J.Z. and his group of radical revolutionaries, he nods at a tall, dreadlocked girl who ambles through the door. As a condition for the interview, I have promised not to reveal his identity nor the location of our meeting. We have been talking about my recent trip to Hay and the revelations of the British liberal elite. He's not impressed.[1]

"Hitchens." J.Z. spits, "He strikes me as someone who believes

---

* J.Z. is a composite of two anarchists I interviewed for the book. The group meeting took place as described but both interviewees asked that neither they, nor any member of their groups be identified "not because we are ashamed, but because of the history of police state brutality against anarchists and dissidents in general."

in power and little else. Intellectuals to govern the rabble. Classic liberal."

More black-clad militants spill into the low-ceilinged room. They glance over at us and J.Z. raises his voice, as if to affirm that he's on message.

"Oxford, Cambridge, Harvard, Yale. Who fucking cares? Establishment liberals have one major function besides the incessant babbling: that is to channel the energy and rage of the masses into a safe arena where popular ferment can be defused and rendered benign."

This is the way he talks. J.Z. is a self-described anarchist and writer known on the internet for an encyclopedic knowledge of radical American and European philosophers; he can quote Chomsky, Bakunin, and Rocker at will. Burly and thick-necked, he looks thuggish in a black long-sleeved shirt emblazoned with scrawled red ink, a quote from Publilius Syrus, the freed Roman slave from the Caesarian era:

Do not turn back when you are just at the goal.

It's the kind of scene that most would write off as extremist ranting by a minority faction from the far, far left. But J.Z. and his "committee" understand their place in history. For them, the roots of American radicalism have their origin in the student movements of the 1930s which, galvanized by the dual crises of the Depression and the rising fascist tide in Europe, spurred the formation of the American Student Union (ASU). It represented the first nationwide student protest movement in American history and, as the situation worsened, quickly mobilized to fight against the looming threat of another world war. In his *Encyclopedia of the American Left,* Professor Robert Cohen explains that the campus activists of the thirties were highly suspicious of Woodrow Wilson's motives for entering World War I. Those students, according to Cohen, "were convinced that the United States had gone to war in 1917 to serve plutocracy rather than democracy; they believed that Wilson's lofty rhetoric had hidden the fact that America had entered the war to safeguard the profit margins of bankers and munitions makers."[2]

Led by a bloc of predominantly Communist and Socialist activists, the ASU organized a series of anti-war rallies. In 1936, over 500,000 students representing half the national student body participated in a one-hour campus strike. But the movement descended into fractional chaos after Stalin green-lighted a non-aggression pact with Germany in 1939, forcing the American Communist leadership to back away from its anti-fascist platform. Perceiving a weakened ideological base, and disappointed with the ASU's reluctance to criticize Russia's invasion of Finland, the membership declined, ultimately collapsing the student movement in the early 1940s. American campuses would not see that kind of spirited, unified agitation against war and social injustice until the early 1960s with the founding of Students for a Democratic Society (SDS).[3]

"The SDS were important. So were the Panthers," J.Z. declares. "Critical. But, in the end, they provide us with no stable model for a radical opposition to the current war. All the really passionate, courageous leaders from the sixties are either dead, in prison or they've totally sold out to the system. Look at Hitchens, he was a '68er, wasn't he?"

J.Z. shakes his head and looks over at his group of 15, who have now assembled the chairs into a circular formation. Standing to begin the meeting, he motions for me to join the circle.

"That's why there's no unified, organized American radical front today. No place for a true youth and student-run movement. What kind of leadership do we have from our elders: [Todd]

Gitlin, [Paul] Berman? [David] Horowitz?" he laughs, "They all grew up and became fucking liberals. Or worse."

Of course, he is exaggerating. There are still some forceful voices in the anti-war left who do not consider themselves liberals and who are just as radical as J.Z. and his group of fifteen activists gathered in this west coast cellar. Turning my chair to face the rest of the circle, I suggest, "Of that generation of political writers, there must be someone you still value as an authentic voice."

The group looks at each other, trading shrugs and doubtful grins. The dreadlocked redhead offers, "As far as people who actually reach the mass public? Alexander Cockburn is the most true to the original spirit. But then, even he's made a devil's pact with the hard-right conservatives like Pat Buchanan."

J.Z. spins his chair, back facing in, and hunches his chest against the frame. Bringing his arms up, he crosses them and sighs. "It's a murky pool, my friends, a murky pool indeed."

The meeting begins. Moving counterclockwise around the circle, each member reports on an ongoing guerrilla war against this or that imperialist power—the most interesting of which, by far, turns out to be an account of the Maoist rebels battling India in Nepal. But, even as inspired and educational as the storytelling is, I can't help but feel that it's only just that. Storytelling. Engaging narratives to keep the flickering flame of a radical socialist revolution alive. These activists are the inheritors of a legacy that has been abandoned by the young student leaders who once drove the American state to the point of retreat and implosion. It's easy to understand why J.Z. feels a little bitter. He is hyper-intelligent and more historically and politically literate than most Gen Xers in the United States. But he's also instinctually driven to protest the government and what he calls its "puppeteer": the military industrial complex. For him and this group, as for the hundreds of other small anarchist groups who meet in similar rooms in cities across the country, all American military action is imperial and profit-driven. They just can't see it any other way. And, he reminds me, there was a time when this was the prevailing wisdom guiding many of the former radicals—both American and European—who hit the streets to battle police and soldiers at the height of the Vietnam War. These were the infamous '68ers, named after the era-defining mass protests in France, Germany, and the United States that make today's anti-war demonstrations look like choreographed Tai Chi sessions for the revolutionary set. Dissatisfied with the outdated, Marxist and labor-centric rhetoric of their parents and the "old left," this "New Left" grounded their ideology in a pragmatic doctrine that sought to revolutionize society from the heights of government to the ground floor of the educational system, remaking it in the image of an egalitarian, humane and socially just democracy.

The movement was greatly responsible for the end of the Vietnam War. But, like its predecessor in the 1930s, it also imploded from the lack of a unified ideological core, ultimately spawning a hybrid of violent revolutionary groups like the Weathermen and the Symbionese Liberation Army who advocated the destruction of the American government.

"You know, the ones that kidnapped Patty Hearst," J.Z. explains. I nod, sympathetically. It is his turn to talk and, instead of briefing us on a current struggle, he's talking about the sixties radicals who went beyond peaceful protest and picked up guns against the state. He lights up a cigarette and blows a cloud of smoke over the heads of the group.

"They were fucking crackers, but their hearts were in the right place."

While the radical militants took center stage in the vacuum that was left in the wake of America's withdrawal from Vietnam, this was not the end of the New Left's influence on the political society. Over the next twenty years, the ideology of the American Left came to be dominated by 1960s baby boom liberalism. They infiltrated and inseminated the Establishment so successfully that today this generation has had a profound impact on Western cultural and political power. Clinton was a '68er—or so he claimed to be—as is the aforementioned Hitchens. German Foreign Minister Joschka Fischer battled police in the streets and was almost unseated when photos of him thrashing a young cop were published in a top German paper. But, J.Z. is careful to remind me, "at one point or another they all stood, united in a countercultural front, against American imperialist aggression in Indochina and the rampantly unjust, coercively acquisitive capitalist system." In the thirty years since their riotous heyday, the New Left mellowed and matured, learned from their mistakes and made peace with the system they had once fought so hard to reform. During Clinton's last year in office, hard-line Croatian conservative Tomislav Sunic summed up what many on the left and right had begun to feel about '68ers' newfound comfort at the top of the political food chain:

"From 1600 Pennsylvania Avenue to 10 Downing Street… Perfectly recycled in stylish Gucci suits, wearing expensive Bally shoes, sporting fine mascara, the '68ers pontificate about the global free market. They have embraced their former foe, capitalist entrepreneurship, and have added to it the fake humanistic façade of socialist philanthropy…."[4]

Of course, world leaders like Clinton and Fischer were never radical in the sense that J.Z. and his group aspire to be. "It's their nature… to compromise," he explains. For these kids, the disappointment lies with the intellectual class, the ones who wrote and spoke the words of passionate anti-war and anti-imperialist speeches, who rode with the Panthers and traveled to

Latin America to follow the revolutionary movements struggling against U.S.-backed counter-revolutionary forces. Gitlin, Berman, Horowitz; these names that J.Z. unconsciously listed are an interesting trinity in their own right. Each has carved out a strikingly different legacy for himself in the post-New Left era. Taken as a group, they represent a fascinating spectrum of destinies—from Gitlin's post-9/11 position as an anti-Nader, anti-protest Democrat, to Berman's prominence as a pro-Iraq liberal hawk, and finally, to Horowitz's transition to scathingly anti-liberal, rabidly pro-Bush, conservative hawk. They all occupy positions of power and influence in the mainstream political culture. All have essentially, and even categorically, turned their backs on the socialist idealism and anti-establishment revolutionary spirit of their radical '60s activism. It's understandable that J.Z. feels a little like a bastard child of the New Left.

Watching him crush his cigarette under the thick sole of his army boot, I see the deep lines in his calloused hands. For the first time I can detect J.Z.'s age; under the revolutionary colors and anarchist slogans is a boy reaching adulthood. I wonder if the vengeful disillusionment he feels for the trinity is just veiled fear of the prospect that he too might share that propensity for caving. Or, like Peter Hitchens, of simply growing up.

In the '60s and '70s, protest culture was all-enveloping. There was a cohesive fabric in the form of a nationwide scene that was a way of life for many people. They lived "in protest" and survived off the infrastructure that had been built up around, and beneath, the movement. But today's radicals are more like lone moose in a deforested hinterland. Mass protests are few and far between, leaving only these small gatherings as fuel for the collectivist fire. Capitalism has divided and conquered the dissidents of each successive culture into neat, adversarial demographic packets, distilling the suspicion and anger at the system into pop songs and iPod commercials. Even Bob Dylan, the authentic "rolling stone" and anointed voice of that rebel generation, recently confessed in his memoirs that upon reaching maturity all he wanted was a "nine-to-five existence, a house on a tree-lined block with a white picket fence, pink roses in the backyard."[5]

Listening as J.Z. closes the meeting, I sense I am witnessing the slow death of a once sacred ritual and it gives me the urge to find the trinity he named: the former radicals Berman, Gitlin and Horowitz. To ask them what had changed. Was it them or was it that radical quotient of liberalism that had first inspired them? Or both? Though I had seen Paul Berman with Michael Ignatieff a year earlier, the idea of speaking to him had never occurred to me. But the thought of it now makes me nervous. And David Horowitz, the legendarily cantankerous despiser of all things left, scares me too. I would have to start with Gitlin, I decide, without realizing the next stage of my journey was just beginning.

THE NEW LEFTER

In the final scene of Philip Kaufman's coming-of-age film *The Wanderers*, Richie, a *Grease*-era Italian-American gang member, follows the beautiful, hippie-esque Nina through the streets of the Bronx. Watching her enter a small café filled with long-haired kids listening worshipfully as Bob Dylan sings "The Times They Are A-Changin'" Richie stops, realizing he has reached an impassable border dividing Nina's world and his own. This was symbolic of America's transition from the superficial, politically ambivalent youth culture of the 1950s to the radicalized, anti-establishment counterculture that defined the 1960s. Set in 1963, *The Wanderers* chronicles the very year that Todd Gitlin, a bright twenty-year-old radical aspirant, took over the presidency of the Students for a Democratic Society (SDS). He was the third president of the organization, which had framed its mission in the 1962 Port Huron Statement, a manifesto written by its then-president Tom Hayden.[6]

Speaking to me from his office at the Columbia School of Journalism, Professor Gitlin remembers that when first read the Statement, in the spring of 1972, he recognized he was part of a movement that would have far-reaching impact for the society. But it was not, he clarifies, something that he would have called revolutionary.[7]

"I would have been pretty fussy and precise about it," Gitlin explains. "Did I feel that I was affiliated with a radical movement that aimed at big structural change in American life? For sure."

In the Statement's introduction, titled *Agenda for a Generation*, SDS placed the New Left in its epochal context. The language embodies the aspirational idealism of a movement caught straddling a moment in American history when "complicated and disturbing paradoxes" forced them to act instead of looking away. It's worth quoting a few key paragraphs of this document, if only to remind us of the gale force winds, to invoke Dylan again, that were blowing through the cloaking veils of American social consciousness:

> When we were kids the United States was the wealthiest and strongest country in the world: the only one with the atom bomb, the least scarred by modern war, an initiator of the United Nations that we thought would distribute Western influence throughout the world. Freedom and equality for each individual, government of, by, and for the people—these American values we found good, principles by which we could live as men. Many of us began maturing in complacency.

As we grew, however, our comfort was penetrated by events too troubling to dismiss. First, the permeating and victimizing fact of human degradation, symbolized by the Southern struggle against racial bigotry, compelled most of us from silence to activism. Second, the enclosing fact of the Cold War, symbolized by the presence of the Bomb, brought awareness that we ourselves, and our friends, and millions of abstract "others" we knew more directly because of our common peril, might die at any time. We might deliberately ignore, or avoid, or fail to feel all other human problems, but not these two, for these were too immediate and crushing in their impact, too challenging in the demand that we as individuals take the responsibility for encounter and resolution. [8]

For Gitlin and the pioneers of SDS, there was a profound sense of fatalism in their work which, they professed, was "guided by the sense that we may be the last generation in the experiment with living." Looking back at the social and political experimentation of the '60s era, it would be hard to argue with that appraisal. In today's buttoned-down, shoulder-to-the-corporate-grindstone world of the post-9/11 Patriot Act paradigm, there is little time or cultural space for exploring new frontiers in living, learning and loving. And this is, in no small part, the effect of a society shaped by the very generation that drew inspiration from the Port Huron Statement.

Perhaps we should not be surprised. A careful reading of the Statement illuminates a focused pragmatism aimed at disabling the establishment critiques of the student movement and its legacy. "It has been said that our liberal and socialist predecessors were plagued by vision without program, while our own generation is plagued by program without vision," wrote Hayden in 1962. In response, SDS sought to draw its membership into a political mode,* one that had the function of "bringing people out of isolation and into community" and, allowing the "individual [to] share in those social decisions determining the quality and direction of his life."[9] Judging by the paths of Tom Hayden, who as a California senator has become a fixture of the mainstream liberal Democratic Party, and Todd Gitlin, who has been a vocal critic of both third party politics ("reckless... specious... irreparable... catastrophic") and radical mass protests ("a [self-indulgent] performance piece that dramatizes the theatrics of rage"), this movement from isolation to community ultimately pointed to an alignment with institutional, establishment politics. It's a position that many young activists see as an acceptance of the very status quo the SDS leaders were once so effective at opposing.

In 2003, Gitlin wrote *Letters to a Young Activist*, another installment in the Art of Mentoring series that published Hitchens's *Letters to a Young Contrarian*. In his correspondence with an anonymous mentee, Gitlin lays out the basis for his "realistic" approach to activism, which is grounded in lessons learned from the failures and successes of the '60s student movement. He warns the young activist to avoid romanticizing his generation's struggle into a "simplistic and seriously distorted" picture, "predicated on a melodramatic tale about those far gone and glorious sixties when moral seriousness entailed spontaneous action and street fighters stalked the land..."[10]

Instead, Gitlin wants his readers to understand that the idealism of the New Left was also its most detrimental aspect;

---

* Elaborating on the core values and mission of SDS, as outlined in the Statement, Gitlin tells me, "[Participatory democracy] was the universal principle that would guide politics... Attached to that were reform proposals [that] represented the left wing of the liberal ideal of the extension of the welfare state, the enlargement of egalitarian economics, the overcoming of the more reckless versions of the Cold War—aspiration towards American participation in the world which would not be driven by the military metaphysic. Affirmation of an end to racism as a social principle."

one that allowed it to drift into narcissistic self-satisfaction while a powerful conservative right was mobilizing under the directive of political realism. According to Gitlin they were "think-tankers in training, who, when they didn't despise us for our softness, condescended to us that we had no idea how the world worked." [11]

That contrast in attitudes and discipline was decisive, Gitlin writes, for while "the academic Left, whose numbers were not trivial, spent an inordinate amount of its time and energy marching on the English department... the Right descended on Washington." [12]

In coming to terms with that legacy of hardcore pragmatism and political positioning, Gitlin's *Letters* concludes with an admonition for the Left to focus its energies on defeating the Republican Party. A mission, according to him, that can only be achieved by realizing "the Democratic Party is the inescapable field where we either win, lose or draw."

Understandably, this position upset many of his younger readers: "Whatever happened to the idea of voting your conscience or fighting for an end to the two-party system whose candidates are barely distinguishable from each other?" asked Kari Kunst on *AlterNet*. [13] "Steal this book... at $22.50, Gitlin's 161 pages aren't worth it," Todd Chretien taunted on *Counterpunch*. [14]

But it was author and anti-globalization activist Naomi Klein who took the hardest line on Gitlin. In her review of *Letters*, Klein tore into the Columbia professor for his "patronizing" commentary, delivered, she argued, not to a young revolutionary aspirant, but, instead, to "a fading memory of Gitlin's younger self." Calling Gitlin an "activist-ologist," Klein summed up his *Letters*'s less-than-radical advice as:

"Don't opt out of electoral politics... Vote for the lesser of two evils. Don't fight the power. Find friends on the inside. Don't aim for revolution. Shoot for achievable reforms," concluding that "if Gitlin had followed this advice in 1964, he wouldn't have been president of SDS at all: He would have been president of the Young Democrats." * 15

Ouch. To be fair, there are parts of *Letters* that aim to encourage ("Openness is one of your virtues, built into your kind of practical intelligence") and inspire ("you live beside others… they are the field of your action"). But in the end, for much of the activist generation to whom the book was supposedly written, Gitlin's *Letters* come off as one too many lectures on what to avoid instead of what to dream about. It seems drastically out of step in a time when activists are struggling to find creative ways of energizing a largely apathetic youth culture and facing a vacuum of potential for organizing on college campuses. But perhaps that is exactly the point of Gitlin's message. That, given the obstacles faced by today's activists, there is, as J.Z. claims, no model to be found in the '60s era movement. These are simply different times.

"No moments of history are stamped out on assembly lines," Gitlin tells me. "The movements of the '60s were not like the movements of the '30s. There clearly are movements today; there is obviously an anti-war movement. It would be a big mistake for it to go out and drape itself in the old costumes. It'll only make it look retro and offensive and plain foolish to the people it's ostensibly trying to appeal to."

Throughout our conversation, Gitlin sustains the vibe of street-smart academic. He doesn't mind playing the spoiler to conventional activist wisdom. Listening to him talk about the weaknesses

---

* Klein and Gitlin clashed on Amy Goodman's *Democracy Now!* a few days before the 2004 Republican National Convention in New York. When Gitlin reiterated his belief that mass protests would be merely "symbolic" and, if they got unruly, serve to "recruit voters for George W. Bush," Klein accused him of playing into the Republican's strategy of scaring people off the streets of New York. "This is a moment for massive courage," Klein declared, "To stand up against all this fear mongering, to say we're going anyway, because we know that there are a lot of problems with this country, but too much dissent is not one of them, okay? And anyone telling people to stay out of the streets, frankly, Todd, has a lot to answer for." Listen to the debate on *Democracy Now!* available at www.democracynow.org/article.pl?sid=04/08/26/1421204.

in old and New Left thinking, no one would doubt that he is being true to his own accumulated wisdom, a product of his well-documented experience in the trenches of the most successful youth movement in American history. And perhaps this is the reason the criticism was so sharp, because of his symbolic value. His status as a respected author and professor at the top journalism school in the country, combined with his legacy as a former SDS president makes him one of the most credible voices from the student movement of the 1960s. But a radical he is no longer. So what is he now?

"I'm comfortable calling myself a liberal, which I certainly wasn't in the '60s," he confesses.*

Prodding, I wonder if he sees that shift as an *evolution* from radicalism to liberalism. And, more importantly, whether it was a slow shift along the ideological spectrum or the product of a sudden realization that one is superior to the other.

"The former," he answers quickly. "Even in the '60s I thought of it that way. When I was president of SDS I came across a quote from Walter Lippman in his young radical phase. I don't remember his exact words... 'Our mission was to make conservatives into moderates, moderates into liberals, liberals into radicals, and radicals into socialists.' Words to that effect. That seemed right to me—it was an affirmation of the continuum idea. There were certainly times in the '60s—from '64, '65 on—when it was very hard to sustain the idea that there was still a genuine liberalism alive as a force. Not a hypothetical theoretical position, but an actual political force in which the liberal ideal still endured. From then on—even from earlier on—I certainly would not have called myself liberal."

---

* Writing in *Salon* in 2000, Gitlin defined his political viewpoint as "frequently critical of Clinton-Gore politics from the left. I think the drug war is a disaster, the Colombia intervention wrongheaded, insurance companies and HMO's cruel and unnecessary punishment, big-money giveaways to media tycoons indefensible, free trade oversold, labor underprotected." Quote from Todd Gitlin, "Unsafe in any state," *Salon*, October 28, 2000.

This conflicted alliance to the liberal project was never more clear than in 1965, when SDS president Carl Oglesby gave what Gitlin calls a "defining" speech, clarifying the movement's position at that point in the escalating Vietnam conflict. In a language and spirit that are absent from the rhetoric of today's mass movements, Oglesby leveled an indictment of "American liberalism," the leaders of which—Truman, Eisenhower, Kennedy, Johnson—had ultimately unleashed the United States military machine onto Indochina.

"They are all liberals. But," Oglesby reminded the crowd, "so, I'm sure, are many of us who are here today in protest. To understand the war, then, it seems necessary to take a closer look at this American liberalism. Maybe we are in for some surprises. Maybe we have here two quite different liberalisms: one authentically humanist; the other not so human at all." [16]

For Oglesby and SDS, "not so human," meant "corporate liberalism." Gitlin, who contributed to the speech, remembers that the delineation between the two liberalisms, humanist and corporate, was still viable in 1965. But, after that, he explains, "it was a wasting commodity, it was a diminishing distinction in the minds of most people in the New Left, largely I think because of the Vietnam War." Liberalism of any stripe had simply become a bad word. I am too young to have experienced the crisis of this era, but as Gitlin explains it, liberalism was like a mirror held up to the face of American society, which allowed its youth to see the pockmarked legacy and disfiguring priorities of the so-called liberal establishment.

Oglesby continued:

> We have become a nation of young, bright-eyed, hard-hearted, slim-waisted, bullet-headed make-out artists. A nation—may I say it?—of beardless liberals.

You say I am being hard? Only think.

This country, with its thirty-some years of liberalism can send 200,000 young men to Vietnam to kill and die in the most dubious of wars, but it cannot get 100 voter registrars to go into Mississippi.

What do you make of it?

The financial burden of the war obliges us to cut millions from an already pathetic War on Poverty budget. But in almost the same breath, Congress appropriates one hundred forty million dollars for the Lockheed and Boeing companies to compete with each other on the supersonic transport project, that Disneyland creation that will cost us about two billion dollars before it is done.

What do you make of it? [17]

Reading it now, in light of the controversially slow federal response to the Katrina flood crisis in the South and the ongoing expense of American lives and tax dollars in Iraq, Oglesby's forty-year-old speech sustains a certain resonance. There's more:

Let's stare our situation coldly in the face. All of us are born to the colossus of history, our American corporate system—in many ways an awesome organism. There is one fact that describes it: With about five percent of the world's people, we consume about half the world's goods. We take a richness that is in good part not our own, and we put it in our pockets, our garages, our split-levels, our bellies, and our futures.

On the face of it, it is a crime that so few should have
so much at the expense of so many. Where is the moral
imagination so abused as to call this just? Perhaps many
of us feel a bit uneasy in our sleep. We are not, after all,
a cruel people. And perhaps we don't really need this
super-dominance that deforms others. But what can we
do? The investments are made. The financial ties are
established. The plants abroad are built. Our system
exists. One is swept up into it. How intolerable—to be
born moral, but addicted to a stolen and maybe surplus
luxury. Our goodness threatens to become counterfeit
before our eyes—unless we change. But change threatens
us with uncertainty—at least.[18]

Concluding, Oglesby directed his focus to the movement's
core membership of "humanist liberals," asking them to make a
choice:

Corporatism or humanism: which? For it has come to that.
Will you let your dreams be used? Will you be a grudging
apologist for the corporate state? Or will you help try
to change it—not in the name of this or that blueprint
or -ism, but in the name of simple human decency and
democracy and the vision that wise and brave men saw in
the time of our own Revolution?[19]

Despite the criticism of his *Letters,* Todd Gitlin clearly chose
humanism over corporatism. Yet, when I ask the inevitable question about his own flirtation with socialism, he is uneasy about
retroactively categorizing his political beliefs during the SDS era.
He first decided he was a socialist in 1958, when he was a fifteen-
year-old student in high school, "reading George Bernard Shaw."

But during his university years, he cringed at the self-identifiers.

"People who went around declaring that they were 'socialist' struck me as sectarian and foolish for the most part. I was a compound of things," he explains, adding, "Would I have felt that I was somehow in the socialist tradition during those years? Yes."

"But today," I ask, "do you still look for alternatives to the capitalist system?"

Gitlin thinks for a moment and then answers, almost solemnly. "If capitalism is the principle of the productive value of private property and the value as well of markets as principles of allocation, then I would have to say about capitalism what has been said about other political economic theories: it is the horizon today. It cannot be transcended today. That's my view. It obviously wasn't my view in the '60s."

Echoing Christopher Hitchens's concession to the revolutionary power of capitalism, Gitlin is weary of "anti-market fundamentalist"* positions to the extent that they exclude the potential for engineering our socioeconomic systems. He has not abandoned the idea that there can be a compromise between free market economics and a form of social justice.

"There are many systems of ownership that are compatible with a market society. One of the mistakes of the old Left—and, insofar as it cared about economic questions, the New Left—was to think that once you said that ownership and markets were the indissoluble elements of capitalism, you were also saying unlimited prerogative for private capital. It doesn't follow. What are the rights of the owners of capital? Do they have utter rights to do as they wish or must they also be responsible to workers, communities, others? Insofar as they have other obligations and you put limits on

---

* Writing in *Letters to a Young Activist*, Gitlin warned, "The remedy for market fundamentalism is not anti-market fundamentalism. We've been down that grim road before." Quote from Todd Gitlin, *Letters to a Young Activist* (New York: Basic Books, 2003), p. 103.

the powers of capital—you've still controlled them in the interest of social values. You can have, in that sense, a society which is respectful of markets—but at the same time incorporate elements of the socialist ethos. It's been a Holy Grail for a few seekers on the edge of socialist tradition."

A Holy Grail, indeed. For a moment, Gitlin almost sounds idealistic. "But you still value those controls in the name of social justice," I suggest.

"Of course, otherwise I wouldn't be a liberal."

It's a long way from the passionate war cry of SDS anti-corporatism. I think back to Hay and my interview with the *Guardian*'s Alan Rusbridger, who admitted that the new status quo for leftists is impotence. "After the fall of the Berlin Wall, the Left just rolled over," he explained. "We can't think of an economic model that is better than capitalism, so we argue about the limits of regulation within it, which is a weak position to be in. It's a rather insipid position to be in."[20]

Speaking to Gitlin, I feel the same way as I did hearing Rusbridger's confession: I am struck by the defeatism of his stance. Not that there is anything wrong with his acceptance of American capitalism, but because it seems so obvious that we now live in an era defined by the world's wholescale rejection of it. If anything, American capitalism has only become more cunning and insidious since the time of Carl Oglesby's impassioned warning against it. And this aggressive acquisitiveness and quest for ever-expanding markets and cheap labor is precisely what young activists like J.Z. believe is the primary engine that drives American armies into the world. Gitlin, who supported NATO's 1999 bombing of Slobodan Milosevic's Yugoslavia and the post-9/11 American attack on the Taliban in Afghanistan, warns against these kinds of simplifications.

"[Young activists] should ask questions. Of course it's good to ask questions about what the motives are, but that doesn't mean signing on to the formula answer. There were people during the Vietnam War who thought that the motive for the U.S. in Vietnam was tin and tungsten and offshore oil. That was nonsense. There were people around *Z Magazine* who thought that the American motives in opposing Milosevic were economic imperialist motives. I thought that was nonsense and continue to think it's nonsense. The case of Iraq is more complicated because of all that black stuff under the sand. But even there I don't think it's the prime motive because as many people have pointed out, whatever government is ruling Iraq has a desire to sell oil to the Japanese or Americans. I don't think it explains what we did in Iraq. Ideology explains this misbegotten war."

Ideology. The very force that, from time to time, claims power over all the world's leaders, pulling them into the ritual of armed conflict. For activists like J.Z., capitalism is just as much an "ideology" as the more nuanced values that Bush, once he got past the WMD and al Qaeda-Saddam narrative, claimed to be fighting for. Even Sergeant Hollis, our tank commander in Samarra, speaks of the larger geostrategic and economic value of American military positioning in Iraq as an ideological campaign. But for establishment liberals like Gitlin, it isn't a motive or strategy that can be gleaned from the statements and writings of foreign policy strategists.

In a 2002 National Security Strategy document, the Bush administration proclaims the "great struggle" between fascism and democracy to be over. Yet it also warns the United States is "now threatened less by conquering states than we are by failing ones."[21] As a response, the nation's leaders must "look outward for possibilities to expand liberty," through a national security strategy that seeks to "make the world not just safer, but better."[22] This language echoes the argument for "liberal interventionism" that guided Bill Clinton and other Western leaders in their bombing of Serbia in 1999.

It is the same principle that drove high-profile New Leftists of Todd Gitlin's generation—Hitchens, Michael Ignatieff, and Paul Berman—to support the invasion of Iraq.

Gitlin cautions, "You have to be very careful. One of the slippery terms in such discussions is 'generation.' If you're looking at Paul [Berman], Ignatieff, Hitchens, they're not representative of a generation. They really aren't. Paul is a good friend of mine. We have big political disagreements, but I know of no reason to believe that Paul's position [on the war]—or for that matter mine, which is quite different—is representative of our generation's position, or even that of former SDS members. I have no reason to think that."

But Paul Berman, the bookish liberal hawk who has built a minor literary franchise on the vivid chronicles and critiques of his generation, holds a fierce conviction that his position on the war is distinctly identifiable as "of his generation." It lies in the radical leftist opposition to totalitarianism and dictatorship, those wordly forces hell-bent on the destruction of Western liberalism. For Berman, this is a struggle that will demand a degree of political courage and a commitment to violence that once fueled the radical youth who became known as the Generation of '68.

THE STREET FIGHTER

For those who had begun the sixties with an earnest desire to transform American society, the seventies were a terrible comedown. Writing in *A Tale of Two Utopias*, his testimonial history of the generation of 1968, Paul Berman remembers the New Leftist concepts of participatory democracy, libertarian socialism and non-violent protest had devolved into "guerrilla mayhem and

Dostoyevskian persecutions, and the specter of left-wing dictatorship arose, and instead of freedom there was havoc. And in these matters, the American New Left stayed in line with the other movements around the world. The worldwide rebellion went down." [23]

And down it went. While some in the New Left saw a political purism—based on the radical Maoist critique of American imperialism and maintenance of the class system through a police state apparatus—in the guerrilla militancy, it horrified the more moderate of their cadre and sent them scurrying away from the ideological socialist foundations of the movement, back to the safety of their middle class values. Where once capitalism had been targeted as an original sin, the lie upon which Western civilization was able to exploit Third World nations and call it progress, now it was a lesser evil. The biggest threat to a just society was authoritarian, reactionary leftists—whose rhetoric echoed the murderous Communist totalitarianism of Stalin and Mao—not the liberal American corporations to whom many would now have to turn in order to make a living in the mellow seventies. Writing in the *Nation*, Corey Robin describes this shift of the generation of '68 as one "from skepticism of to faith in US power, and from faith in to skepticism of popular movements." [24]

In their retreat to the status quo, many of the most prolific and influential of the New Left began a critical re-examination of their generation's political legacy. While Todd Gitlin focused on evolving and mainstreaming the movement for social change past the debacle of the early seventies, Paul Berman took a more controversial path, setting himself up as the New Left's resident contrarian. Unafraid of challenging the conventions of institutional leftist thought, Berman dedicated himself to a singular brand of revisionist journalism that has often placed him in the center of the most legendary political ideological shitstorms of the post-sixties era.

Berman's first major provocation of the establishment Left ignited a high profile editorial battle that spilled out of the small offices of *Mother Jones* magazine and into the mainstream media. On September 27, 1986, the *New York Times* reported that the "radical" *Mother Jones* had fired Editor-in-Chief Michael Moore for refusing to print a report by Berman, which painted Nicaragua's leftist Sandinista government with a Red ideological brush.[25] Writing from Managua, Berman described the Sandinista leaders as disciples of Che Guevara, "whom they adored," and practitioners of Leninist doctrines who had "never really turned against Moscow." These were ideas, Berman explained, that American leftists did their best to ignore. Instead of reality, the Left chose idealism and self-deception that led to a "temptation to recreate [the Sandinistas] in the image of our own ideas." For Berman, idolizing the Sandinistas smacked of the very same Utopianism that ruined the sixties radicals, and he became the messenger of a bitter pill that few leftists wanted to swallow.[26]

It's important to place Berman's article in its temporal context. As one of the few truly independent socialist revolutions in the Western hemisphere besides Cuba, the Sandinistas were a cause célèbre of the American Left. Though it was commonly understood that Reagan was behind the right-wing Contra rebel army in their guerrilla war to overthrow the Sandinistas, it was still a few months before the Iran-Contra scandal—which proved Oliver North was covertly backing the Contras with illegal drugs and arms shipments—would publicly discredit the Reagan administration's alignment with the counter-revolution. In other words, it was a time of fierce ideological warfare and the embattled Left was no match for Reagan, who was exploiting the ever-dependable hot-button fear of Communism to drive American support behind the Contras. So when Michael Moore read Berman's dispatch from Managua, he decided to cut the story for the simple reason it would add fuel to Reagan's argument that Nicaragua was a critical front in the Cold War fight against Communism. It was a decision that would ultimately cost him his job and launch him on his own path to glory as one of America's most celebrated dissidents.[*]

With Michael Moore gone—and now engaged in a full-scale public relations battle with the magazine—*Mother Jones* founder Adam Hochschild published Berman's story in the December 1986 issue. He prefaced the feature with a short editor's note, reiterating the magazine's commitment to provide Berman with "space for a full, uncensored report on his impressions."[27] No doubt, the Republican ideologues cheered its evenhandedness. Berman, a former SDS militant who had supported the Black Panthers, studied under Palestinian radical Edward Said and ran with leaders of the Paris '68er rebellion, had become a passive eye, a working journalist capable of filing stories that could grant comfort to America's warmongering conservatives. Like so many of his generation, Paul Berman had grown up and away from his radical roots.[†]

Or so it would seem. Speaking to Berman by phone late one night in New York, I ask him if he experienced a transition from radicalism to skepticism; if there was, to quote Peter Hitchens, a Damascene conversion.[28]

"There never was for me," he replies. "I never had the feeling that I've made some dramatic transition. I've always been radical

---

[*] The Berman imbroglio had fortuitous consequences for Moore, who packed up his things and returned to Flint, Michigan, where he began filming his breakthrough documentary, *Roger and Me.*

[†] Berman is one of the few leftists who still calls himself a socialist, though he does it with some qualification: "I continue to speak of myself and to think of myself as a socialist, but I don't like to beat too heavily on that particular drum, the socialist drum, because, so few people understand these philosophical questions in a useful way. In other words, what I'm saying is that the old-time socialists had many valid ideas, which continue to be valid, but there's something about the rhetoric of socialism that after a while turned out to have misled many people."

and, also, skeptical. And I've always thought or known there was something wrong with the mainstream of the Left."

For Berman, skepticism and radicalism are not mutually exclusive, they are interdependent. One can never become so satisfied with the mantras of their political cult that they lose the skill of deconstructing its inherent biases and delusions. Yet, despite his agnosticism, Berman has remained a faithful adherent to the leftist *weltanschauung*.

"I've always felt there is something in the tradition and culture of the Left which is very deep and profound and which I've never, for a moment, thought of abandoning or leaving. But I have had many moments when I've looked around me at other people who consider themselves part of the Left and I've wondered: 'what are they dreaming of?' That they, in my eyes, seemed to have marched off a cliff."

"Can you give me an example of one of those times?" I ask, pushing him toward familiar territory.

"Well, like when I realized that most people who consider themselves on the left did not want to overthrow Saddam Hussein. I thought that was shocking. Now, we had good reason to worry about the Bush administration. We had many reasons to worry. But the basic goal of overthrowing Saddam and coming out in favor of the majority of the Iraqi people... all that was, to me, by definition a principle of the Left. To my mind, anti-fascism is a really fundamental aspect of the Left. And I think a huge number of people on the left have abandoned that. So, I just sort of wonder, what are their deep values? What are they *for*? Why do they consider themselves on the left?"

While Berman meant the question for the Left in general, I took it as a direct challenge to my own bearing as a leftist. In truth, my opposition to the war was never influenced by a consideration of Saddam's fascism. Rather, it was driven by a suspicion of the

Bush administration's latent authoritarianism and manipulation of truth and public opinion to get the United States military onto Iraqi soil. That was the fascism I was fighting, even if it was tame in comparison to that of Saddam and his security forces. For many of us who opposed the war, it was impossible to dissociate the legacy of political actors like Bush and Cheney from the action they were taking in Iraq. They both stank to high heaven.

When I first saw Paul Berman in person—at the Overseas Press Club in New York discussing the Iraq War with Michael Ignatieff—I was struck by the bespectacled, scholarly man who sat upright in his chair, arguing that we need to strike a balance between "a realistic response to actual dangers" and "moral perfectionism." Seeing him there, it evoked in me that well-tread suspicion: that those most eloquent and seductive in their arguments for war were always the least capable, or ready, to charge out with gun in hand to wage it. It was our generation that Berman's writing would most impact, the soldiers I met in Iraq who had not seen their families for a year and professed confusion about the real reasons for their presence in the dreaded Sunni Triangle. These are the soldiers fighting Berman's "liberal war": the poor and lower middle class Americans, many of whom had only signed up for service to get a cheap education or as a ticket out of the ghetto. Had this one-time radical and his "American social-democratic heart" really become so ignorant to the realities of military service in this country?* Didn't he know that it was just as much

---

* National Priorities Project, a nonpartisan research group that analyzed 2004 recruiting data by zip code, found that the military is leaning heavily for recruits in "economically depressed, rural areas where youths' need for jobs may outweigh the risks of going to war," the *Washington Post* reported. More than 44 percent of U.S. military recruits come from rural areas compared to fourteen percent which come from major cities. Nearly half of all recruits are from lower-middle-class to poor households with nearly two thirds coming from counties in which median household income is below the U.S. median. Quote and information from "Youths in Rural U.S. Are Drawn to Military," November 4, 2005, *Washington Post*, p. A01.

about class and color as the "evacuation" of New Orleans?

I remember leaving that night with a deep-seated contempt for the intellectualization of the conflict. How easy it was for the writer to sit at his Brooklyn desk, urging on the battle when he had no direct exposure to the risks of its prosecution. Why, I wondered, could Mr. Berman not employ his considerable intellect and power of persuasion to convince the warring societies to enter a form of rational conversation, in which both could admit their long-standing cultural and religious prejudices, their economic needs and insecurities and the more recent military and diplomatic blunders that had been driven by an instinctual fear of "the other?" Instead, after embracing a radical skepticism of state-sponsored war during the end of a century that will be remembered as the most violent in human history, at the dawn of the twenty-first century he chose war as resolution to the vast problem of this ideological conflict.[*]

When I ask him how he deals with this kind of reaction, which must greet him from time to time when young people attend his public lectures, he admits, half-jokingly "I have had talks with people like that and I throw up my hands in despair."

But when I push him to comment on the real problem of having George Bush and Dick Cheney as the authors and leaders of his liberal war, he relents.

"That's all understandable. I think the real culture of the Left is weak in the country. People don't have an independent body of

<hr/>

[*] Quoting Corey Robin from the *Nation*: "Paul Berman has called the war in Iraq this generation's Spanish Civil War. Berman's own biography, of course, makes mincemeat of the analogy. Spain's civil war demanded, in Stephen Spender's words, "a very personal involvement." But unlike George Orwell, André Malraux or any of the other writers who fought for the Spanish Republic, Berman has yet to pick up a gun to defend the Iraqi government. Martha Gellhorn claimed that Spain's foreign fighters "knew why they came, and what they thought about living and dying, both. But it is nothing you can ask or talk about." Yet all Berman can do is talk... and talk and talk. Meanwhile, the only international volunteers who seem to believe that Iraq is worth fighting and dying for are joining the other side."

knowledge to draw on. So one is victim of the TV news—Bush comes on TV with his horrible face and it's just natural to assume that, whatever he's saying, the truth must be the opposite. But the whole purpose of having the Left is to try to maintain one's own cultural or political traditions. To keep them alive, which is to say not go on screaming chants against LBJ. It's a struggle to do that."

Berman pauses and then laughs, "The idea that most college students are wrong is not one that shocks me. Most college students have usually been wrong. At the same time, I can understand why people end up with this view. I can understand the appeal of people marching in Washington. Some of it seems to be entirely wholesome and admirable. Just sometimes it's the most primitive civic stance which I applaud—like: terrible things are happening; one wants to have a say; one sees that Bush is a bad guy. And so one goes off and protests. That's better than a lot of other people who sit at home and do nothing."

"So the problem is one of identification," I offer, "They've associated Bush with the action and they can't dissociate the two."

"Yeah, and there's the problem of an insufficiently broad view of the world," he reiterates. "One can easily allow himself to define the world by George W. Bush; if the world is defined by Bush then of course whatever he's for I'm against."

But for Berman, who has spent a great deal of his intellectual energy on precisely this task of dissociation, the mission has been one of redefining the reasons to wage it; of selling the war in terms of its humanitarian and anti-fascist principles. And this didn't just start after 9/11.

Five years after his controversial report for *Mother Jones*, the *New York Times* served as the vehicle for Berman's next major assault on the left. It was January 1991 and, just a few months earlier, Saddam Hussein had invaded and occupied the neighboring country of Kuwait. The *Times* published an op-ed by Richard Nixon, weighing in on George Bush Sr.'s plan to engage Iraqi forces and drive them out of their oil-rich southern neighbor. Framing his argument on old-school foreign policy realism that was the trademark of Henry Kissinger, his one-time secretary of state, Nixon urged the American people to back the war, not for "democracy," but to protect American "credibility" as a world power and preserve its "vital economic interests."[29] Nixon's editorial conflicted with Paul Berman's '68er social democratic perspective. Berman looked across the world at the Middle East and saw Saddam's dictatorship which gassed and tortured people. He worried about the Iraqi nuclear scientists, who would surely make their bombs someday. The more he thought about Saddam, the more he realized how dangerous a force he was. That he needed to be destroyed. But for very different reasons than those prescribed in the Nixon editorial.

So Berman wrote a rebuttal to Nixon, published in the *Times*, reframing the war as a "progressive" campaign of liberal democracy against totalitarianism.[30] At a time when Christopher Hitchens was still a fiery socialist chucking scathing indictments at the hawks from his pedestal at the *Nation*, Berman was one of the first major New Leftists to come out as "pro-war, left-wing." And he paid the price for it, facing the kind of wrath that only the Left can mete out, one typically reserved for the great traitors of humankind. Writing about the position his leftist peers took toward Iraq, Berman lamented, "those people tended to oppose the war altogether. Opposition was instinctive for them. They worried about America's imperial motives, about the greed of big corporations and their influence on White House policy; and could not get beyond their worries. War, to them, was always the Vietnam War, a debacle in the making."

Paul Berman was eighteen years old in 1968. He can authentically claim to have come of age in that cataclysmic year when, each month, hundreds more young men of his own generation were being returned to their mothers in body bags. It's no wonder that for many of his peers, war could only mean disaster and heartbreak. I ask Berman if he was really that surprised by the opposition he encountered when he turned hawk in 1991. Wasn't Vietnam such a scarring moment in the life of his generation that it would leave a wound on the collective consciousness, one that would shroud any unilateral war in a kind of deep, restless suspicion?

Berman takes a deep breath. "Yes. I think it has a lot to do with Vietnam. And that was a scarring moment. And I understand why that was a scarring moment. But I think that many people on the left failed to be scarred by the next moment, which should also have been a scarring moment. Which was what happened after the United States withdrew from Vietnam. And, of course, what happened is that a half million Vietnamese fled into the sea in little boats and there was a genocide in Cambodia and there were horrors far beyond those that had occurred during the war.

"So the American actions in Vietnam were horrendous. But the consequences of American defeat in Vietnam were also horrendous. And so there should have been two scarring moments. One, if there was anybody who thought that whatever the United States does was by definition good, anyone who held that belief, should have been scarred by the war itself, which was the plain indication that the United States was perfectly capable of doing perfectly dreadful things. Not that one ought to have needed Vietnam to demonstrate that, but there were people who needed to be shaken out of that naivety. But then there should have been the second scarring moment, where people should have realized that just because the United States is against something, that thing the United States is against is not automatically good. It might be really, really bad. And that there is something more in the world than the crimes of the United States. And in the modern world, one of the principle things has been the crimes of sundry totalitarian movements."

In the traumatic post-9/11 political vacuum, Berman seized the opportunity and upped the ante for liberal aggression. Flanking the Bush administration's avenging neoconservative militarism with a '68er's leftist humanism, Berman became one of the war's most articulate and aggressive liberal backers. For him, 9/11 represented the exploding cyst of a long-festering conflict between Western liberalism and Muslim fundamentalism, one that could only be ignored at our peril. Channeling all his intellectual heat into his bestselling *Terror and Liberalism*, Berman unleashed a forceful, liberal argument for the War on Terror.[31]

Berman wrote *Terror and Liberalism* looking out from his Brooklyn study at the cavitied Manhattan skyline. In the months after the attacks, he had sequestered himself, reading the texts of radical jihadists like Hassan al-Banna, founder of the Muslim Brotherhood in Egypt, who, according to Berman, "expressed a considerable admiration for the Nazi Brownshirts." But it was not the specter of al-Banna that most terrified Berman. That power was reserved for Sayyid Qutb, another Egyptian who is considered Islamism's most influential thinker. Qutb had lived in America and could put his rhetorical finger on the most insidious and damning perversity of the Western world. It lay in the very foundation of liberal society, the separation of Church and State, which he deemed the "hideous schizophrenia" of modern society. More, he felt that liberalism was a poison that could only distract and pollute the Muslim world.* In this way, Qutb presented Berman with the model villain for his narrative. For, unlike the fantasist

* Berman quotes Qutb's *In The Shade of the Koran*, choosing a passage that echoes the leftist critique of capitalism's destruction of society's communitarian fiber: "We must not be deluded by false appearances when we see that nations which do not believe or implement the Divine method are enjoying abundance and affluence."

anti-war protesters, who see capitalism and U.S. foreign policy as the ultimate provocations for Islamist rage, Qutb's jihad was driven by ideological absolutes. It was liberalism itself that he despised; a system that sought to penetrate Muslim culture with ideas that, if unleashed, would "exterminate" Islam. As Berman recounts in *Terror and Liberalism,* Qutb called on the Arab vanguard to fight the jihad as a religious war against liberal society.[32] Thus, Berman implies, the war on liberalism is not one that can be avoided by simply softening U.S. foreign policy or intensifying our diplomatic efforts. It is by definition, totalitarian, and must be fought with the same ferocity summoned to defeat Adolf Hitler. The first target would be Saddam Hussein.

But, again, Berman found himself staring into the reactionary abyss of the anti-war left. Saddam Hussein may well be a dictator, they admitted, but he was not marching on France, nor did he present a credible threat to Western freedom. In this argument Berman identified the worst elements of liberal society. And no person was more stagnant in his thinking than the protesters' totemic leader, Noam Chomsky, who seemed stuck in a time warp of sixties anti-imperialism and ignorance of the true nature of the terrorist threat.* Berman could barely veil his contempt. In refusing to see the Muslim jihadists as the true threat to America, the protestors had, instead, chosen to champion them as victims. For the anti-war left, the jihadists were a movement, wrote Berman, parroting his targets, that had "stuck a well-deserved pin in the sides of the rich and powerful." Blinded by their hatred for Bush, the peaceniks had failed to investigate the pathological roots of the Islamist jihad. Either that, or they saw it and were simply in

---

* Reducing the anti-war left's Chomskyite position, Berman wrote: "[Their] arguments showed that, if 9/11 was bad, America itself was ultimately responsible. World events could be rationally analyzed. The greed of American corporations, and the long history of American greed in the past, sufficed to explain every last astounding act of suicide terror." Quote from Paul Berman, *Terror and Liberalism* (New York: Norton, 2003), p. 151.

denial of its criminal nature. Then, they chose appeasement over engagement.

In Berman's narrative, the post-9/11 American society is comprised of heroic, courageous figures who have taken a stand against totalitarianism by backing the War on Terror, and their opponents: naïve idealists and fascist apologists who can't see the forest through the trees. The concept of using preemptive, unilateral force to promote humanitarian principles is the foundation of what has become known as "liberal interventionism." A product of the same kind of DIY, take-it-to-the-streets revolutionary pro-activism the '68ers showed in Chicago, Prague and Paris, it first took hold of the mass political imagination during the 1999 bombing of Serbia. At that time, many on the left in Europe and the United States were split over whether to support NATO's planned military campaign to halt Milosevic's alleged genocide of ethnic Albanians. While Serbian soldiers raped and pillaged their way through Kosovo, Berman remembers that many leftists were still caught up in the fears of old, worrying about the evils of American hegemony instead of the mass killing of civilians. But Kosovo was a watershed moment for the radicals who supported a vision of liberal rescue.[*]

While many on the left were ready to support military action in Kosovo and champion the cause of liberal intervention, it was

---

[*] The concept of liberal interventionism was inspired by Bernard Kouchner, the physician turned activist who founded Doctors Without Borders. Kouchner is a '68er who built his legacy on the kind of direct action that once characterized the generation's rebellious period. When thousands of Vietnamese fled into the ocean on handmade rafts, Kouchner did not wait for any politician to give him permission. He converted a ship into a mobile hospital, staffed it with volunteer doctors and raced to the rescue of the drowning refugees. It was a form of humanitarian direct action that did not seek the approval, nor legal sanction, of the State. And it became the inspiration for the kind liberal war that Paul Berman has been writing about since he took on Richard Nixon in 1991. One that essentially declares liberals can't afford to wait for permission from archaic bureaucracies like the United Nations to rid the world of fascism, coalitions of the willing should strap up and move in under the banner of liberal democracy.

not an argument they were willing to extend to the invasion of Iraq. Todd Gitlin stood beside Paul Berman in supporting the bombing of Serbia and the American overthrow of the Taliban in Afghanistan after 9/11. But when it came to Iraq, Gitlin could not support the invasion under the banner of a liberal intervention. For him, this form of unilateral military action is not something that can become a templated response. Rather, as he told me, it's "a puzzle, it's a conundrum that has to be thought through." He admits that it is not something he is opposed to "either by the coalitions of the generally willing or on occasion unilateral intervention... But Iraq was really an idiotic proposition for U.S. power."

Though Gitlin is as militantly against Islamism as any other pro-war liberal, and equally condemnatory of Saddam Hussein, the administration's justification for Iraq didn't win him over.

"I never thought there was going to go well for Iraqis one way or the other. I thought the choices stank. I thought the decision to let the Saddam government persist was an agonizing decision and I felt agonized about it—but I still thought it was necessary. Because I don't think politics is pretty. And I think Paul thought something more glorious was possible."

THE SECOND THOUGHTER

Of the three former radicals cited by J.Z. during our meeting in the small church basement, David Horowitz had the genetic and intellectual pedigree most suited for lifelong leftist activism. As bona fide red diaper baby, Horowitz's parents were schoolteachers and members of the Communist Party who brought him up under a strict Marxist ethos. Writing in his engrossing memoir, *Radical Son*, he describes an adolescence split between two wildly disconnected worlds. The first was the ordinary, inescapable realm of popular culture, populated with material symbols like *Ozzie and*

Harriet and *The Lone Ranger*. But the second was sheathed within the politics of Marxism-Leninism. There, his icons were writers from the communist *Daily Worker* and folk singers, the most influential of whom was his hero, Paul Robeson. In 1948, when he was 9 years old, Horowitz marched with his parents in the May Day parade. Five years later, he attended the death vigil for Julius and Ethel Rosenberg in Manhattan's Union Square Park.

"Looking back, I see that there is a way in which my entire youth was a form of quarantine," he writes in *Radical Son*. "There was the protective environment of our political community itself, a kind of hospital of the soul. We were embattled, surrounded by enemies, and this made the members of our tribe like family." [33]

But like many in his generation. the young Horowitz quickly grew out of the flimsy rationalizations of Stalin's totalitarian doctrine. In 1956 Stalin's successor, Nikita Khrushchev, issued a secret report to the Twentieth Party Congress on Stalin's crimes and the cult of personality that was the antithesis of Marx's socialist dream. The report was widely disseminated and shook the foundations of the global Communist party structure. While many old school American Communists, unable to transfer their socialist vision to the new Russian leadership, refused to completely abandon the old order, their children carried no such baggage. They saw value in the Marxist ideology that had been so perverted by the murderous authoritarianism of Stalin and reclaimed it for themselves under the rubric of the New Left. Tapping his deep indoctrination into socialist philosophy, Horowitz asserted himself as one of the most prodigious and brightest lights of the intellectual set. Commenting on Horowitz's chosen form of radical action, one-time collaborator Art Goldberg writes that "he almost never went to demonstrations. He was always too busy writing." [34]

Indeed, Horowitz sold over 25,000 copies of his 1962 book, *Student*, a seminal text on the New Left that delineated their poli-

tics from those of the communist Left; namely, a more progressive
commitment to democratic principles. Based in Berkeley during
the riotous downfall of the movement that had so haunted Gitlin
and Berman, Horowitz was not repelled by the collapsing moral
superstructure of the New Left. Instead, he waded into it, orches-
trating an overthrow of journalist Robert Scheer's editorial hierarchy at *Ramparts* magazine and forming a close relationship with
embattled Black Panther Party (BPP) leader Huey Newton.[35]

When David Horowitz was first introduced to Huey Newton,
the Panther cofounder and de facto leader was in Oakland being
retried for the 1968 murder of a police officer. Writing in *Radical
Son*, Horowitz remembers a muscular, bare-chested Newton
standing in his posh apartment that had been provided by Hollywood insider Bert Schneider, producer of the Monkees and Jack
Nicholson's pivotal film *Five Easy Pieces*. When Newton bragged
that he had just returned from an audience with the Chinese
Premier, Horowitz challenged him over China's status as a police
state. The argument was so intense Horowitz thought Newton was
going to hit him.[36]

Energized by their mutual ideological ferocity, the two became
friends and Horowitz began putting together financing for one of
Newton's pet projects, the Oakland Community Learning Center
for inner city youth. At this point, Horowitz admits, he should
have been more suspicious about the internal problems of the
BPP. Newton was widely reputed to have a cocaine problem and
had expelled his co-founder Bobby Seale from the party over a
ridiculously trivial matter. More, there was a steady flow of reports
that Panthers were involved in attacks on both police and civilians and the BPP's reputation in the Oakland community was so
bad, Horowitz was having difficulty bringing other progressive
blacks into the organization. But none of this deflected Horowitz's commitment to the school project. He even stayed on when

Newton fled to Cuba after being charged with shooting a young prostitute.

Facing a party in turmoil, the new Panther leader Elaine Brown asked Horowitz to find someone to manage the party finances. In June 1974, he brought in Betty Van Patter, an old associate and bookkeeper at *Ramparts*. Six months later, Van Patter disappeared from a Berkeley tavern and was never seen again.[37]

Writing in his column on *Salon* on the twenty-fifth anniversary of her death, Horowitz agonized over the murder of his friend, whom he had brought into the organization. "By the time the police fished her battered body out of San Francisco Bay in January 1975, I knew that her killers were the Panthers themselves." *[38] While he grieved Van Patter's murder, Horowitz seethed at the support the Panthers were still receiving from mainstream political entities like the Democratic Party, trade unions and, of course, the same New Left radical groups he was involved with. But it was the latter who were most guilty because they were closest to the Panther culture and had even come to idealize and celebrate the criminal element in the Panther leadership as a form of rebellion against the corporate capitalism that was, they believed, in itself a form of theft. The left's belief in the lie protected the Panthers and, ultimately, had endangered Betty Van Patter. For this, Horowitz could never forgive himself or the "progressive" movement.[39]

With her death, Van Patter took Horowitz's Utopian ideal to the grave, initiating a period of deep self-investigation and ideological revisionism that far exceeds that of Todd Gitlin or Paul Berman. The description of his loss of faith comes as close to a Damascene conversion as any that I have read by a person of his generation.

---

* Though her murder is still unsolved, it is widely believed Van Patter had discovered some degree of corruption or fraud in the BPP finances.

"For the first time in my conscious life I was looking at myself in my human nakedness," he writes in *Radical Son*, "without the support of revolutionary hopes, without the faith in a revolutionary future... For the first time in my life I confronted myself as I really was in the endless march of human coming and going. *I was nothing.*" * [40]

He never looked back. Speaking to him by phone from his home in California, I begin by asking about the violent dislocation he experienced from all his youthful idealism and political Utopianism. Before I can finish, he cuts me off. [41]

"Let's start with this: Idealism kills."

He pauses for a moment, as if to make sure I have understood the gravity of his charge.

"In the name of an impossible dream, any crime is justified. And that's why the Left has committed the worst atrocities of the twentieth century, because it's intoxicated with this fantasy that it can remake the world into a place where there's something called 'social justice.' "

Horowitz uses the Biblical metaphor of the Garden of Eden to describe the Left's perversion of free will, it's idolatrous quest for the forbidden fruit.

"Adam and Eve, in a way, were leftists," he tells me. "Erich Fromm once wrote a book, *You Shall Be As Gods*; that's the siren song of the Left. That's what the snake says to Adam and Eve in the garden, that's the whole point of it. They had better than Socialism, right? They didn't have to work, they had food drop-

* A confessional as much a generational history, *Radical Son* is a great read, but it ultimately serves as a rolling indictment of the values and ideals that he once held so dear. Favorite targets are *Ramparts* editor and Horowitz arch-enemy Robert Scheer (a lazy authoritarian chauvinist), SDS honcho Tom Hayden (a duplicitous, violent endangerer of other people's lives) and New Left spiritual guru Michael Lerner, who, according to Horowitz's account, abandoned his young child for the hippy lifestyle of Berkeley and expressed shock when Horowitz told him he hadn't tried acid: "David, you *have* to take LSD. Until you've dropped acid, you don't know what socialism is."

ping from the trees, they didn't die. But that wasn't enough for them, they had to know evil, they had to have that knowledge, they had to be like God, they wanted control of their own destiny."

According to Horowitz, it is the yearning for the impossible maxim of Earthly perfection that makes the Left dangerous. "So, in the name of that, the Left supports monsters."

Of course, he is talking about Stalin, Mao and Castro. But the question begs, if the support of monsters is a leftist tendency, how does he explain the Republican's support of Saddam Hussein throughout the 1980s?

"You know the United States did tilt towards Iraq in the Iran-Iraq War. It's not because we supported Iraq but because we didn't want the Iranians, who were four times as big, to win the war because they were all chanting 'Death to America!' That was radical Islam, Khomeini. So it was just a classic balance of power politics. But the Left has to go way beyond that: 'The United States loved Saddam Hussein, they *supported* him.' That's what gets the cheers. So it's just anything to hate America—radical hate and very close to fascism. Fascism is misunderstood as a right-wing phenomenon, but it really isn't."

Rather, Horowitz explains, fascism is the result of failed expectations. This was the lesson of the post-Vietnam period in which all of the radical dreams had funneled into a churning vacuum of ideological violence.

"You have ideas that don't compute with reality," he explains, almost wistfully. "For some people the reality breaks through and for others it doesn't."

For Horowitz, the reality finally broke through during the 1984 presidential election, when the Nicaraguan Sandanistas were a major campaign issue. Up until then, he had been in a dormant phase. After the death of Betty Van Patter he dropped out of all political life, turning his energy to co-authoring (with his

Ramparts co-editor Peter Collier) a series of crowd-pleasing books on American political dynasties: *The Rockefellers*, *The Kennedys*, and *The Fords*. The biographies made him famous and wealthy. In the late seventies he slowly resurfaced, turning his attention to presidential politics and voting for the Democratic incumbent Jimmy Carter in 1980. It was the first presidential vote he had cast since 1964 and one of the factors that drove his support for Carter was the genteel president's 1979 decision to allow the leftist Sandinistas to take power in Nicaragua.[42]

But the Republican juggernaut of Ronald Reagan proved too enticing to the America electorate and Horowitz's candidate lost. During the next four years, Reagan's support of the Nicaraguan Contra rebels dominated the American scene and divided the nation. When Horowitz finally looked under the hood of the Sandinista engine, he, like Paul Berman, discovered "Marxist protégés of Castro who had announced their intention to turn Nicaragua into another Cuba." This time, Horowitz could not allow the radicals to get their way and turn another Latin American country into an authoritarian economic basket case. With the issue of Contra support shaping up as a major campaign issue—some Democrats were threatening to cut off aid to the guerrillas—Horowitz made up his mind, walked into the voting booth and marked an X for Ronald Reagan.[43]

Hearing that Horowitz and Collier had both gone Republican, the *Washington Post* asked the team to write an article about their defection from the left. Still not complete converts to Reaganism, Horowitz and Collier were, however, ready to publicly swear off from their New Leftist idealism, writing that their vote for Reagan represented a disavowal of "the self-aggrandizing romance with the corrupt Third Worldism; to the casual indulgence of Soviet totalitarianism; to the hypocritical and self-dramatizing anti-Americanism which is the New Left's bequest to mainstream politics."[44]

Horowitz hit the speakers' circuit and began developing the thesis for his new political alignment with the conservative cause. It took the form of a narrative, one that recounted his process of political transformation and ultimately inspired Horowitz to self-identify as a "second thoughter." * At first, Horowitz classified himself more as *sui generis*—anti the Left—than *for* anything else. But soon he began reading conservative magazines like *Commentary* and found that he had far more in common with the Reaganite Republicans than his old radical comrades, let alone the moderate leftists in the Democratic Party. He began to investigate the writings of an older generation of second thoughters he had once despised and accused of treachery. These were the neoconservative thinkers Irving Kristol and Norman Podhoretz, former liberals who had become disillusioned with the failed promise of the Left and carved out a new approach to radical intellectual rightism. He couldn't help but admire their courage. Upon meeting Horowitz, Podhoretz warned him, "When you were on the left, you got away with everything. Now that you're on the right, you'd better be careful, because they won't let you get away with anything." The words turned out to be prophetic. There was a price to pay for his disloyalty.

"The one thing that really struck me, after I had my second thoughts," Horowitz admits, "was when I lost all my friends, every single friend that I had ever made. You're a young person, but you can still imagine what it would be like to lose all your friends and be hated by them. That keeps people in line."

Today Horowitz, like Peter Hitchens, sees conservatism as a

* Writing on his website in 2002, Horowitz distinguished between himself and the left-wing intellectuals whose "blood still warms when they hear the word "revolution." We second thoughters, on the other hand… are impressed by the fact that in the long run the counter-revolution produces more compassionate results. In terms of the proletariat, conservative, free market solutions are actually best." Quote from David Horowitz, "The Destructive Romance of the Intellectuals," TownHall.com, July 29, 2002.

natural destination for the conscious political disciple. The only force that can obstruct the individual from making the leap is the primeval fear of abandonment. "I realized that I never thought about this while I was a leftist. You know, you always want to kid yourself into thinking you've come to the conclusion for perfectly honorably and reasonable reasons but there are certain things that are just unthinkable if you're in the left…. the unthinkable is really that you're going to lose your whole community."

Twenty-five years after he first arrived in Berkeley as a radical anti-war agitant, Horowitz returned to address a group of pro-Sandinista students. He was shouted off the stage. The text of the speech was reprinted in *Commentary*, which finally put Horowitz's new conservatism on a solid footing. In response, the *Village Voice* published an article attacking Horowitz's ideological bi-polarity, characterizing him as a quasi-religious born-again in the cloak of Judas: "He doesn't correct; he converts. What he denounced before, he announces today." The writer was Paul Berman.

Horowitz responded with his own article in the *Voice*, "Better Ron, Than Red," chronicling the murder of Betty Van Patter and attributing his second thoughts to the realization that "the best intentions can lead to the worst ends." It was the beginning of a minor literary feud that would reach its dramatic climax in the fall of 1987 when both writers were in Nicaragua, albeit for very different reasons.

In October 1987, Horowitz and Collier had been recruited by the U.S. State Department and sent to capital city, Managua. Their mission: to train the Sandinista opposition to "stir up trouble" deploying the same anti-authoritarian tactics they had used against the U.S. government as New Leftists. Berman was there reporting on the Sandinista revolution for the *Village Voice* when they ran into each other in the lobby of the Intercontinental Hotel. Though the two had sparred publicly, Horowitz felt encouraged by Berman's controversial *Mother Jones* article, published the previous year, that had so divided the left. So he invited him to lunch. Sitting in the dining room of the hotel, they began to argue over the Sandinistas. Despite their flaws, Berman still believed in the potential for a progressive Marxist economic program. Horowitz became enraged and made a scene. Aware that Sandinista agents were probably among those in the room, he raised his voice defiantly. "For the sake of the poorest peasants in this godforsaken country, I can't wait for the Contras to march into this town and liberate it from these Sandinistas!"

From that point on, Horowitz took the "second thoughter" theme and made it central to his platform as the left's primary *antagoniste*. A few months after the scene in Managua, he and Collier organized a Second Thoughts Conference in Washington. "We only had two criteria," he explains, "one, that they were opposed to Communism. The other, that they were opposed to the Sandinistas." In 1989, they published their "second thoughts manifesto," *Destructive Generation*, a critical memoir that deconstructed the "destructive legacy" of the New Left, and their former selves. Their radicalism, Horowitz and Collier claimed, was inspired "not by altruism and love but nihilism and hate."[45] This confession, of course, was a blanket indictment for the entire left. So the left bit back. Horowitz had ugly run-ins with Christopher Hitchens and David Rieff and was the target of spirited attacks in the *Nation, Washington Monthly,* and the *New Republic.* One of the most damning was that of Horowitz's old nemesis, Paul Berman, who tacitly imputed the rise a "criminal-intellectual left-wing culture" in the San Francisco area to the influence of Horowitz's own radical *Ramparts* magazine.[46]

When I asked him to clarify his statement Berman explained that there was "a cult of criminality for a while in the New Left. 'You should be a thief, you should be a criminal.' It was a bit of a Jean Genet thing, 'we're going to be super-rebels.' Some of this was in the Black Panther Party, where people celebrated their criminal backgrounds—they'd been in jail for holding up people and raping women. The cult of the Black Panther Party owed a lot to David Horowitz, [who] is hugely responsible for creating that cult; he created it and then blamed everyone else."

Though they have both ended up on the same side of the Iraq War debate, Berman disavows any linearity to Horowitz's dramatic conversion.

"To me, on one hand he's a guy who went through a Damascene moment as you say, but on the other hand, he's a guy who didn't at all. I don't think I went through a Damascene moment where I converted ideologically. I do think I've grown older, more subtle, more sophisticated, more capable of making points that might have an aspect of ambiguity or ambivalence in them, which you get to do more skillfully as you get older. Horowitz is a guy who never did that. I think he's a fanatic who figured out a way to continue being a fanatic. He used to be a Communist fanatic—which he denies—and now he's a right-wing fanatic. He just enjoys the fanatical moment."

When I press Horowitz on his legendary combativeness and rhetorical pugilism, he confesses to being an instigator. But only out of a reaction to the battle being waged against him by the reactionary left.

"I'm under such furious attack all of the time, and my pugnacity was, in some sense, charactological and in some sense, calculated. When I woke up, as it were, I began to be able to feel how the other guy feels and look at the attacks that we made on people. I just said I was going to address the left the way the left addresses everybody else. Give them a taste of their own medicine. Of course, I've been doing it now for a very long time, I had set out to do that initially, but I'd been under such attack all the time that I think it's somewhat affected my tone."

In fact, Horowitz can be extremely incisive and almost violent in his written critiques of the left. Talking to him is a wholly different experience. He comes across as a person who genuinely wants to be liked, but who can't help playing a little rough, rubbing dirt in the eyes of his opponents. Now, after all the kids have fled the ideological sandbox, he doesn't understand why they don't want to play with him anymore.

I asked Paul Berman how he feels sharing the pro-war platform with David Horowitz. He answered dryly, "Oh well, you know, I see all kinds of terrible people with positions like mine, but then I see all kinds of terrible people with positions against mine. Life offers alternatives."

One of the terrible people who shares Berman's pro-war position is George Bush, whom he described as "the worst president the U.S. has ever had." For Horowitz, this was more proof of the "narrow-minded, self-righteous, arrogance of the political left." Responding to Berman's deprecation of Bush, Horowitz wrote on his website, "By no stretch of any reasonable imagination… can Bush be judged anything but a leader who… belongs in the rare circle of Franklin Roosevelt, Harry Truman and Ronald Reagan as wartime leaders. Why can't Paul Berman summon the grace to concede this—or at least to acknowledge Bush's achievement without attacking Bush with such mean-spirited frenzy as to make himself look unhinged? The answer is that Berman is afraid to look in the mirror and see a man who has praised a defender of American capitalism and a man of faith or to give him his due."

In this response, Horowitz grants a rare insight into the conservative mindset. While most commentators promote the argument that Bush overthrew Saddam because he posed a threat to American security, Horowitz focuses his praise for the action on an economic platform. For him, in attacking Iraq Bush was, in part, acting a "defender of American capitalism." This falls perfectly within the thrust of the analysis that Sergeant Hollis's gave me in Iraq ("When Americans say liberation, we mean capitalism"). If this is true, then it certainly isn't something that has passed through the lips of any neoconservatives, let alone pro-war Republicans. I repeat the quote to Horowitz.

"That's encouraging to me," he replies, adding definitively, "There are no free societies that aren't capitalist and there never will be."

"But you could never get George Bush to talk that way," I prod.

Horowitz pauses for a moment before answering. "Well, capitalism is not a romantic story; it's a pragmatic one. And politics is about romance. If you're leader of a country like Bush is, you've got to give them romance. And that's why it was so smart of him to be a compassionate conservative. Very smart of him to sell democracy. Don't talk about capitalism. Very hard to defend a system that makes losers resentful."*

I can feel Horowitz smiling into the phone. He laughs to himself again, "That's well put, I like that." Then he turns serious and asks the $64,000 question: "How can you sell a war—who's going to give their lives for capitalism?"

Hollis, for a start. When I asked the young tank commander whether he was willing to die for capitalism, he shrugged. "Is capitalism worth fighting a war for? There's many reasons to fight a war. Land, resources, religion, patriotism, nationalism. Capitalism. Yes."

---

* Despite his explanation of the need for politicians to obfuscate the economic factors in war, when I asked Horowitz if Iraq was fought for economic goals, he snapped back into form, at least partially, replying: "No. Look, there's a reality. God played a very mean trick on everybody by putting the oil underneath these bozo's territories. And we need to get free of it. One thing the left has done, they have prevented us from having nuclear power plants so we're dependent on oil."

But, like David Horowitz, the soldier understands why this will never be offered as an official justification for war. "Can you tell mothers and daughters and sisters that your sons are dying for the American way of life?" he asked rhetorically. "Can you say that they're dying for capital goods? No, you cannot. So you have to make sure that whenever you fight, you fight for moral and ethical reasons. This is what the public buys."

What both Horowitz and Hollis are saying is while the mission to perpetuate capitalism is reason enough to wage a war, this is not something that can be explained to the American people. Instead, it must be proposed as a romantic, humanitarian adventure. The same kind of argument that pro-war liberals put forward for the military attacks on Slobodan Milosevic's Serbia and Saddam Hussein's Iraq. Yet, when I asked Paul Berman and Todd Gitlin, neither would concede that either of these campaigns were driven by economic concerns. So who's right?

Perhaps they both are. The fact is that spreading classic American values of individual freedom and democratic pluralism has been a core goal of U.S. foreign policy since the end of World War II, when Democratic President Harry Truman's proposed his "Truman Doctrine" in 1947. At that time, Truman was petitioning the U.S. Congress to put money toward helping countries that were fighting Communism, to stem the potential of a domino effect that would eventually reach American shores. Naturally, everyone understood he meant that they needed to bolster capitalist enterprise, but no U.S. leader has ever expressed their international objectives in terms of establishing free markets. Yet, in those nations that are considered success stories, it is the development of capitalism that is the major legacy of U.S. intervention. Look at Japan, Germany, Indonesia, Greece and Turkey. So even if the liberals choose to view the intent of military action as humanitarian, if the net outcome is a new market for American companies to sell products and find cheap labor, everybody wins. Except, of course, for the target nation, which has traded its autonomy for the exploiting hand of the free market. It's the classic case of good cop, bad cop.

A few weeks after my interview with David Horowitz, the final member of J.Z.'s trinity, I phone the young revolutionary to thank him for the inspiration. It turns out that a lot has changed in his life since we last met in the small church basement. Tired of waging his battle from the political margins, he enrolled in film school and is working on scripts to bring his radical ideas into the mainstream through fictional dramas.

He asks me where I am headed next, and I tell him that I have a film playing in Munich and that I am going to use the trip to do a little research into the impact of liberalism in the former East German and Yugoslavian socialist republics.

"Well you're going to the root of it then," he says.

"Glad you approve," I laugh. It reminds me of something he wrote to me in an email before that first meeting. "As a revolutionary the only way you can evaluate an action is through its outcome. Intentions, stated or otherwise, mean nothing in politics or war. It's through the result that we measure the success of an action."

4

The Liberals' War

It became necessary to destroy the village in order to save it.
— An American major (after the destruction
of the Vietnamese village Ben Tre)

FUKUYAMA'S HISTORY

A cloud of blue-tinged smoke wafts elegantly above the heads of
Germany's film and television elite. A chatty bunch, I watch as
they alternately draw from cigarettes and glasses of champagne to
fill their mouths between thick-accented declarations.

We're in the marble-pillared courtyard of a modern museum
for the opening night gala of the Munich International Film
Festival. Spotlights caress the sky as VIPs pull up in chauffer-driven
BMWs to make their well-timed entrances. Rail-thin starlets and
models mix it up with barrel-chested, tuxedoed Bavarian men.
White-shirted waiters wend their way through the crowds carrying
small orbs of sorbet suspended in crystal martini glasses. In one
corner, near a fountain, two women take a few last hits from a joint
and then kiss deeply before walking back into the fray.

Though it is not the country's premiere film event—Berlin
wins that contest—Munich is still one of Europe's best festivals,
especially noted for its American independent film program
curated by the legendary Ulla Rapp. I first met Rapp at Sundance

after a screening of my low-budget feature film *This Revolution*. As soon as the lights came up, this black-clad woman with a great mane of grey-streaked hair emerged from the milling audience and beamed at me. Speaking in a deep, lyrical German accent, Rapp introduced herself, urging, "You *must* come and show your film to the Germans! Will you come to Munich? Yes, yes, you must!" She then handed me her card and disappeared back into the crowd, undoubtedly to catch one of the 100-plus films she sees each year at the festival.

Six months later, I scanned the immaculate Munich streets from the backseat of a brand-new BMW 7 series sedan. This is the irony of filmmaking, that the director of a cheap little movie about anarchists who want to destroy America ends up staying in one of the plushest hotels in Germany. But instead of schmoozing, I am already planning my exit. I have decided that one area of liberalism that I want to explore is the ideological battle between American capitalism and Eastern bloc Communism. And this Munich trip gives me the chance to plan a larger expedition into two of Europe's more hotly contested battlegrounds in the post-war expansion of liberalism: Germany and the former Yugoslavia.

Germany, of course, was the initial epicenter for Cold War hysteria. It was in the capital city of Berlin that Russian-backed East German communists built a wall that came to symbolize the Manichean paradigm of the post-war era. For forty years, the Soviet Union engaged the West in a nuclear showdown from behind the Iron Curtain that scarred the German countryside and segregated a third of its population behind communist lines. But, despite a heavy propaganda campaign, it soon became clear that the armed borders were designed to keep East Germans *in* rather than West Germans *out*. The Wall ruined any chance Communism had to become a dynamic challenge to liberal democracy. Instead of working to develop a Marxist system within the changing world, the communists turned inward, creating the perfect living model of George Orwell's totalitarian nation state. With so much of their money and energy spent jealously keeping their population from seeking refuge in the West, the communist bloc languished and failed. Bankrupt and facing mass revolts in their central European states, in the mid-1980s Russian president Mikhail Gorbachev began to dismantle the autocratic machinery of the USSR. On November 9, 1989, the East German government officially reopened the border, initiating what would become the end of the Cold War. The world cheered, but nowhere was the victory of western liberalism more pronounced and widely celebrated than in Germany, which would reunite after forty years of imposed segregation.

So momentous were the events leading up to the final destruction of the Berlin Wall that in the summer of 1989, a few months before the East German government would surprise the world by opening the border, American scholar and policy analyst Francis Fukuyama predicted the end of history as imminent. Of course, he did not mean that history, as the progression of recorded events, would terminate. Rather, he predicted that the evolution of human social and political systems had reached its zenith.

"Are there," Fukuyama asked in his article published in the *National Interest*, "any fundamental 'contradictions' in human life that cannot be resolved in the context of modern liberalism,* that would be resolvable by an alternative political-economic structure?[1]

"No!" came the resounding reply from conservatives and neoliberals alike. And when the Wall came down that November, Francis Fukuyama seemed prophetic. No longer could anyone

---

* By liberalism, Fukuyama is referring to the system of constitutional democracy and free market capitalism championed by America's conservatives and liberals alike as the antithesis of Communism. It is the very system that so many young '60s era radicals fought to inculcate with their values of social equality and economic justice but ultimately failed.

question the supremacy of the Western model as a template for realizing the highest form of individual freedom. Communism had collapsed like so many chunks of concrete in the streets of Berlin, and now it lay in rubble. Two years after Ronald Reagan had scolded Gorbachev to "please tear down this Wall," the people had done it themselves. Now all that was left was a graffiti-covered slab in the heart of Berlin, a vibrant memorial to a dark legacy.

But, Fukuyama explained, at the end of history it was not necessary for all societies to become liberal ones, just that "they end their ideological pretensions of representing different and higher forms of human society." [2] The fall of the Wall had simply proved, once and for all, that liberal democracy was the killer app. All the free world needed was to plug it into the various hardware terminals of state political and economic systems and they would soon be humming at their highest socioeconomic potential. But now, twenty years after his declaration, many of the most hard-won battlefields are scenes of a resurgent nostalgia for the socialist dream.

TERRA TERRIBILIA

Axel Schmidt banks his car through a long corner that cuts through a thicket of lush green trees. The Volkswagen's wheels track noiselessly over the pavement, which is perfectly flat and bisected by crisp yellow lines. Axel guns the engine and shoots me a worried look in the rearview mirror, "I'm sorry, I should have warned you on the phone. Uncle Manfred can be... difficult."

I smile back, reassuringly, not wanting to upset his mother, Margreth Schmidt, who is seated next to him in the front seat. The two have journeyed from Margreth's small hometown of Bad Köenigshofen to pick me up at the Schweinfurt train station, 180 miles north of Munich. A few minutes after I got in the car, Axel dropped the bad news that his uncle Manfred had gone back on his word to grant me an interview about life under the old communist system. Despite having traveled six hours to get here, I am undeterred.

"You have to understand," Axel continues, "people from the East are very skeptical of Westerners. Especially Americans. Manfred doesn't like to talk about the past. I think it's very painful for him."

In his younger years, Axel had a lot of questions about uncle Manfred and the border that divided them. Most perplexing was why his uncle would never come to see them in Bad Köenigshofen. When Axel got up to the courage to ask Manfred—careful not to let his parents hear him—the tough talking cop shrugged and replied, "We have everything we need here. Why would I want to go to your side?"

Axel smiles wryly, "He was a product of the system. To this day he'll still tell you the Wall was built to keep people *out.* He would never accept that anyone but the criminals or naïve youth would ever want to leave the East side. You couldn't do better than they had it in the GDR [German Democratic Republic]. Everything else was just a lie, an illusion propagated by American imperialism."

Speaking to Axel by phone before I left for Europe, he explained that uncle Manfred has not changed his view of the West. In fact he is just as steadfast in his condemnation of liberal economies and the havoc they wreak on their people and communities. For many in Manfred's generation, forced reunification has only brought economic hardship and social crisis. Pressured by forty years of American propaganda, he does not blame the East German people for craving the fruits of capitalism. But now, nearly two decades since the Wall came down, the former East Germany is only a shadow of its communist self. New buildings—built with the investment and subsidies earmarked for the reconstruction—stand empty, the economy too slow to bring in new tenants. Worse, the free market system that disposed of the state's central planners attracted the worst kind of scavengers, buying up the government-owned businesses and selling off the machinery for a quick profit, leaving the Easterners—those who stayed—unemployed and crime-plagued. Today a dozen workers line up for a single job posting. Political and economic freedom have been realized, Axel's uncle Manfred is willing to admit, but at great cost to their social fabric and individual pride, which has been pummeled by the condescension of West Germans who feel the reunification has dragged them down.

Nearly two decades after reunification, the gap between East and West Germans is expanding. While there was an initial, collective euphoria at the death of Communism and new life under the liberal market economy, the honeymoon did not last. Forty years of cultural and political estrangement had divided Germany into two distinct peoples and the work of bringing the socioeconomic standards of the East to par with the West would not prove to be as easy as Chancellor Helmut Kohl had hoped. Instead of the "flourishing landscapes" he promised for the East, unification put such a strain on the West that resentments began to develop between the two sides.

Presented with an historical opportunity to convert the East's centrally planned socialist economy to a decentralized free market, Chancellor Kohl reached far beyond his fiscal grasp. First, he ordered an at-par exchange of East German marks for the much higher valued West German deutschmark, a move that ultimately devalued the currency and drove up interest rates, depressing economic growth. To prevent another drain of man and brainpower to the West, Kohl increased East German wages despite significantly lower rates of productivity from the former

Communist workers.* He also offered to bring Easterners into the West's social welfare system, granting them health benefits, unemployment insurance, and old age pensions.

"Something very basic went wrong with German unification," wrote Professor Norbert Walter, chief economist at the Deutsche Bank Group, in 2001. "Instead of offering helping hands, an open mind and a sympathetic heart, West Germans opened their checkbooks. While the money helped materially, it did no good at the human level. In the west, taxpayers developed a condescending attitude. In the east, the status of 'poor relation,' of permanently receiving help, damaged self-confidence. Some people even stopped trying to help themselves. The situation encouraged dependence. Practices, which would have seen both sides contributing to the common table of the future, were not nurtured."[3]

This observation could have been written about any liberal society and its approach to aiding its poor or disadvantaged. In the United States, the liberals have built their legacy on battling to open federal coffers for their various social causes. But as we have seen, it did nothing to bridge the gap between the lower classes and their wealthy champions, neither on economic, nor human terms. It is the nature of a free market society in which its citizens are, first and foremost, competitors pitted against each other in a way designed to bring out "the best" in them.

Axel guns his engine as we zoom through the former East German town of Meiningen, once the epicenter of nineteenth century European repertory theatre. I feel a sense of exhilaration. It's not just the pace at which Axel drives past rows of badly weathered neoclassical housing, lined mere feet from the narrow roads. More, it is the sense of being in alien territory, a place that was once

---

* To give a sense of how drastic an adjustment this was, in a study for American University in Paris, Gabriel Issa reports that: "In 1991 the East German wage level was on average 55 percent of the West German level with a productivity level of only 30 percent of the West German industry." Quote from "German Privatization Program," Spring 1995.

cut off from the rest of the world. In ancient times, mapmakers used the term *terra terribilia* to identify what was beyond their knowledge of the Earth. The connotation was negative, meant to induce fear in the hearts of those whose curiosity extended beyond the perimeter of the kingdom, to lands that remained unconquered by their imperial masters. Meiningen, with its mix of Baroque architecture and decaying Communist-era facilities still has the look of old East Germany. It feels like a land frozen in time, ossified proof of Fukuyama's edict that history has ended and all that remain are the scars of the Communists' misbegotten geographic surgery. I can't help wondering if towns like this serve some higher purpose, as if to remind us that the only true challenge to liberalism was a failure of incalculable proportions, never to be attempted again.

Eventually, we pull up outside Uncle Manfred's small row house in the town of Dietzhausen. Axel throws me a skeptical look as he walks toward the gate. I nod to confirm that I am still determined to engage his uncle. Just as Axel is about to knock, the door swings open. Uncle Manfred pokes his head out and gives me the once over. I smile at him. He shrugs and turns back into the gloomy house.

Manfred leads us out into in his back yard and over to a makeshift gazebo. A small table has been set with china teacups and saucers. Manfred's wife come out behind us carrying a teapot and a large soft drink bottle. As we take our seats in the wooden structure, Manfred asks if we'd like tea or, he points to the bottle, "Vita-Cola."[4]

I choose the cola and Manfred smiles warmly, handing it to me. I wink at Axel, signaling that I think I might be off to a good start. Axel laughs and explains that at the outset of reunification, many East Germans abandoned the state-produced food brands in favor of Western ones. Under the communist regime, Vita-Cola was the only soft drink available in the stores and so as soon as the border went down Coca-Cola became the brand of choice. But when the economy began to falter, East German resentment funneled into the marketplace. Vita-Cola suddenly enjoyed a resurgence in popularity. For Manfred, Axel tells me, this is an obvious source of pride.

I ask how he felt when the Wall came down in 1989, "Was it traumatic for you?"

Axel puts the question to his uncle. Manfred drags pensively on his cigarette, avoiding my eyes. "I wouldn't describe it as traumatic, but we had very mixed emotions about the whole thing." Manfred flicks his butt nervously. "Before unification was technically established, Kohl said nobody in the East will do worse than they are now, but a lot of people will do better. Those were words we held on to. You have to understand, our entire world was changing. Everything I had been brought up to believe in, they were saying it was a lie. And my generation, the ones who were born into it, who knew nothing else, we were considered the problem… the ones who would be most difficult to integrate. But we tried."

"Did you ever consider moving to the West?"

I watch Manfred wince slightly as Axel translates the question. "No. Why should I? This is my home. But I didn't think it would ever get this bad. At first it was acceptable. They built the roads and the shopping centers. They adjusted the currency. But over time the negative aspects grew. Crime, drug addiction, poverty in the streets; things which we never had to deal with before suddenly became major problems. The West just sold us out. They opened the door for capitalists who never cared about us or the history of our state corporations, and they fed on us like carrion."

For older, unskilled East Germans like Manfred, the impact of privatization was felt immediately. Unprofitable companies were closed and their assets sold off, leaving thousands unemployed.

Those that did survive had to make drastic changes to become competitive in the world market, laying off workers and cutting many of the social benefits that had been provided by the state-owned companies.

Manfred, who had left the police force and gone to work for a bicycle manufacturer, was forced into retirement four years after unification. "They made be quit at 55 and take my pension. It is 860 deutschemarks [$530 USD] per month," he shakes his head angrily. "After 46 years of work."

A national poll conducted by *Stern* magazine in 2004 reported that twenty percent of Germans feel the country would be better off if the Wall were back.[5] I ask Manfred if he's one of them.

"Yes," he answers quickly, "But it's not so much the border that I miss, as the system. We should have held onto some of our accomplishments, the values that were the good part of Communism. Instead, we let it all slip away... All in all, there was a better sense of camaraderie," he says. "If a matter needed to be sorted out, people put their heads together and resolved it. Likewise with the social structure. In our community, for instance, the kids wanted a swimming pool. So the local people got together with an engineer and created the plans and then for the next two months we used whatever we had, from our hands and wheelbarrows to bulldozers and cement trucks to get it built. But nowadays that's not the case. It's every man for himself and I'm not able to live in that way."

Manfred excuses himself and walks into the house to get some matches. While he is gone Axel tells me that he has never heard his uncle this conciliatory. "Manfred has softened quite a bit since when I was younger," he explains.

When Manfred returns, cigarette gripped firmly in his mouth. I decide to push my luck.

"During the communist era, the government argued that the

border was designed to keep people out of East Germany. But today we know that it was actually for keeping them in. How do you look back on that type of propaganda? Do you wish that the state could have been more honest with its people? Would that have prolonged its existence?"

At first Axel is reluctant to translate the question, perhaps fearful that his uncle will detect that I have been told of his own fervent belief in that doublespeak. But I press him and he agrees. Axel fumbles for words for a few moments and then blurts it out. Manfred's expression switches immediately from passive interest to stern disapproval. He looks at me and shakes his head.

"You don't know what you're talking about," he says, pointing at me with his unlit cigarette. "Of course there was propaganda. Every country uses propaganda during a time of war. But this is the problem, you are too young to see this border in its military perspective. We had NATO on one side and the Warsaw Pact on the other side. Both had acquired huge missiles that could have destroyed all of Europe and Russia and they were positioned on either side of the Wall. So of course the border was meant to keep them out of here. In one way, it was a demonstration of strength to show, 'Okay, we can block you. We can keep you outside.'"

Scratching a match on the rough wooden table, he lights his cigarette. "Many countries have built walls to protect themselves. Look at the Israelis and the wall they are building. Are they keeping Palestinians out or locking Jews in? Or locking Palestinians in and keeping Jews out? It depends on who you ask. In East Germany, the system was still Stalinist and very rigid for some people. And if they wanted to leave, there was always a way to go. But now, as we have learned, it didn't matter whether the system was communist or capitalist, Germany was going to have to undergo a drastic change. Even if we had never been divided, all of this would have happened. Today they say our system is liberal and the fence is gone, but still the young people are all leaving the East. So what is the difference between the two systems?

"The capitalists don't build a physical wall. Theirs is mental. It is a wall of shame that the citizen feels when they are made useless in a system that is based on the individual and not the whole. And that wall keeps people locked into a system that forces them to work at jobs that have no integrity and at a cost that is far below that of a dignified person. Tell me, whose wall is more dangerous in the long run?"

Manfred looks up at Axel's mother for the first time in our conversation. "Margreth used to come here and complain about the Wall. She always said, 'This is one country. Why do we need a fence?' But I knew that Germany was no longer one country. We didn't need a wall to understand that. Once the communists incorporated us into their system, most of us lost interest in trying to keep up with the West. We wanted this system to work because we knew that theoretically it was more fair and humane. And now, there is not one Germany. The East is simply one quarter of the West, that is how we feel. That is how we are treated, like the poor cousin. You can see why some of us want the Wall back, at least it would protect us from their pity and scorn."

"But didn't you ever sense that the West was more free?" I ask, "That liberalism was a more progressive political system?"

"Of course we knew they had better products than us, if that's what you mean. They were more free to consume. But what does freedom truly mean? As far as I am concerned, being free means that I have the freedom to make a decent minimal living. And be free not to worry about my future and who will take care of me when I am old. In that sense, we're less free now than we were with the border."

"But the communist system was totally bankrupt," I argue. "Eventually it was going to be unable to keep providing rent and social benefits and pension. So isn't liberalism a better long term system?"

"In the way that Americans apply liberalism, we don't want that at all. The meaning of the word has so many applications, it can be used in so many ways. There's not one particular meaning. If you are going to talk about it, you need to clarify it."

"Okay," I answer, "liberalism as a system that is based on protecting the rights of the individual and which is dedicated to providing every person with the opportunity to reach their highest potential."

"Is that what you think liberal means in America?" Manfred asks, "America is not liberal in that sense of the word. They have a class system and the people who are poorest, the lower class people, are worth nothing to the government. Where are the rights in that? I don't see how it can be enough for you to live in a slum and not have anything and just claim, 'at least I'm free.' To me that would not be enough. I cannot see why it would be enough for anyone else. I don't have an explanation for why Americans think that way."

Walking out to the car, Manfred seems despondent. We stop at his front gate and I turn to shake his hand. Manfred raises his finger and says, wistfully, "Something happened to us with that Wall. East Germans were forced to become a new type of person. For those, like me, who were born into the communist system, it was not a problem to adapt. It was all we knew. But for the others, who had lived under the capitalist system before the communists came, it was more difficult. The government told us that those who had experienced the capitalist system would never be able to lose it from their minds. So education was very important for them, so they could be taught how to think. Everything we did was based on the philosophy of communism. In Germany now, they do not care how the Easterners think. There is no emphasis on education about the new system. There is no philosophy of capitalism. It is just a way of living to make money. And that is why it won't last."

Driving back toward the West side, I keep thinking about Manfred's last words; this idea that capitalism does not have a philosophy, that it lacks an ideological core. I wonder if he is just parroting the teachings of his childhood, if this was part of the broader Soviet belief system. If so, it shows how badly they misjudged both the foundation of liberal society and human nature. By forcibly cutting off their citizens from the West, not only did they create a hunger in people to experience the forbidden, but they also gave the soulless capitalists something to fight against. If nothing else, it was the rise of communism as a world force that shaped the liberal ideology of the Cold War period. Which in turn fueled the capitalist engine that dedicated itself to outproducing, outfeeding, outclothing, outsatisfying, outlasting its totalitarian competitor.

In the post-Cold War era, there was no longer a justifiable cause to wage war against non-liberal systems. And so a new rationale was developed, one which empowered the West with a cause to wage unilateral military action. It was liberalism itself.

COLLATERAL DAMAGE

Two days later I am in Serbia, the battleground republic where American liberalism fought one of its most historic battles at the end of the twentieth century. This was the moment when unilateral warfare was justified in the name of "humanitarian interventionism." And while the economic dimensions of the conflict are rarely discussed except under the tainted banner of conspiracy theory, I am going to see for myself just what the impact has been on the society and economy.

Ostensibly this war was waged for humanity; to cripple a dictatorship that was ethnically cleansing a secessionist minority.

And while few would argue the virtues of standing idle while mass murder is being committed, it is worth asking why some genocides are more pertinent than others. Bill Clinton chose not to respond to the tragic drama that unfolded in Rwanda five years earlier, when 800,000 people were massacred. Perhaps, as some liberal interventionists explain, Serbia was his way of making up for the failure to act in Rwanda. Or, maybe there were simply better incentives.

In the case of Serbia, the mission was to end a brutal dictatorship with liberal and humanitarian intervention. But if the net result has been the establishment of a free market along with reforms implemented by neoliberal economists, then Serbia will provide an object lesson in kind of bait-and-switch gamesmanship that is played by wolves in sheep's clothing.

"One thing I heard was that it was a test to see if America was strong enough to defy the United Nations and declare its own war on humanitarian grounds," Miki Milakovic says distractedly, "They wanted to test the strength of their power."[6]

A waitress walks up and plunks down a large plate in front of us. Miki immediately sets to work, pouring olive oil on the colorful spread of diced cucumbers, onions and tomatoes. Next, he begins scooping pinches of pepper from a small dish. Looking up, he asks, "Do you want pepper on it?"

I nod, warily. Beside me, Miroslava Stojanovic blows smoke out of the side of her mouth and points at the vegetables. "It's Serbian salad. Have you ever had it before?"[7]

I had only been in Belgrade for a few hours before the two young artists invited me to experience some traditional Serbian cuisine. But I am more interested in their views of the 1999 NATO bombing campaign that decimated Serbia's civilian infrastructure and ultimately led to the fall of their president, Slobodan Milosevic.

Before the bombing, Miki worked at a petrochemical plant

in Pancevo, one of Serbia's big industrial cities. He remembers the missiles hitting their targets with pinpoint accuracy. "They destroyed parts of the plant but not the reservoirs full of gasoline. If they had hit those, it would have wiped out a third of the city." Chomping on raw cucumbers, he laughs, "For them, it was a demonstration of power. For us, it was a demonstration of powerlessness."

Of course, that was the point of the campaign, to force Milosevic to retreat from the Serbian province of Kosovo where his troops were engaged in a war against secessionist Albanians. It was the fourth major battle between the Yugoslav security forces and independence seeking ethnic minorities since Slovenia declared independence in 1991. Like the other conflicts in Bosnia and Croatia, Milosevic's troops were being accused of ethnic cleansing in the region, and this finally proved too much for the Western democracies. NATO hit Serbia's cities and bridges with bombs for over eleven weeks until Milosevic was forced to withdraw from Kosovo.

I ask the kids if the outcome of the bombing served its ultimate purpose, of protecting the Albanians.

Both of them shake their heads. "More Albanians were killed and evacuated during the bombing than before it," Miki says.

"The only thing that came out of the Kosovo war is the NATO base there. Those people didn't get their independence." Miroslava adds.

Noting their cynicism, I ask what they think the purpose of the war was, if not a humanitarian rescue operation. Miroslava shrugs her shoulders. "Yugoslavia was a large, powerful country that had to be split up. They invented a word for it; this is what they call Balkanization."

"But isn't there more freedom now that Milosevic is gone?" I ask.

"Well, what does free mean?" Miroslava asks. "The government is more free to use their position to make their own people wealthy. They are just as free to be corrupt as during Milosevic. We are more free to see it, but not more free to stop it."

Miki pushes the salad away and lights a cigarette. Smiling, he says, "That's the free market, I guess."

Back in 1999, as NATO planes pummeled the Balkan landscape, American liberals were engaged in a heated debate over the actual goals and merits of the military campaign. For some A-listers like Christopher Hitchens and David Rieff, Kosovo represented the inaugural campaign for "liberal intervention," which would later become the rallying cry for pro-war liberals who backed the overthrow of Saddam Hussein. Writing in the *Nation* two months into the NATO campaign, Hitchens—who, self-admittedly had been slow to put his support behind the bombing—justified the campaign as an option of last resort, "when the sheer exorbitance of the crimes in Kosovo became impossible to ignore."[8] Likewise, Rieff chastised the reluctant, anti-imperial liberals who "would prefer to see genocide… and the mass deportation of the Kosovars rather than strengthen, however marginally, the hegemony of the United States."[9]

Others questioned just how humanitarian the impulse to bomb Serbia could be, especially considering the Clinton administration's decision look past the mass slaughter of the separatist East Timorese by U.S.-allied Indonesian troops, not to mention the ongoing Turkish repression of the rebel Kurds and the 1994 Hutu massacre of Tutsis in Rwanda.* In America's sudden willingness to aid the Albanians, these critics saw other forces at work. Making his case for the bombing, Clinton put it in distinctly economic terms.

---

* While NATO was bombing Serbia, Indonesian troops were perpetrating the Liquica Church Massacre, in which 200 East Timorese civilians were killed. This was just the final chapter in two decades of brutal, genocidal violence which took between 100,000 and 250,000 lives between 1975 and 1999.

America was spearheading the new globalization movement* and, Clinton declared, "If we're going to have a strong economic relationship that includes our ability to sell around the world, Europe has got to be a key.... That's what this Kosovo thing is all about." [10] Arguing against the intervention in Kosovo, the *Nation's* Benjamin Schwarz and Christopher Layne wrote that Clinton, "thus seems to argue that the United States is fighting a war in Kosovo to make the world safe for capitalism." They found similar themes in the words of Defense Secretary William Cohen, who told business leaders that NATO's role in Eastern Europe would bring stability to the region. "And with that spread of stability," he vowed, "there is a prospect to attract investment." [11]

Like the dispute between liberals that erupted over the first Gulf war four years later, the NATO bombing divided people into camps based on their interpretation of the true aims of the military action. Was it humanitarian or economic? Reading commentaries from both sides of the debate, one is led to the conclusion that the two are mutually exclusive. It's either one, or the other. But for kids like Miki and Miroslava, the question isn't so incomplex.

Over the past fifty years, Yugoslavia had developed one of the more dynamic and resilient forms of state socialism. That posed a challenge, at least ideologically, to the globalist liberals who were now staking their claim to the world markets. But at the same time, the rise of a genocidal nationalist force within Yugoslav politics, and Europe's inability to deal with it on their own, had invited the NATO aggression. In the short time since the last NATO bombing, Serbia has been transformed into a liberal democratic prototype,

---

* During the global economic crisis of the 1970s, Yugoslavia was vastly over-extended and had no choice but to turn to the IMF and World Bank for a bailout. Sensing their opportunity, the economic hit men stepped in and funneled money into the country on the condition that their program of "structural adjustment" be adopted. Throughout the 1980s, Yugoslavians were subjected to various blasts of economic shock therapy. The result was massive unemployment and inflation which ultimately pitted the republics against each other, revitalizing old ethnic rivalries.

forced to accept the economic and political reforms that will qualify it for eventual inclusion in the European Union. While the economic and political elite understand these measures are necessary if Serbia is to be a player in the world economy, for many average working Serbs the loss of the socialist model has meant the loss of their national identity and their history.

NATO's military campaign, and the ensuing electoral defeat, arrest and extradition of Milosevic for war crimes, forms just a small part of Serbia's long and complicated struggle toward self-determination. The capital of the former Yugoslavia, Belgrade has been the scene of invasions, ethnic strife and territorial haggling that dominated the Balkan Peninsula for most of the twentieth century. Yugoslavia, itself, was never more than a collection of ethnically diverse peoples, ruled by a series of dictatorships that began at the end of World War I. In its largest incarnation, the country reached from the northern border of Greece to the southern borders of Hungary and Romania. During that period it was known as the Kingdom of Yugoslavia and ruled by King Alexander who held together an uneasy alliance of Serbs, Croats, Bosnians, Albanians, and Macedonians; all of whom had, at one point in their histories, been hated enemies of the others.

But with World War II, Yugoslavia became a prime target for Hitler and the Axis powers. In April 1941, Belgrade, along with several other major cities, was bombed by the German Luftwaffe and, after a brief fight, Yugoslavia was forced into a truce. Hitler promptly split up the country and began an ethnic cleansing program that ultimately wiped out over ten percent (1.7 million) of the population. Hitler and Mussolini also inflicted brutal collective punishment tactics on the Yugoslavians, sometimes shooting or hanging as many as 100 innocent civilians for each German or Italian soldier killed during the occupation. As a result, much of the bitter ethnic rivalries dissolved as the people threw their support behind Yugoslavia's guerrilla resistance army. Led by the communist Marshal Tito, the resistance started without the backing of any major Allied powers. And though, over time, Tito's fiercely brave fighters won the support of Britain, which set up a small force of RAF planes to supply the insurgency, the guerrillas were mostly left to their own devices. This offered Tito a rare quotient of autonomy from the victorious Allies, one that he used to his advantage at the end of the war. In 1945, when Russian troops marched into Belgrade to officially liberate it from the fascists, Tito quickly decided that he did not want Yugoslavia to turn into another Soviet satellite state and expelled them.

At the end of World War II, Tito used his troops—and war hero status—to establish control over the splintered Yugoslavian nations. In 1946, a new constitution was signed, reconstructing the country into six republics: Serbia, Croatia, Macedonia, Montenegro, Bosnia-Herzegovina, and Slovenia. Though Tito did not renounce Communism, his rejection of Stalin's overarching vision of a unified, Soviet-controlled bloc of communist states, or Cominform, led to a split between the two countries.* Tito sought to create a new form of socialism that would alchemize what he saw as the best aspects of Russia's centrally-planned economy and the West's free market system. He called it "worker's self-management." Like in Russia, the Yugoslav Communist Party maintained a monopoly over political affairs of the state, but it did not seek to control all aspects of local government and economic activity. Instead, workers were organized into cooperatives that set goals and managed finances of their respective operations. Through the

---

* Tito's rejection of both the Soviet Union and NATO led him to officially form the Non-Aligned Movement (NAM) in 1961. Together with leaders of India and Egypt—along with those of 25 other countries—Tito convened the first NAM summit in Belgrade, where the members asserted their desire to be independent of the Cold War struggle between Russia and the capitalist West. Today the NAM is comprised of over 100 nations that represent over 50 percent of the world's population.

cooperatives, the workers had a direct say over the allocation of profits and were provided with benefits like medical care, education, housing and pensions.

After Tito's death in 1980, a collective presidential leadership took over. But they were unable to provide a vision for the nation's future. Without any dominant, central patriarchal figure, Yugoslavia's long-festering ethnic tensions floated to the surface, threatening to dissolve the fragile conglomerate. For the Serbs, who held a dominant role in the national government despite the relatively small size of their population, the threat of losing the federation was too great a risk. Fiercely nationalistic, they worried about the fate of ethnic Serbs living within the borders of republics like Croatia, which had collaborated in the Nazi slaughter of Serbs during World War II.

Out of this vacuum emerged Slobodan Milosevic, a fast-rising Communist Party member who became president of Serbia in 1989. His immediate focus was to rein in the Republics of Slovenia and Croatia, which had begun a move toward democracy and liberal economic policies. Their leaders—no less nationalistic than Milosevic—sought more autonomy from Yugoslavia and proposed that the country become an informal confederation of republics. Milosevic, with the backing of the Yugoslav Army, refused, arguing that ethnic Serbs in Slovenia and Croatia should not be separated from their own people. But the two republics, which had supplied most of the economic growth during Tito's regime, were tired of taking orders from Belgrade.

On June 25, 1991, Slovenia and Croatia declared independence from Yugoslavia. For ten days Slovenian militia battled the Serb-controlled Yugoslav Army, ultimately driving them out of their borders. Croatia was not as successful. Ethnic Serb guerrilla fighters, though comprising only twelve percent of the population, were able to control key border regions. They backed up the national Army, attacking Croatian police and civilian targets and the region was thrown into a terrible civil war that lasted into the winter. Slowly, news began to filter out of Croatia that forces in the Serb-controlled areas were ethnically cleansing the non-Serbian population of Croats and Muslims.[*]

In January 1992, after the Serbs had succeeded in gaining control of a third of Croatia, a UN-brokered truce was signed by Milosevic and Franjo Tudjman, the Croatian leader. To protect the agreement, the United Nations created its UNPROFOR peace-keeping force and moved them into the region. But they proved to be wholly ineffective in disarming the Serbian guerrillas and returning the Croat refugees to their homes. The world slowly began waking up to the nightmare that was unfolding in the crumbling Yugoslavia.

Then all hell broke loose in Bosnia. In a larger-scale repeat of the Croatian war, Bosnia's Serbs fought the majority Muslims and minority Croats to keep the republic from winning its own independence. It was later revealed that Milosevic, upon realizing that Croatia and Slovenia were preparing to secede, began funneling money and arms to the Bosnian Serbs to prevent the Bosnians from separating. The ensuing conflict raged for three years and embroiled all parties in the violence. By the end of 1995, neither the Croat nor the Serb forces could claim innocence in the slaughter of civilians. A conservative estimate puts the total number of dead Bosnians at 200,000. While the Croats gave as good as they got: burning, looting, raping and murdering their way through Serb-controlled regions, the enduring image of the war is centered

* The Balkan conflict is one of the most controversial military struggles of the twentieth century. In this short recap, I have attempted to remain as neutral as possible while simultaneously elaborating those aspects of the conflict that became key justifications for NATO's bombing of Serbia. It is critical to understand that many of the leaders who ascended into the vacuum left by Tito used their power to agitate ethnic and nationalistic passions. For example, many neutral observers claim Croatian president Franjo Tudjman is as much to blame for the eventual bloodshed within his and Bosnia's borders as Milosevic.

in the small Bosnian mining town of Srebrenica, where, in July 1995, Serb forces massacred over 7,000 Muslims and Croats. It was the Srebrenica slaughter, targeted at non-Serbian, non-combatant males, which exposed the genocidal strategy pursued by Milosevic's forces. And it was this narrative that eventually drove America's liberals to support a military-backed, humanitarian intervention to overthrow the regime of Slobodan Milosevic.

By the end of 1995, the international community had had enough of the Bosnian War. President Bill Clinton, challenged by Republicans who claimed he was being soft on the Serbs, and realizing that only formally negotiated and militarily binding terms would end the fighting, made resolution of the Bosnian conflict a centerpiece mission to end his first term. In November 1995, Serbia's Milosevic, Croatia's Tudjman, and Bosnia's Alija Izetbegovic met in Dayton, Ohio to engage in the U.S.-sponsored peace talks. After three weeks, the Dayton Accords were drafted and prepared for final signatures in Paris later that December. Apart from the ceasefire, the agreement carved up Bosnia-Herzegovina, giving half to the Croats and Muslims and half to the Serbs. More importantly, Dayton replaced the UN peacekeeping forces with troops from NATO, which would soon engage in its first full-scale military conflict since its founding at the end of World War II.

After he signed the Dayton Accords, Milosevic was quickly rehabilitated to the status of international statesman. U.S. sanctions, which had been in effect since 1992, were lifted, breathing much-needed oxygen into the Yugoslavian economy. More importantly, American officials openly credited him with bringing peace to the region, which Milosevic used to help him win the Presidency of Yugoslavia. But this was just a fleeting moment of quiet before the final storm. In 1998, in the southern Serbian province of Kosovo where the ethnic Albanians had long suffered under Serb rule, armed guerrillas began agitating for secession.* This time it was the Kosovo Liberation Army (KLA) that led the struggle for independence. Newly enthroned in the office of president, Milosevic sent in Yugoslav security forces to engage the KLA and revisited the same ethnic cleansing tactics that had been used in the Croat and Bosnian wars, massacring Albanian men and driving hundreds of thousands of women and children out of the province.

Watching his much-lauded Balkans peace project fall to pieces, Clinton dispatched U.S. Secretary of State Madeleine Albright to Rambouillet, France to broker an agreement between the Serbs and Albanians. The crux of the deal required that Milosevic—who had watched the Yugoslav Federation be reduced to the single Republic of Serbia and its two provinces of Kosovo and Montenegro—grant a degree of autonomy to the Kosovars. Predictably, he refused. In March 1999, NATO went on the offensive, beginning an 78 day bombing campaign of Yugoslavia that, according to the EU, set the country back 50 years.

"I was sitting in my parent's house, hearing the sound of the planes diving toward Belgrade, wondering if they would hit our building," remembers Valentina Macura, a young broadcaster on Serbia's B92 radio network. "And all I could think about was, 'what kind of future is there for me?'"

We're sitting in an outdoor café in Belgrade early on a Saturday morning. As with so many of these young Serbs, I am struck by the pragmatism and political maturity that the crisis inured in them. They are able to recount all they endured without ever slipping into the kind of self-pity or anger that might be expected of people who

---

* The crisis in Kosovo did not emerge from a vacuum. The Kosovar Albanians, who comprised 90 percent of the Serbian province's population, had enjoyed considerable autonomy under Tito's regime. But during Milosevic's 1987–88 surge for the Serbian presidency, he focused his nationalistic rage on the issue of Kosovo, eventually stripping it of "provincial status." An apartheid-like police state was imposed, forcing hundreds of thousands of Albanians to flee. The rise of the Kosovo Liberation Army in 1997 was largely a reaction to these policies.

saw their whole country torn apart by their parents' generation.

Macura was twenty years old when the NATO planes started bombing the Serbian capital. Despite the threat of the nightly raids, she and her friends would take the perilous walk downtown and converge at discos or house parties. The fear and tension gave way to euphoric, cathartic releases in the form of dancing and making out. It was all they could do to keep their sanity during the seemingly endless parade of fighter jets zooming across the Serbian skies. Worse, they were counter-terrorized by Milosevic's state-controlled media apparatus, which never failed to report on the regular instances of civilian injuries and deaths from the high altitude bombing.

In order to protect their planes from Yugoslav anti-aircraft defenses, NATO ordered its pilots to fly three miles above ground. At this height, the targeting of bridges and military installations was left to high-tech missile guidance systems that made several tragic errors, including three separate strikes in April that killed at least 30 people, including eleven children in the village of Surdulica when their homes were hit by a 2,000 pound bomb.* By the end of the war, Human Rights Watch estimated that over 500 innocent civilians—both Serbs and Albanians—had been killed by errant ordnance.

"They invented this word, collateral damage, you know?" Macura explains. But I get the sense she means more than just the mortality rate. The bombing had an effect on the entire society, whether they were for or against the NATO action. Betrayed by their leader and the West, Macura and her friends turned inward.

* Most infamous of the NATO gaffes was the May 7 bombing of the Chinese Embassy which killed three journalists and injured twenty diplomats, setting off a wave of anti-U.S. protests in China. While president Clinton apologized for the "tragic event," the UK *Observer* reported that the bombing was a deliberate attempt to halt Chinese rebroadcasting of Yugoslav military communications. The *Observer* reported that "a source in the U.S. National Imagery and Mapping Agency said that the [official] story was 'a damned lie.'" See "Nato bombed Chinese deliberately," *Guardian Unlimited*, October 17, 1999.

When I ask her whom she blamed for bringing on the terror of the attacks, she balks at the simplification, explaining the situation in Serbia with Milosevic and America was not so black and white. "We hated Milosevic. But when the bombing started, we hated NATO as well. How can you say you are here to help us but then bomb us as well?"

It's a good question. Even Dr. Bernard Kouchner, the founder of Doctors Without Borders and originator of the concept of "humanitarian intervention," could see it's inherent contradictions. Writing in his book, *The Warriors of Peace*, Kouchner admitted, "Intervention—the word was frightening, it seemed synonymous with rape. But," he reasoned, "nothing is more consensual, so long as intervention always responds to a cry for help." [12] For Paul Berman, this cry for help was amplified by the failure of Europe to deal with its own affairs. And so it was left to the Americans to do it for them. Or, at least, to America's liberals. Kosovo was, he explains in *Power and the Idealists*, also known as the "Liberal's War, because it was the liberal idealists, more than the conservative realists, who were keen on intervention." [*][13]

Of course, he is right. One need only read some of the right-wing commentary from the period to see how the war split Americans along ideological lines. For conservatives like *Foreign Affairs* editor Fareed Zakaria, it did not matter so much that the bombing of Yugoslavia did not receive United Nations approval. Nor that it was being ordered by a philandering Democratic president. In those days conservatives were still isolationists who could not support the liberal desire for "nation building." Writing in William F. Buckley's

---

* Perhaps no liberal was more "keen" than the *New York Times*'s Thomas Friedman who gleefully called out the dogs of war, writing, "It should be lights out in Belgrade: every power grid, water pipe, road and war-related factory has to be targeted... [W]e will set your country back by pulverizing you. You want 1950? We can do 1950. You want 1389? We can do 1389." Friedman quoted in Norman Solomon, "Thomas Friedman, Liberal Sadist?" *Common Dreams*, July 27, 2005.

neoconservative *National Review,* Zakaria lamented the wholesale destruction of the nation's civilian infrastructure, the rebuilding of which was pegged at $50 billion. Worse, wrote Zakaria, "Yugoslavia has been turned into a Third World country" of which "NATO is now a colonial power." As the new security force in Kosovo, NATO was now the sole obstruction to the Kosovar dream of independence. "An odd role," Zakaria wrote, "for an alliance that has made the promotion of democracy one of its new goals." [14]

But, in the end, liberal democracy is exactly what the NATO bombing delivered to Yugoslavia. In June 1999, with several minor mutinies on his hands and no end to the NATO bombing in sight, Milosevic ordered the majority of his troops out of Kosovo. Ignoring an indictment for war crimes by the International Tribunal in the Hague, Milosevic called for elections in September 2000. When initial results showed an opposition victory, Milosevic refused to concede defeat. But his opponents, emboldened by the Western media's now-rapt attention to their drama, could smell blood. Hundreds of thousands of Serbians took to the streets in what became known as the October 5 protest. A general strike was called as opposition supporters stormed the Parliament buildings and took over the state television network. On October 6, after a thirteen-year run in which he presided over the breakup of Yugoslavia, Slobodan Milosevic officially stepped down from office. Five months later, Serbian police forces surrounded Milosevic's villa and arrested him on charges of embezzlement and corruption. With the U.S. pressuring Serbia's new leadership to extradite Milosevic to the Hague or be denied millions in critical aid money, the Serbs caved and snuck their former dictator out of the country in June 2001. After a long and protracted trial for crimes against humanity, Milosevic died in his cell on March 11, 2006.

In his absence, Belgrade settled into the peace, quietly becoming one of Europe's hottest tourist destinations. The narrow, serpentine downtown streets are crowded with young, strikingly beautiful Gen X and Y-ers hanging out in the public squares or drinking coffee at one of the ubiquitous outdoor cafés. Women outnumber men two to one and are as fashionable as any Parisian or Milanese trendsetter. I watch them from the terrace of a small café where I sit with Serbian philosopher Branimir Stojanovic and his translator. Searingly intelligent, Stojanovic cuts the perfect profile of an East European intellectual, cocking his shaved head, cradling his sharp chin in his right hand, and using his left to bludgeon the air with his ideas.

Finishing a long rant, Stojanovic tells me, "From the West we have a pressure to forget the era of socialism."

I wonder what other kinds of pressures the Serbian people are feeling. "Has Serbia been more impacted by American values and culture since the fall of Milosevic?"

He shakes his head. "Actually, Serbs were more Americanized during the 1960s and 1970s than they are today. During the Milosevic era there was this kind of bizarre folklorization of Serbian culture."*

"A reactionary impulse?" I ask.

"Yes, very reactionary. But during Tito's era, Americanization was a very interesting thing."

"I'm surprised Tito allowed it."

"It was a promotion of elite American culture," he explains. "I remember when some Yugoslav painters went to the United States and their style changed from socialist realism into something quite different. So it was state-encouraged. For example, I remember they did a comparison between Sunday TV programming in Ireland

---

* The "folklorization" that Stojanovic refers to actually had a name: *turbofolk*. It was epitomized by the busty singer Ceca who was married to Arkan, the genocidal Serb warlord. Her fusion of pop and Serbian folk music became a soundtrack for the garish gangster elite which ruled Serbia in Milsoevic's time. Arkan was eventually gunned down in Belgrade in 2000 and Ceca went on to play packed stadium concerts.

and Belgrade and it was the same, we were both watching the same movies—John Wayne movies—on Sunday. So it was very funny."

Stojanovic crosses his legs and leans toward me. Speaking in hushed Serbian, oblivious to the translator who strains to hear, he continues. "When you speak with people who spent their youth in the real socialism—the Soviet kind of real socialism in Bulgaria and other countries that were behind the Iron Curtain—they know nothing. They don't know who Marilyn Monroe is. I mean, they know her name, but they've never seen her movies. They don't know Velvet Underground or Brian Eno, or whatever. But these were common cultural knowns in Yugoslavia."

I ask him about his youth. Unlike most kids in the U.S., he grew up with a simultaneous love for the American avant-garde culture and an intuitive understanding that it was a reaction to capitalism's exploitive tendencies. As a student, he decided to focus all his energy on the study of psychoanalysis, which he pursued for fifteen years, until the start of the NATO bombing campaign. Up to that point, he had wrestled with the idea of becoming a clinical psychologist. But once the attacks began, those pursuits felt trivial.

"Everybody in Serbia had to suspend the idiotic doubts they had during the Milosevic era."

"What doubts?" I ask.

"The doubts of whether one should do this or that," he explains with a flick of his hand.

I ask him how the bombing affected other people, psychologically.

"My father died shortly after the NATO intervention," he says matter-of-factly. "My mother became demented during the NATO intervention. So the population hardest hit by the war was the oldest one. They were indirectly pushed into death. Their world was dying."

Sipping his espresso, Stojanovic adds, "It was the last vestige of the illusion that died then."

"Describe that illusion though," I press him. "What idea died at that point?"

"Independence. Socialism."

"Has capitalism replaced socialism?" I ask.

He shrugs, smiling for the first time. "The situation in Serbia is interesting because in Serbia all the basic political structures and all the basic political foundations for the past 100 years have refused to enter into capitalism. Or, at least, used this concept of trying to take all of the good of capitalism and throw out all the bad."

Of course, he's talking about Tito's model of worker's self-management, in which the society was based on a classless system that was also flexible enough to reward individuals for their unique talents and contributions. The nation was a family, a worker state, united under the strong patriarchal figure of the leader. But with the death of Tito, that fragile, egalitarian holograph began to flicker and mutate. With no gravitational force to remind them of their value as a whole, the once-bounteous Yugoslavian constellation was returned to a mere collection of states. And Milosevic was the Frankenstein born from that period. Under his rule, nationalism became genocide. Politics became war. Soldiers became gangsters. Ethnicity was suddenly the most valuable possession of all, or the biggest liability.

"Were you worried that the NATO bombing would destroy Yugoslavian socialism for good?" I ask.

"Milosevic's socialism was a total negation of Tito's socialism, so there was no complaint, really. But I also could not support the NATO intervention, in a certain way."

"Do you agree with the argument that it was a front for the incursion of a neoliberal agenda that was essentially designed to expand American global economic hegemony?"

"Of course it was," he replies.

"So what did you make of the official argument that the bombing was done for purely humanitarian reasons?"

"I agree with that."

"You agree with that assessment?"

"Yes."

"But you just said it was about economics."

"Yes, humanitarianism, like profit, is a liberal ideology," Stojanovic says, looking past me into the street.

With that, Stojanovic leans forward and lights another cigarette. Admittedly, I am puzzled. Yet, despite my disorientation, I can feel his logic, his desire to provoke me to think. While American pro-war liberals refuse to admit the bombing's economic dimension, the Serbs have enough history to embrace its complexity. *Of course there was something in it for them.* But still, his ambivalence is surprising.

Ignoring my confusion, Stojanovic continues. "The Albanian question in Serbia is something that is traumatic for me personally because Serbs didn't find a way for the whole of the twentieth century to integrate Albanians into its political and state structures. I cannot guess America's geostrategic or financial needs that they had coming into the conflict. What was very important for me was the end of the opportunity for the Serbs, from time to time, to sadistically massacre Albanians." He thrust a thumb into his chest, "For me."

"So it was good, for you."

"For me, yes. But not for all Serbs."

"They enjoy massacres," his translator adds, laughing.

"The things Milosevic did at the end of his own regime really couldn't be stopped from inside," Stojanovic continues. "All Serbs were for it, in other words. So, from my perspective, the NATO intervention was inevitable, for that reason alone."

"And the end of Yugoslavian socialism, was that inevitable as well?"

He looks at me, and opens his hands. *Of course.*

There is no trace of remorse in his eyes. He looks at me to see if I am satisfied. I nod and he bangs the table and says in his own simple English, "I must go now."

Later that night, unable to sleep, I leave my hotel for a stroll through the quiet city. A warm wind blows off the Sava River and draws me towards it. Energized, I walk across the bridge that extends over the wide channel of water, leaving the old city behind me for the twinkling lights of New Belgrade.

Approaching the other side, I see a large, well-lit billboard hanging over the road. Shimmering with golden skin, a wide-eyed woman looks down at me. From her eyes, she emits the perfect simulation of uncaring ambivalence. Printed in white under her perfect neck is one word: *Envy.* It reminds me of something Branimir Stojanonic told me near the end of his interview. I had asked him how the new liberalized economic system would change his country. "Socialism," he answered, "and even Milosevic's national socialism, is the order of love. Love towards the leader, love for your neighbor, your nation. And capitalism is the order of desire." Standing here, now, under this billboard that would be hardly noticeable in New York or Los Angeles, I feel a wave of melancholy. In the liberal marketplace of North America, where citizens are treated as consumers, we have become accustomed to these unmasked attacks on our human fabric. After all, it is envy and jealousy, the feeling of not having enough that drives an entire economy.

Walking back across the bridge toward my hotel, I wonder if the Serbs are ready for the rugged individualism of the free market system. The pitting of each against the other in competition for material goods. Unlike East Germany and the other former Soviet republics which were liberated into it, Serbia had to be bombed into acquiescence. Even if the people hated Milosevic for what he had done to the country, they did not identify his madness with the socialist system. For many, he was an aberration that only made them more nostalgic for the social and economic egalitarianism they had experienced under Tito. And this has presented a profound challenge to the new architects of Serbia's neoliberal economic policy.

The next afternoon, I sit across from Sonja Drljevic at a large meeting table in the office of AWIN, her women's support organization in Belgrade. Now in her sixties, Sonja is telling me about her experiences under Tito's worker-managed socialism. Or, at least trying to. Every few seconds, she is interrupted by the black-clad, heavyset kid with a full Marx beard sitting to her left.

"So her position is," explains Ratibor Trivunac—or Rata, as he introduced himself, "that in Yugoslavia—"

Sonja shoots Rata an impatient stare. "Can I explain my position, and you will explain yours?"

Rata sighs and looks at me resignedly. "She is my aunt."

Turning back to me, Sonja continues. "I understood it as an experiment. It was, let's say, a family of socialistic ideas. Anyhow, it produced, from my point of view, some very good results for the majority of the people."

Sonja recounts her days as a young engineer with a large, worker-managed construction firm. When she arrived in 1965, the company paid for two years of further education, for which she was obliged to work two years in exchange. Starting as a junior engineer, she continued her studies at the on-site schools that were set up by the company wherever they had bridge or tunnel projects. With their profits, the company first paid its taxes to the central government, which provided each citizen with medical insurance, old age pensions and basic education for the youth. Any leftover money would be allocated by the Workers' Council to build housing for the employees and fund special projects that were voted on by the group.

Sonja remembers the first collective building she lived in. "We had six families from my company. Two of us were engineers, two were administration, and three were workers. And one woman was there because her husband died at work. Immediately after that happened, the Workers' Council made the decision that she would have a flat for her two children and disability from her husband's death."

She looks at Rata, who nods affirmatively. "And I think these little things were very important for people like me," Sonja continues, "Because I am not a philosopher, not a scientist. I am just like the others. But we had this social security. And I knew when I arrived that I was going to stay there. I could see my life from twenty, when I started to work, to the end. It was completely clear."

"But," I interject, "some people would say that that is horrifying. Some would say they want to have a life where they have a choice."

Sonja shakes her head. "There was a choice, I could see if I wanted to stay there. But if I wanted to do something else, I could. For example, when I finished my study of building, I wasn't satisfied. So I studied economics, which would then allow me to work somewhere else. Nobody pressured me to stay all my life in one company. But we had this certainty that the society would take care of us, and it gave me the security to develop myself."

"This is the difference between the socialist system and the capitalist system," Rata begins, but Sonja cuts him off.

"I remember when one worker had some terrible disease," she says wagging her finger at him. "And the government's social insurance couldn't afford to send him to Paris to a specialist. So he came and asked the Council to help get him this operation. And so we voted and we pulled from our fund for special situations and sent him to Paris, and paid everything for him.

While this utopian, workers' paradise is a wonderful memory, it was also the product of an authoritarian system. While Sonja and her comrades were hard at work building the country, the Communist Party was acting exactly like the ruling class they claimed to have abolished. Tito was famous for his fleet of luxury cars and lavishly furnished residences. But when I suggest that there was a double standard, Rata bristles.

"Tito, no—it wasn't his own. It belonged to the state. His kids are now poor living in some shack in ex-Yugoslavia."

"Really?" I ask.

Rata nods. But, he explains, this was exactly the reason for the wars that broke out after Tito's death. The Communist bureaucracy, prevented from exploiting the state during Tito's rule, suddenly saw an opportunity to create private wealth. Playing what Rata calls the "wild card" of nationalism, Milosevic and the communists understood that war would be inevitable. And in war, there were vast opportunities to create private wealth outside of the state apparatus.

"These wars were used as a method of creating a new ruling class of the thieves who were stealing and smuggling oil and ciga-rettes and weapons," he explains. "And, after the war, the dream of every criminal is to become legal, which they were able to do under the Milosevic regime. Now they own the place."

"But the official justification for NATO's involvement was to end this nationalism and to open the system up beyond this gangster elite," I argue. "So, in this respect, you could have seen it as a good thing."

Sonja suddenly stands up. "You will understand how we see

it," she says, walking toward the bookshelf.

I look over at Rata. "It's a book full of nasty little photos," he explains.

Reaching up, Sonja pulls two thick white bound volumes from the top shelf and brings them to me. On the top cover, written in black text, is the title,

N.A.T.O. CRIMES IN YUGOSLAVIA
Documentary Evidence
24 March–24 April, 1999

The second is the same, only the period spans from April 25–June 10, 1999. Silently, Sonja turns page after page, showing me the photos of burned and disfigured bodies, crumbled buildings and collapsed bridges. "Here is bombing, here is bombing. Here is humanitarian bombing."

Rata explains that these are comprised solely of police reports, objectively documented at the scenes of the deaths. Quickly scanning the pages, I see detailed lists of injuries and damage reports. Viewed this way, as an administrative report, it is shocking.

"This is all NATO?" I ask.

"Yes, and what you can see on your TV as a target," she answers, referring to the video game simulations of the bombings shown on CNN, "that's what happened here. Nobody in the West understands what happened. They saw the poor Albanians flee to Albania, and then the good American target bad Serbians."

Sonja opens the second book to a well-worn page and points at a wrecked bridge. "This is the bridge my company made." She flips the pages, pointing to several more. "Thirty-two bridges destroyed. Two thousand people killed and five thousand people injured. All this in three months."

"So what do you think were the motivations of the attacks?"

"It was a reason to gain control on this part of the world, from that empire," Sonja replies, firmly. "It was nothing about human rights."

Rata shakes his head. "I don't believe it."

"Fine, you don't believe it." Sonja raises her eyebrows. "The Albanian people—the Americans said they fought for their rights, or something. They got nothing."

Rata looks over at Sonja to see if she has finished. "I want to say that I don't agree with Sonja," he says. "Of course, the Americans didn't do anything because of human rights. Let us make this clear. But there were problems with human rights in Kosovo. The people in Kosovo were living in apartheid, under the control of Milosevic... Of course, this was only the explanation why they bombed, not the reason."

"So what don't you agree with?"

"There is no single Empire where the center is the United States. That's too simplistic. America does not control Serbia now, it doesn't need to. As long as the economy is opened to Western business, then they have succeeded in their mission."

Echoing the words of Sergeant Robert Hollis, the young tank commander I met in Iraq, Rata believes military actions have a direct link to economic needs. He argues that the bombing campaign was the product of a nation operating from a position of weakness, not one of strength. Seen from this perspective, Rata tells me, the rationale for the bombing is multilayered. First, the war provided a fundamental boost to the American economy, which has a strong military industrial sector. Second, the establishment of bases in the Balkans—"you have military bases all over the Balkans: in Kosovo, Bosnia, Greece, Bulgaria"—is a critical facet of America's long-term goal of protecting strategic markets. Third, the Serbian economy has now been opened completely to foreign capital, many of the large national industries have been closed down, privatized or sold off to smaller foreign companies.

"The market is totally liberalized now," he declares.

"And this is a direct result of the bombing?"

"Of course!"

But this is not the most painful outcome of the attacks. Worse, he explains, is that the new Serbia is now being run by many of the people who were once far left dissidents. His heroes, in other words.

"Like this guy, Privo Indjic, who's now the [foreign policy] advisor the president of Serbia. He was an anarchist."

Listening to Rata, it feels like déjà vu. Sitting there in his dark clothes, listing names of one-time far left rebels who have sold out to capitalism, he reminds me of J.Z. in his church basement headquarters. Only, instead of castigating leftist turncoats like Paul Berman, Todd Gitlin and David Horowitz, it's Svetozar Stojanovic—whose Praxis Group was a collective of Marxist university professors who criticized Tito's regime for its censorship, bureaucratic elitism and fiscal mismanagement—and Privo Indjic. I wonder if they, too, had come to the conclusion, as did the SDS student leader Todd Gitlin, that capitalism was simply the only choice left. That while socialism had once represented a beautiful vision, it had faded away into a hazy daydream of conquered hopes. That capitalism was now the only "horizon."

Rata holds his hands in fists on the table, slowly opening them as he speaks. "All of them now are totally out of radical politics and we are living in a society made by these former dissidents. And this is the horrifying realization. Especially for me, as an anarchist, because they were critical of the communist system, and now we can see they have made something that is a billion times worse."

But in Serbia, it is not just the former radicals who are steering the neoliberal course. Working diligently on the sidelines, a new generation of laissez-faire economists now have their hands on the wheel of federal policy. One of the most influential of these is Dr. Miroslav Prokopijevic, the director of the Center for Free Trade in Belgrade. In a short interview, Prokopijevic explained that under the previous socialist regimes, he had been branded a heretic for his liberal views—a "Taliban" as he described it to me. He believes the failure of socialism lies in its desire to mix egalitarian, philosophical goals with fiscal policy. In a 2002 report on economic reform, Prokopijevic actually omitted the results of a study which incorporated civil and political liberties—"freedom to earn a living, non-discrimination in employment, etc."—in its evaluation of a nation's economic freedom because, as he wrote, it is "biased."

When I asked him if this purist approach to capitalism might not risk producing a society void of social and humanitarian standards, he shook his head. "No. Because simply, the more economic freedom you have the more successful you are, both in terms of individual and social gains." Reading this quote aloud to Rata and Sonja elicits an immediate reaction.

"This is moronic," Rata nearly shouts. "If you remove political and social freedom—then the freedom he is talking about is in fact the freedom to exploit. He is claiming that the more freedom somebody has to exploit the workers, the more it will benefit individual freedom. This is moronic. And it's not only moronic, it is also..." Rata looks over at Sonja for a moment. "If you say he is a moron and not educated enough, that is not good enough, because it is a way to say it's not his fault. But the point is these people are creating the society that we are in. He is creating public opinion. And I am radical, and if I were big enough he would be the first one on our list for being shot down!"

"Nobody will be shot!" Sonja bangs her fist on the table.

"Do you believe in violent revolution?" I ask, wondering how far he'll go with what I figure is a bluff.

"Of course, I believe in extremely violent revolution," Rata answers. "This is the point, there is this tendency to say that anarchists are for violence, which doesn't mean anything. Because what does it mean that you are *for* violence? That you enjoy violence? No. It is something completely different. It is understanding that we are living in a violent system. Capitalism is a violent system. Today there was a worker who died in the petrochemical industry because his bosses failed to provide safety equipment. This is violence. In Serbia, you have mines which are now owned by Canadian and American companies where people have an average life expectancy of 45 because of the working conditions. This is violence. And you are living in dream world if you are saying that it is horrible for somebody to be violent while we are in violence permanently."

Rata stares hard at me until I turn away. It is not a gesture of animosity nor bravado but, rather, one of indignation. In so many ways, that look sums up everything that I have encountered so far in Belgrade. Even from the neoliberals like Miroslav Prokopijevic, there is an overriding sense of helplessness, of having no control over their national destiny. No matter what side of the political and economic equation they defend, Serbians see their modern history as one of constant intervention by outside forces. For most observers of this scene in Sonja's office, Rata could easily be dismissed as an idealistic radical, much like those who defined the American social and political revolution in the 1960s.* As

---

* When I asked him what alternative he would offer to the privatizing and downsizing of Serbia's bloated state-owned corporate sector, Rata questioned the very premise that it was overstaffed. "What does it mean, too many employees?" he barked. "It is all in the system, where you have an eight hour day. If you have a four hour day, there are no more workers than are needed."

"But," I asked, "how would people survive if they only worked four hours a day?"

"You know there is an old communist slogan—from each according to their ability, to each according to their need. In globalization you can say there are too many workers but in the society we are asking for, it wouldn't matter. You can have a four-hour day, you can two-hour day. People work as much as they can, they will all be taken care of."

history proved, they were unable to implement any truly lasting socialist policies because the alternatives had been exhausted. There simply was no realistic way to bring American society back toward a socialist model; average Americans were terrified of it. The very idea of egalitarian economic management had been stigmatized and desecrated by the anti-communist movement that lasted from the 1950s right up until the fall of the Berlin Wall. But for the Serbs, it is still a lingering possibility, and this is something that Western liberals see as the most vital challenge to reforming the Serbian economy and, perhaps more importantly, the Serbs themselves.

One of the longest-serving American pro-democracy non-governmental organizations is the Freedom House. Dedicated to promoting "the expansion of freedom in the world," Freedom House was founded in 1941 with a goal of stemming the rise of Nazism and Communism in Europe. Over time, the organization has dynamically readjusted its focus to countries that are trying to escape the "debilitating legacies of tyranny, dictatorship, and political repression."[15] Reading their mission statement, the emphasis is clearly on social and political freedom with only one mention being made of attention to free market economics.*

Yet, in 2003 Freedom House funded a study that looked at the prevailing attitudes of poor and lower middle class Serbian workers toward economic liberalization. It reported results gathered from a survey of Serbs categorized as the most potentially resistant to economic reform. The language of the study is fascinating. Here is an excerpt from a description of the "target group":

---

* Running down the list of Freedom House's Board of Trustees, it includes former and current Fortune 500 executives (Nancy Lane at Johnson & Johnson, Kathryn Karol at Eli Lilly), U.S. ambassadors (Mark Palmer), billionaires (Steve Forbes), neoconservatives (Jeane Kirkpatrick) and American hegemonists (Samuel Huntington). Its chairman is Peter Ackerman, an investment advisor who, as director of International Capital Markets at Drexel Burnham Lambert, he led structured deals for some of the largest and most complex leveraged acquisitions in the 1980s.

Certain social groups, in particular unskilled laborers, suburban dwellers, rurally-based workers who also manage their land holdings and elderly people in general were seen in the past decade as the main opponents of Serbia's modernisation and linkage with neighbouring western Balkan countries and the international community as a whole.[16]

In other words, working class people who have historically been opposed to globalization. The report continues—using terminology that would not, itself, be out of place in a Nazi handbook—to describe these people as a "biologically and economically uncompetitive strata whose attitudes are... characterized by outdated communist egalitarianism, ethnic nationalism, xenophobia and an anti-market bias."[17]

Of these attributes, clearly ethnic nationalism and xenophobia are destructive and can be exploited by leaders like Milosevic who seek to galvanize support for undemocratic programs. So no one can fault the Freedom House for wanting to focus on combating those negative attitudes. But, as it turns out, those polled for the report showed no earnest desire to fight the old ethnic battles, leading to the conclusion that "ethnic questions are history." Furthermore, while half of those polled thought the United States was hostile toward Serbia, this wasn't a major contributing factor to their opposition to free market reform. What the report discovered instead was that the biggest obstacle to winning public support for full economic liberalism was the people's belief in "egalitarianism," defined as a policy in which the ratio between highest and lowest personal incomes should be flat or, at best, no more than three to one. For the authors of the report this was clearly troublesome for, as they explained, "an absolute majority in our target groups support an extreme left-wing economic option rather than reforms; this finding should make only communists and crypto-communist happy." [18]

And here is where it gets interesting. What the survey discovered was that the sector which showed the strongest support for egalitarianism was the employed, unskilled workers. It was the unemployed people, more desperate for any chance to make a living, who were willing to consider American style capitalism. This, according to the report, proves the "liberal thesis" that those who are the most insecure in the resource market are also the most open to taking risks:

> Unemployment appears here as a factor undermining egalitarianism and in a sense beneficial to the process of carrying out reforms. This is also worth thinking about. By far the biggest supporters of egalitarianism are employed unskilled workers; those unskilled laborers who have no jobs appear far more ready to accept new rules of the game. Attention should perhaps be paid in the practical actions to this last and less privileged group, endeavoring to win their support for reforms.

> Employed unskilled workers are once again seen here as a factor blocking reforms, and unemployment also reveals itself as a school for reform, hence also a remedy for social problems and not just a problem...[19]

Unemployment as a remedy for social problems. Barely veiling its call to exercising social engineering on the Serbs, the report goes on to suggest that the unemployed workers, who represent 30 percent of Serbia's viable workforce, might be the best chance pro-market liberals have to sell their reluctant peers on the new system. Hence, it is implied, workers are more valuable when they are jobless. Or, as the report states, "unemployment appears here as a factor undermining egalitarianism and in that sense is useful for the purpose of implementing reforms." The report goes on to recommend that "minimising resistance will only be achievable through a broad media campaign adapted to the receptive characteristics of the aforementioned target group."[20] And now it is clear just what those "receptive characteristics" truly are. It is their weaknesses and desperation. Hardly the kind of humane leadership one would expect from something called Freedom House, nor from the leaders of the world's reigning liberal democracy. Or, perhaps it is.

THE RELUCTANT REVOLUTIONARY

One of the most popular conspiracy theories in Serbia is that the anti-Milosevic revolution which swept through the universities and unions, and which ultimately galvanized the popular voters to dethrone him in 2000, was orchestrated by American intelligence officials. I could hardly get through a conversation without it being mentioned: this notion that while American-led NATO planes bombed from the sky, CIA agents were financing and training dissidents to wage a peaceful ground war to destroy the socialist regime forever.*

Calling themselves *Otpor!*, or "resistance" in Serbian, this highly motivated and well-branded student movement emerged

---

* I had read about the backing American intelligence had given to the anti-Milosevic forces in far left American journals in the years after 2000. During my interview with Branimir Stojanovic I referred to it as "a commonly held belief." A supporter of the revolution that toppled Milosevic, Stojanovic nevertheless responded: "It's not a commonly held belief, it's a historical fact. It's like asking someone in Tehran if the Americans brought down the 1953 democratically elected government. Yes they did. It's not just an opinion, it's true. All Serbian opposition leaders received American education in Budapest and Otpor!, the student movement, was financed by these institutes."

just as Milosevic began to plan his repression of Kosovar Albanians in 1998. Armed with cell phones, spray paint and a list
of catchy slogans—"Resistance until Victory" and "Slobo, save
Serbia: kill yourself!" among them—Otpor! led the massive street
protests that ultimately forced Milosevic to accept the 2000 electoral defeat that paved the way for his arrest and extradition. But,
according to Srbijanka Turajlic, the University of Belgrade engineering professor who became Otpor!'s unofficial godmother
and appointed spokesperson, the movement did not emerge
from a vacuum. It was the product of a collaboration between the
Serbian students and "outside forces."[21]

In 1998, Turajlic, along with a small squad of activists, began
to make weekend trips out to the countryside, hosting coffeehouse
meetings with groups of rural Serbians who politely listened
to their calls for democracy. At first, Turajlic felt the operation
was totally hapless. She describes the meetings, which rarely
numbered more than ten people, as "the most silly thing I ever did
in my life." With Milosevic's state intelligence and security forces
monitoring all opposition groups, there was no way to bring in
money to finance their activities. And people were scared to help
them. When Turaljic's car broke down, a close friend agreed to
lend them hers, but only under the condition that they lie to the
police if they asked who it belonged to.

But the meetings were having an effect. Slowly people were
beginning to respond to the message and the audiences began to
grow. The group made tapes and began circulating them to local
democracy groups that were sprouting in the outlying regions.
And then it all stopped. When NATO inaugurated its bombing
campaign, Turajlic's student-collaborators disappeared and she
did not see them again until the summer of 1999.

In their absence, Turajlic worried that all of their progress would be lost. Sitting at an outdoor bar on my last night

in Belgrade, she explains that the initial effect of the NATO bombing was negative.

"It didn't help anybody. It didn't help us as the opposition, because we had been going around Serbia saying, 'we have to have democracy.' And then suddenly democracy is bombing them. It was kind of a strange thing."

Eventually, however, the sustained bombing began to have its desired psychological effect on the Serbians. They were no longer living in a cocoon, protected from the consequences of Milosevic's policies. Turajlic admits that the 78-day campaign forced people to question where their leader was leading them.

"However," she adds, "I would have preferred that they managed to find some other way to raise awareness."

As it turns out, Western groups were developing a corollary strategy to transform Serbia's political scene. But Turajlic didn't find out until her students reappeared in Belgrade in May 1999.

"What exactly was happening during the [bombing] campaign, I couldn't tell you. But something was happening, because when we came out of it, those same guys were suddenly extremely well organized. They knew exactly what they were doing, how they were doing it. And I honestly think that before the bombing, somebody, somewhere, recognized: here is a group of guys willing to do something, but they're rather clumsy, and don't know exactly how to do it."

Now the movement had a name (Otpor!), a well-designed logo (a black clenched fist highlighted in a white circle) and catchy slogans ('He's finished!'). But most of all, there was now an infusion of cash that enabled the movement to galvanize and channel the Serbian public's outrage against Milosevic. It soon became obvious that the young revolutionaries had received some outside help.

"They picked, among those students, a few who they recognized as possible leaders," Turajlic tells me. "And obviously they trained them."

"Did you know who was helping them?" I ask.

Turajlic shakes her head. "I knew that money was coming from the outside. If I had asked, they would have told me. My students were always honest with me. Later on I realized that I didn't really want to know."

What she later learned was that her students had made covert trips to Budapest in neighboring Hungary. There, they were coached by Colonel Robert Helvey, a thirty-year veteran of the Defense Intelligence Agency who specialized in political subversion and covert ops in Southeast Asia. Prior to his arrival in Budapest, he worked with dissidents in Myanmar and China, training them in the art of "strategic non-violent struggle" against their own dictatorships. Now installed as the president of the Albert Einstein Institute (AEI), Helvey became the point man for America's political overthrow of Slobodan Milosevic.

"It was a very organized effort," Turajlic remembers, "and at the same time still a movement of the students. It looked that way, but was really not so. Nothing is spontaneous. All movements are organized by somebody. The question is if you are going to learn who organized what. It took me years to realize who was organizing the protests, even in Belgrade, where I was supposedly one of the leaders. Later on I realized I was manipulated."

As Michael Dobbs wrote in the *Washington Post*, "U.S.-funded consultants played a crucial role behind the scenes in virtually every facet of the anti-Milosevic drive... training thousands of opposition activists. U.S. taxpayers paid for 5,000 cans of spray paint used by student activists to scrawl anti-Milosevic graffiti on walls across Serbia, and 2.5 million stickers with the slogan 'He's Finished,' which became the revolution's catchphrase."[22]

Despite the sudden transformation, her first reaction was pride, not skepticism. "I mean you know, when you are an old professor, you are always crowded with students. So I was proud that they were doing it so well... they had symbols there, but the whole campaign, type of campaign had changed."

I ask Turajlic if she would have been upset to know her kids were being financed by American-backed sources.

"Well no, because I really had had enough," she says. "At that time, I was absolutely ready to make a pact with the devil if necessary just to get rid of Milosevic."

By the spring of 2000, hardly a wall in Belgrade was free of graffiti or posters emblazoned with the distinctive clenched fist. The Belgrade-based Human Rights Law Center estimated that over 2,000 people were beaten or arrested for plastering banners or wearing t-shirts with Otpor! slogans. Now the students were ready to expand Otpor! to a broad-based popular movement. At that point, Turajlic explains, "We decided somehow that we had to take part of the responsibility from the kids."

In May, a meeting was organized in one of Belgrade's opposition strongholds. It was resolved that they would create an organization to front the student's political movement. When it came time to appoint a leader, Turajlic remembers, "everybody looked around, and everybody looked at me, and I ended up being the president of the student movement."

I smile at the accomplishment but Turajlic shrugs it off. "My role was really to put the stamp here and there and merely to sign things. They were organizing things, and they just needed a name. They needed somebody who was not a student."

By summer, Otpor!'s membership had swelled to over 40,000. Apart from the nominal leadership provided by Turajlic and some other civil rights leaders, the organization was strictly non-hierarchical. It's primary objective was to engage the society in a bottom-up dialogue, one in which Serbian youth would mobilize the older generations to become actively involved in creating a Serbia that could provide them with a future.* It was a broad strategy that would soon be given a catalyzing point of focus.

For Milosevic, the stakes were high. Losing control of the government to Victor Kostunica, his moderate challenger, would place him in danger of being extradited to the International Criminal Tribunal in the Hague. So, in the run-up to the 2000 election, he turned up the heat on his challengers, arresting and brutalizing the Otpor! activists, shutting down pro-Kostunica radio stations and raiding the offices of independent political organizations. Still, on election day, close to 70 percent of Yugoslavia's 7.25 million voters turned out to cast a ballot. Initial results gave Kostunica 53 percent of the vote to Milosevic's 35 percent.

The people waited, but Milosevic did not make any public acknowledgement of his defeat. Then, after several days of silence, the Federal Election Commission announced that Kostunica had only taken 49 percent of the vote, not enough for a victory. The September 24 election results were annulled and a runoff election was called; Milosevic was stalling for time. But it was too late. Otpor!'s populist message had reached past generational barriers and energized the once-comatose Serbian electorate. Five days after the election, workers at the Kolubara mine 30 miles outside of Belgrade went on strike. A critical supplier of Serbia's electricity, Kolubara became the scene of a standoff between police and miners that only deepened Milosevic's crisis. When authorities offered the miners double wages to keep working, they refused, with one yelling, "This is not about money. It's about votes."

Back in Belgrade, the Democratic Opposition of Serbia

---

* One of Otpor!'s more memorable propaganda devices was a postcard featuring the faces of 16 children. Under them, a caption read: "Greetings from the Future of Serbia." Over 100,000 copies were distributed throughout Belgrade and peripheral towns.

(DOS) called for mass protests on October 5. Srbijanka Turajlic joined the crowd of people, which eventually reached 500,000, outside the Parliament building. Looking around, she saw parents standing beside their kids waving Otpor! banners. When soldiers began launching the tear gas, she knew victory was close. "There was a sense, a collective sense, that it has to be finished this day," she later told reporters, "You could feel that this crowd was going to finish things." As the world watched Milosevic's fate unfold on CNN, protesters broke through the police barricades and stormed the Parliament, lighting it on fire. Next, a man driving a bulldozer broke through the door of the state-controlled radio and television building. It too went up in flames. The crowds cheered triumphantly. The national socialist era of Serbia's history was over.

The next day, Milosevic appeared on television to congratulate Kostunica and accept defeat. Five months later, after the new government handed Milosevic over to the International Tribunal, $1 billion dollars in aid was given to Serbia, most of which was already earmarked to repay loans made under the Milosevic regime. In the three governments to hold power since the 2000 election, successful capitalists from the Serbian diaspora returned to lead the ministries of economy, privatization, finance, energy and industry. The stated goal of the neoliberals is to complete the process of privatization by 2008 and to return the nation's GDP to the same level as 1990—just before Milosevic fought the first of his four wars against the separatist republics. It is estimated this will not be realized until 2014.

In the meantime, Serbia's economy is in shambles. Based on statistics for 2005, unemployment grew to fourteen percent while inflation hit eighteen percent. The average monthly salary was around $300. But the black market is booming and, Serbian academic Marko Popovic explained in an email, "the number of private and state companies that manage to skip paying taxes is overwhelming. As a result, the feeling of social injustice is very high among the Serbian population. This effect has been a sense of resignation among ordinary people, which reflects in small exit numbers at the elections."*

Perhaps this is the most tragic outcome of the new liberal paradigm: the enthusiasm for politics that brought so many into the streets in 2000 has fallen off drastically. In November 2003, Serbians failed for a third time to elect a president due to low voter participation. In response, the Parliament was forced to repeal the 50 percent turnout requirement.

As for the young activists who led the Otpor! insurgency, they received funding from Freedom House and the U.S. government to establish the Center for Nonviolent Resistance in Budapest. Their mission: to train and outfit pro-democracy groups in other Balkan and former Russian republics. And they've been busy. Movements in Georgia (*Kmara!*), Ukraine (*Pora!*), Belarus (*Zubr!*), Albania (*Mjaft!*) and Russia (*Oborona*) have all been branded with catchy names and the slick trademark paraphernalia. Despite a setback in voting out the government of Belarus President Alexander Lukashenko in September 2001, two other Otpor!-backed liberal revolutions succeeded in deposing authoritarian regimes. In November 2003, the peaceful "Rose Revolution"—led by opposition groups financed by George Soros's Open Society—unseated Georgian President Eduard Shevardnadze. One year later came the famous "Orange Revolution" which overthrew Leonid Kuchma and installed Viktor Yushchenko as president of the Ukraine.

While the majority of these liberal revolutions were ignored by the American public, the apparent poisoning of Ukraine's insurgent leader, Yushchenko, brought worldwide attention. He

---

* Another outcome of this widescale dissatisfaction has been the resurgence of nationalism on the political scene. In the January 2007 elections, the Serbian Radical Party (SRS), whose leader Vojislav Seselj is being tried for war crimes in The Hague, won 28.5 percent of the vote—the largest of any other single party.

may have come to regret it. Five months after he formed his new government, a newly liberated media began poking into the excessive habits of the president's son, Adriy. When a Ukranian reporter asked Yushchenko how a young student was able to afford a $120,000 BMW M6, not to mention personal bodyguards and a $30,000 platinum Vertu mobile phone, the president shot back, "Act like a polite journalist and not like a hit man."

Considering one of the key promises of the Orange Revolution was to fight corruption, the question was hardly out of line. Especially in lieu of the president's reported annual salary of $56,000. But that was only the start of Yushchenko's troubles. A few months later he was forced to fire the entire government after a top-level organizer of the Orange Revolution quit, citing mass corruption. He said the situation was "even worse" than under the former president Leonid Kuchma, which is saying a lot. Kuchma was caught on audio tape in 2000 ordering the murder of an opposition journalist.

A few weeks before our interview, Srbijanka Turajlic visited Ukraine's capital Odessa. There she met with three economics professors at Odessa University who had helped with the revolutions in Georgia and Ukraine. They told her that at first they were excited about the changes, but then, after seeing the results of Yushchenko's presidency, they have begun to have second thoughts. Ironically, she tells me, the very people who had championed the advent of free market liberalism—economics professors—are now turning back to Russia for protection from American-style neo-liberalism.

"They are becoming more and more pro-Putin because they are tired of importing revolution," Turajlic explains.* "They were

---

* Viktor Yushchenko's slide in credibility resulted in the election of pro-Russian Prime Minister Viktor Yanukovych in March 2006. It was telling that just two years after winning the presidency, Yushchenko was forced to create a coalition government with the very man who was beaten by the Orange Revolution.

all very much engaged in the revolution in Georgia, and they really believed that they were helping Georgian students. Then after a few months they realized that Georgia didn't do anything but install the guy who is for America, and then it started to happen in Ukraine."

"But isn't the Russian system worse, as far as corruption and propaganda are concerned?" I ask

She shakes her head. "Look, we spent two years in America back in the '80s. Even then I had the impression that the society was slightly dangerous, more unpleasant than the Soviet society at that time. And I'll tell you why. Because the Soviet propaganda was very open at that time. So if you had some brains, you were absolutely able to detect what they were doing to you. In the States, it is more refined, so you really have to have some experience to watch slightly from the outside, to be slightly detached to understand what they are doing to you. Maybe they just want a less sophisticated type of lie."

The next morning, sitting in a cab on the way to the airport, I flip through a thick black book that contains the notes I have taken throughout this journey. On the second page, I find a quote from Michael Ignatieff's *The Lesser Evil*. It reads, "It is a condition of our freedom that we cannot compel anyone to believe in the premises of a liberal democracy. Either these premises freely convince others or they are useless. They cannot be imposed, and we violate everything we stand for if we coerce those who do not believe in what we do."

Have liberals really adhered to this well articulated maxim? If the new U.S.-backed revolutionary movements in the Balkans and former Soviet states are any indication, Western liberals have not been content to allow their principles to "freely convince" anyone of anything. It is not simply a case of presenting a living example of such unparalleled human freedom that others organically move toward it like stars to a black hole. Instead, it takes massive levels of grassroots organizing and the indoctrination of a new generation of neoliberals to engineer the overthrow of "fragmentary" leaders.

And while I am certain that many of those young revolutionaries understand that American free market liberalism is not the perfect model, they know that the best way to catalyze the pro-liberal movements is through the mass marketing of an image of America as the land where anything is possible. A place where anyone can go from zero to two hundred in five seconds flat. They have manufactured the ultimate product, the myth of unlimited potential. It's called the American Dream. And for many people, this was enough for them to leave everything behind just for the chance to experience the sensation of self-determination. Of rags to riches success. Of a true participatory democracy. And still they come.

But is that what they're getting?

5

The Shining City

Give me your tired, your poor, your huddled masses yearning to
breathe free; send these, the homeless tempest-tossed,
to me; I lift my lamp beside the golden door.
— *The New Colossus* by Emma Lazarus
(inscribed on the Statue of Liberty)

A STRANGE DEATH

Flying on another plane back to New York, I read the last pages of a book given to me by the owner of a Belgrade bookstore. He's a retired political science professor from the university and, when I told him about my book, he led me to the back of the shop. Stuffed on a dusty shelf with a few old *Life* magazines and a bundle of *Encyclopedia Brown* paperbacks was an old hardcover of H.W. Brands's *The Strange Death of American Liberalism*.[1]

"This will give you something to write about," he told me, stuffing the book into my bag. And then I forgot about it until my connection took off from Frankfurt early this morning. Suffice it to say, he was right.

In a style that is piercing in its sensibility, Brands explains that American liberalism reached its maximal form during the Cold War when the nation was fighting against Communism. The battle was two-fronted, he argues, at once military and ideological. And because of the latter dimension, which meant a struggle for hearts and minds, America had to become the ultimate liberal system. Its leaders understood that the victory of democracy over Communism could only be delivered if the United States could present "a powerful example of a society that offered hope and opportunity to all."

And so government, that civic force for which most Americans hold only the deepest skepticism, was allowed to expand. President Johnson's Great Society program was initiated and with it came the extension of voting rights to African-Americans, financing for public education, the arts, health care and urban development. There was even a War on Poverty to provide for those excluded from the capitalist dream.

But then came Vietnam and with it, according to Brands, the death of liberalism. "When the Cold War cracked up in Vietnam," he writes, "it shattered the consensus, ravaged popular faith in government, and scorched the earth from which the liberal agenda had sprung." With each revelation of gross military blunders and government deception, the people pulled back their trust until there was nothing left but the hollow shell of the American liberal project. And when the Soviet Union collapsed, there was no longer any reason to maintain the illusion. All that was needed was one true patriot to put a death to the lie, and his name was Ronald Reagan.[2]

The lesson of the Cold War, as even Russia's Mikhail Gorbachev understood, was that "government must step out of the road and let people apply their personal energies to achieving their individual destinies in their own ways." And so, American politics became dominated by those who believed that less government is more, and that competition is the ultimate determiner of social value.[3]

Brands closes by admonishing those who naively believed that Reagan's conservatism an anomaly, merely a fleeting swing of the political pendulum. Those idealists who pinned their hopes on a reciprocal swing that would bring back the liberalism of old were wrong. Because, as Brands concludes in his final pages,

> "It was the liberalism of the Cold War that was the anomaly. The appropriate image wasn't a pendulum but a balloon, one held aloft by the confidence in government the successful prosecution of the Cold War inspired. When Vietnam destroyed that confidence, the balloon deflated, and expectations of government descended to their traditional low level. Pendulums swing back on their own; balloons require refilling." [4]

Reading these words, I feel a creeping sense of sadness. So much of what I have learned on this journey affirms what Brands is saying. The old school New Left radicals who were the inheritors of that Cold War liberalism traded it in for a new millennial realism that has more to do with territorial conquest than individual freedom. And despite what the voters are told, Democratic presidential candidates from Bill Clinton to John Kerry bear no resemblance to the liberals who gave that party its identity. As Clinton said, mimicking his hero John F. Kennedy, "We must not ask Government to do what we should do for ourselves... We have to cut yesterday's Government to help solve tomorrow's problems." [5]

But then I am pulled out of my small moment of despair. Flying over New York, the pilot announces that below us is "one of the most beautiful sights in global aviation." I look down at Manhattan's skyline. It reminds me of the famous words once uttered by John Winthrop. A distant relative of John Kerry's, Winthrop stood on the deck of the good ship *Arbella* as it set sail from England to the Massachusetts colony in 1630, urging his fellow Puritans to make their future home a place that would serve as an example to the rest of the world. If they didn't, Winthrop warned, then they would pay a heavy price for failing to live up to that promise:

"For we must consider that we shall be as a city upon a hill, the eyes of all people are upon us; so that if we shall deal falsely with our God in this work we have undertaken, and so cause Him to withdraw His present help from us, we shall shame the faces of many of God's worthy servants, and cause their prayers to be turned into curses." [6]

While Winthrop, who became the first governor of Massachusetts, hoped the new colony would become a symbol of religious sanctity, modern politicians have used his words to inspire in their people the vision of America as the beacon of liberal democracy. In his last public speech as president, Ronald Reagan referred to the United States as "the shining city upon a hill... teeming with people of all kinds living in harmony and peace; a city with free ports that hummed with commerce and creativity. And if there had to be city walls, the walls had doors and the doors were open to anyone with the will and the heart to get here." [7]

In the 350-year span between Winthrop and Reagan, the city on the hill became the most coveted destination for migrants who hoped for a new country that championed human liberty and individual freedom before all else. America became the global model of liberalism and democracy with its bicameral legislative process, authentically competitive political parties, vibrant economy and tolerance of ideological dissent. More, it offered its citizens the ultimate promise in the form of a sanctified dream, the American one, that any person who was willing to work hard and obey the rules could escape the shackles of class, making a better life for their children than they had had for themselves. But today, many people, of all generations, openly question whether America truly is still that shining city on a hill.* Or if it ever was.

MIGRANT MANIA

I am glued to the television in my hotel room, watching a lone motorcyclist racing up the freeway, weaving through traffic at 140 mph. Only in Los Angeles can you turn on the six o'clock news to see a high-speed chase that has more drama and sensory danger than a Spielberg movie. The rider is so skilled on his bike that even the newscasters, who are doing their best to project a stern level of disapproval, betray their amazement when he corners beautifully onto an exit ramp, splitting oncoming traffic to get onto another freeway. I find myself rooting for the rebel biker who fleetingly represents the daredevil in all of us: a lone individual, running against the grain of the social order, betting against incredible odds that he will reach the other side, intact and alive.†

According to Peter Whybrow, director of the Neuropsychiatric Institute (NPI) at UCLA, this is exactly the type of risky, thrill-inducing behavior that is to be expected from Americans. They are, Whybrow explains in his engaging book, *American*

---

* In the summer of 2006, a poll by UK research firm YouGov asked Brits if they "regard the U.S. at the moment as a beacon of hope for the world?" 77 percent said "no," 12 percent "didn't know" and 11 percent said "yes." Even more relevant to the thesis of this book was the following question: "Do you think [President Bush] genuinely wants to create a more democratic democratic world, or is what he says merely a cover for pursuing American interests in the world?" To which Britain responded: 15 percent democratic world, 72 percent American interests, 12 percent didn't know. Cited in "Pox Americana," *Vanity Fair*, October 2006.

† As it turned out, the rider, Alvaro Rodriguez, was able to outrun the California Highway Patrol and escape the aerial surveillance of the network choppers by exiting the Ventura Freeway and then racing through the city on surface streets until he reached the Glendale Galleria mall. Once there, he zipped into the parking garage and fled on foot. The next day, Rodriguez was arrested when, in a ploy designed to divert suspicion from him as owner of the bike, he tried to report it stolen. He was immediately sentenced to two years in prison for perjury and evading arrest.

Mania, "mavericks who run at the edge of the human herd... a self-selected band of seekers—those of adventurous and curious mind—who in their restless approach to life lie at the extreme of the bell-shaped curve of behavioral distribution."[8]

Whybrow is an expert in the field of human psychology and one of the few neural academics who can actually translate the science in a way that lay people understand it. One night I was flipping through the special features on the DVD of Martin Scorsese's *The Aviator.* I stopped on a discussion on obsessive-compulsive disorder, from which Howard Hughes, the subject of the film, suffered. Whybrow, who is world-renowned for his study of mood disorders, moderated the panel that featured Scorsese, Leonardo DiCaprio, and Whybrow's associate at NPI, Jeffrey Schwartz, who worked with DiCaprio to prepare for his role as the billionaire eccentric.

With the camera trained mostly on Scorsese and DiCaprio, Whybrow's unpretentious intelligence was relegated to a few introductory comments. But a few months later, when he and I were serendipitously paired in a public debate on American foreign policy, I immediately understood how he had risen so far in the academic realm. Not content with relegating his observations and analysis of human psychology to individual or group behavior, Whybrow takes pleasure in challenging the way political and economic theorists explain our society. In all affairs of the human species, he sees neurobiology as the primary driving force. It can be a controversial stance. During our debate—which was staged for a European crowd eager to hear nasty put-downs about the United States—Whybrow refused to play ball. Instead, he tracked a path onto the high ground, describing America as a "state of mind" rather than a geographic location. Speaking in his quiet, faded British accent, Whybrow concluded, "I think of America as a temperament rather than a place. Expansionism is at the root of the collective mythology."

When he was challenged by a few angry Brits, who claimed he was intellectualizing and, thus, displacing the very real threat of U.S. military aggression, Whybrow responded calmly, explaining that in order to discuss the role the United States is now playing in the world, we must first understand the mythology Americans have created for themselves. Because it is this narrative that fuels their adventures into the world beyond U.S. borders. Speaking like a practiced clinician, Whybrow was simply stating the obvious: in order to design strategies to curb the behavior, we first have to get to its psychological root.

If that analysis did not transform the crowd's anger into curiosity, it piqued mine. In the months after I began writing this book, data began to flow through newspapers and economic journals indicating that, contrary to the great promise of the well-marketed American dream, the United States was as entrenched in a class system just as rigid as any in the developed world. Gauging by the statistics, there is very little real hope for the majority of Americans to ever move beyond the economic tier into which they were born.* I began to wonder what effect this socioeconomic entrapment would have on the myth of America as the shining city on a hill. I wanted to find someone who could offer a scientific analysis of the impact of a failed dream on the wider public consciousness; how would it

---

* Of these major media reports on class in America, the *New York Times* ten part series, "Class Matters" was the most insightful and will be covered later in this chapter. But to give you an idea of the kind of statistics I am talking about, the *Economist* cited a report by The Economic Policy Institute, a Washington think-tank, that declared: "between 1979 and 2000 the real income of households in the lowest fifth (the bottom twenty percent of earners) grew by 6.4 percent, while that of households in the top fifth grew by 70 percent. The family income of the top one percent grew by 184 percent—and that of the top 0.1 percent or 0.01 percent grew even faster. Back in 1979 the average income of the top one percent was 133 times that of the bottom twenty percent; by 2000 the income of the top one percent had risen to 189 times that of the bottom fifth." See "Ever higher society, ever harder to ascend," *Economist*, December 29, 2004.

affect their health as a society? Reading about Whybrow's work at the Institute and then in *American Mania*, I realized he was my ticket.

According to his website, Whybrow's work at UCLA is devoted to "the understanding of complex human behavior, including the genetic, biological, behavioral and sociocultural underpinnings of normal behavior and the causes, phenomenology, and consequences of neuropsychiatric disorders." [9] In *American Mania*, which was published in 2005, Whybrow expands the perimeter of his research of individual psychology to that of the American population at large. His analysis is thorough and damning: America is comprised of highly-motivated, fearless migrants who, driven by the promise of unlimited personal freedom to achieve their loftiest ambitions, uprooted themselves and their families and left everything behind. Faced with the rugged and unforgiving landscape of the frontier, they harnessed their will and ambition and pushed west to the Pacific, taming every geographic and living opponent in their path, until there was virtually nothing left of the New World except its memory. Now seated on the throne of world power and surrounded by every material comfort, they have crashed with the realization that America cannot fulfill its promise. While the very few will reach heights of great personal wealth and fame, the majority remain in the middle strata, spending money at a rate they cannot afford to experience the meager fruits of an elusive dream. The result: a society under a collective spell which, as Whybrow explains in *American Mania*, is a "*dysphoric* state of activity—from the Greek *dusphoria* meaning "discomfort"—that begins with happiness *but lies beyond it* in a tumult of anxiety, competition, and social disruption." [10]

Speaking to me by phone from his holiday on the California coast, Whybrow reiterates his thesis. "If you look at America as a temperament rather than as a place, then most people come here because they are dissatisfied with the place in which they originally found themselves. Although, obviously, the distribution of human beings across the face of the earth is all driven by migration, what has happened in contemporary society is that America has turned this into a mythology, a cultural mythology, where people come to America to dream of the future." [11]

That future is encapsulated in the American Dream: a highly branded concept that became woven into the national, if not global, consciousness. So that America is now not so much a geographic location as it is, in Peter Whybrow's thinking, a state of mind. Yet, the dream is not for everyone. Whybrow describes Americans as a very rare breed of migrant. In fact, very few—two percent—of the world's population ever leave their birth cities, while the rest die within fifty miles of where they were born. "It's a self-selecting process," he tells me, "and if you look at the temperament of the migrant, these individuals are optimistic, risk-taking, belligerent to some degree, self-centered, and tend to see the future as something they can grasp and make their own."

Unlike most of our dreams, Whybrow tells me, the American version is not some abstract fantasy. For those who have crossed the oceans, it's as real as the moon and the stars.

"They don't see the dream as something ephemeral, they see it as a tangible thing they will eventually achieve. And of course this gets translated, in modern America, as a material dream. A bigger house, a larger car, more power in the social hierarchy. More money. That is a consistent background to the American experience. If you look back to some of the persons who characterized America in its early years, especially Tocqueville, you find that he describes exactly the same temperament, exactly the same type of behavior in America, as we see now. There's really no change whatsoever."

French aristocrat Alexis de Tocqueville spent nine months traveling through the country from 1831–32. Originally tasked by the French government to study the American prison system, he soon grew bored with the repetitive research and turned his focus to the burgeoning republic and its experiment with representational democracy. Four years later, Tocqueville recorded his observations in *Democracy In America*, which became an instant classic for its perceptive account of America's sociopolitical prototype, and the people who inhabited it.* [12]

"They [Americans] find prosperity almost everywhere, but not happiness," he wrote. "For them desire for well-being has become a restless, burning passion which increases with satisfaction. To start with emigration was a necessity for them: now it is a sort of gamble, and they enjoy the sensations as much as the profit." Evoking themes that would later become core virtues of American-style capitalism, Tocqueville observed that Americans approach life "like a game of chance... or the day of a battle." [13]

Reading these excerpts of Tocqueville's account, it is easy to forget that America was formed out of a revolutionary desire to create a new liberal society, free from the religious and social constraints of monarchial Britain. But, according to Whybrow, that is just historical fantasy. The New Worlders were pragmatists and businessmen, and their migration was inspired by a far less romantic cause.

"The notion of freedom of markets was more driving than the abstract concept of freedom," he explains. "It was not so much

* Tocqueville traveled to America with his close friend and fellow magistrate Gustave de Beaumont. Six months into the trip, Beaumont wrote to his father about their waning interest in the original mission: "The prisons have pretty well bored us. We always see the same thing. We have now no, or very few, observations to make, and if we always inspect the prisons of the cities where we go, it's solely to fulfill a necessary formality."

political repression as it was the need to be able to get out from under the yoke of the taxation systems and the other mercantile dominance that England exerted on its colonies."

In speaking about markets, we have to remember that revolutionary America of the eighteenth and nineteenth centuries hardly resembled the fiercely competitive marketplace that we see today. Early American society was still mainly agrarian and the market functioned as a vital hub for the community, where farmers and tradesmen could meet as free agents and exchange their wares. For the highly devout Christians of the new American capitalist class, commerce was a vaunted form of human interaction where the maxims of a virtuous and free society were always in play. "The constraints of the social order were hand and glove with the marketplace," Whybrow tells me, "If you were selling bad meat you didn't stay a butcher for long, and your shoes had to wear well otherwise nobody would come back and buy them from you. In this sense, America has always been the great market experiment in the Adam Smith context."

This interplay between self-interest and "social order" was, as Whybrow points out, the brainchild of Scottish professor Adam Smith. Smith's seminal *The Wealth of Nations*—a book I'd contemplated at the Hay festival—was published in 1776 and argued that the market has its own innate system of self-regulation, or "invisible hand," which ultimately, magically, guides the self-concerned actions of businessman to promote the welfare of the community as a whole, and thus does not require government interference. For a burgeoning commercial sector that, for the first time, was functioning independently of the monarchy, there was a great need to codify a system of rules that would protect the individual from harm. But herein lay the dilemma: the whole purpose of the liberal revolution was to escape authoritarian structures imposed by outside forces. Hence Smith's quasi-religious model for the market provided the perfect solution and *The Wealth of Nations* quickly became enshrined as the definitive philosophical model for the "laissez-faire" governance of markets. Published in the year of American Independence, this vision became central to that of the American colonists and Founding Fathers who had finally yanked the chains of British imperialism off their necks.[14]

In the two hundred years since *The Wealth of Nations* was published, Smith's theory remains the cornerstone of the free market system. Despite its spiritual, unscientific quality, modern economists still view the invisible hand as a valid explanation for market activity. But something happened along the way: the invisible hand was gutted of its moral mechanics and slowly became appropriated by economists who saw it as a vehicle to justify the most ruthless of competitive practices. According to Whybrow, this manipulation of Smith's visionary legacy represents a failure by modern economists, who have little desire, or motive, to understand the basic concept of the invisible hand, to grasp the totality of his philosophy. Worse, they know nothing about mission and intent of its author.

"Adam Smith's philosophy was a psychological theory. He was a professor of moral philosophy who taught at Glasgow in the mid 1700s," Whybrow states matter-of-factly. "His famous book, *The Wealth of Nations*, was preceded by *The Theory of Moral Sentiments*, in which he puts forth the idea that a market society will be self-regulating because the balance to that self-interest was the notion that we all want to be loved by other people, and we want to be loved more than we want to be seen as greedy. So we would give up self-interest to a certain point in order to be part of the community, part of the social context."

To explain this quality of human nature, Smith preceded the invisible hand with another philosophical concept which he named the "impartial spectator." Introduced in *Moral Sentiments* in 1759, Smith used the impartial spectator to illustrate the quotients of empathy and altruism required to fulfill the potential of any commercial market. Writing in *Moral Sentiments*, Smith declared, "The man whom we naturally love the most is he who joins to... his own original and selfish feelings, the most exquisite sensibility... and sympathetic feelings of others."[15]

Viewed as an integrated symbiotic whole, Whybrow explains, the invisible hand and impartial spectator fuse into Smith's vision of a "market-driven humanitarian culture." But taken alone, he argues, the invisible hand is incomplete; a yin without the yang. Yet, this is precisely what has happened. The humanitarian aspect of Smith's writing has been all but abandoned by the modern liberal economists for whom the empathetic impartial spectator has no place in the modern, unregulated marketplace.* And so, where once each participant in the market was to be accorded the dignity and respect of free and equal men in a communitarian society, now each would be pitted against each in brutal competition. According to Whybrow, this represents a critical break in the evolution of the American dream and provides substance to his claim that the dream now being marketed and sold to the world is a fraudulent copy.

Modern economists needed the invisible hand theory to give credibility and historical sanction to their idea of unregulated markets, free of government interference. So, like high school essayists, they simply took the parts of Adam Smith's theory that they needed and omitted those that conflicted with their beliefs. Noam Chomsky describes reading the University of Chicago's

---

* Despite my own limited exposure to economics, I had never heard of the impartial spectator before Whybrow explained it to me. It's not hard to see why. When I Google the four key words: "Adam Smith invisible hand," the browser returns 40,400 individual responses. By contrast, "Adam Smith impartial spectator" returns just 43. It is almost as if the concept has been scrubbed from the wider public record.

bicentennial edition of *The Wealth of Nations* and discovering that, in his introduction, Nobel Prize-winning economist George Stigler distorted the meaning of Smith's text, portraying Smith as being in favor of the division of labor, when he was, in fact, opposed to it.

It shouldn't come as a surprise that the University of Chicago's department of economics—also known as the "Chicago School"—would alter Smith's writing to serve a specific vision of laissez-faire capitalism. As America's most influential institutional proponent of the free market, the Chicago School has a mixed history: most notably its infamous gang of "Chicago Boys" who acted as economic advisers to Chilean dictator Augusto Pinochet, ultimately establishing a free market system under the regime which tortured and killed its political opponents. When Milton Friedman, another graduate of and professor at the Chicago School, won the Nobel Prize for Economics in 1976, demonstrators picketed the ceremony in protest of his involvement as an unofficial advisor to the regime.

Ironically, Friedman had risen to prominence for arguing that capitalism and political freedom were inextricably linked. His classic 1962 book, *Capitalism and Freedom* was heralded as the seminal text for neoliberal thought. In it, Friedman attacked Keynesian economics and its offspring, the welfare state, which had dominated American fiscal policy since the Depression. He took great issue with the champions of government interventionism—emblemized by the New Deal and Great Society projects of the Democratic Party—who had "corrupted" the term "liberalism," marginalizing the classic liberal belief in maximum individual freedom by pushing it under the "conservative" banner. Outraged at this revisionist manipulation—and by the fact that he was considered a conservative!—Friedman sought to redefine liberalism, returning it to its rightful heirs whom, he argued, were "suspicious of assigning to government any functions that can be performed through the market, both because this substitutes coercion for voluntary co-operation in the area in question and because, by giving government an increased role, it threatens freedom in other areas." * 16

To prove his point, Friedman cited the writing of Adam Smith and specifically the invisible hand that would, under the right framework, allow men seeking their own self-interest to simultaneously promote the greater welfare of all. He echoed Smith's belief that a stable, progressive liberal society must have a "basic core of value judgments" that are intuitively recognized by the majority of its citizens.[17] But Friedman stopped short of describing these value judgments and rebuked those who had made it a fashion for business leaders to accept a certain degree of "social responsibility." Herein lies the fundamental break of modern free market liberalism and Adam Smith's philosophy: while Friedman and Smith were aligned with their vision of the market as a central communitarian platform for the society, in Friedman's version there was no obligation for its major actors to provide moral or ethical leadership.

By attaching the impartial spectator to his economic philosophy, Adam Smith was directing the capitalist class to construct a system of ethics that would govern interactions between market players. He saw the development of a conscience as crucial to the success of liberal societies which had been unleashed from the control and authority of the state. Without a moral foundation, the invisible hand would simply become another whip for the powerful to rule the powerless. But in the ruggedly individualistic capitalist system championed by Milton Friedman, there was

* Though Friedman gets most of the credit for reversing the tide of "welfarism," it was Friedrich Hayek's 1944 book *The Road to Serfdom* that launched the first major challenge to the prevailing "liberal" fiscal ideology.

no room for an imposed moral code.* Especially when profits depended on maximizing the division of labor, which allowed businesses to pay some workers less than others depending on the color of their skin. Reading *Capitalism and Freedom* now, over forty years since it was first published, is a fascinating study in the deployment of euphemisms. Friedman tries hard to mask his views on minority labor, but fails spectacularly on a few occasions. In one memorable passage, he exalts the capitalist system which forces its participants to look beyond the "characteristics of the individual," meaning their race or religion. Seeking to eradicate government imposed hiring quotas, Friedman argued that discrimination was bad for business and that the invisible hand of the market would punish those who excluded African-Americans from their payrolls because, as he put it, there is "an economic incentive in a free market to separate economic efficiency from other characteristics of the individual;" here economic efficiency means low cost of employment. Hiring African-Americans was a virtue for the true capitalist and had direct benefits in that those who were color-blind, wrote Friedman, "can buy things more cheaply as a result." [18]

While Friedman paid lip service to Adam Smith's classical liberal belief in the dignity of the individual, this did not necessarily extend as far down as the lowest rungs of the working class. Primacy remained with the players at the top of the pyramid who, after all, were the target audience for Friedman's book. It was not long before the new, or neoliberal, interpretation of Smith's invisible hand became a standard for the free market capitalists who sought to overthrow the welfare state, claiming government intervention in the economy went against classic liberal philos-

---

* In their obituary for Friedman, who died on November 16, 2006, the *New York Times* helped sustain the lie of Friedman's direct theoretical lineage to Adam Smith, describing him as "the grandmaster of free-market economic theory" and "a spiritual heir to Adam Smith."

ophy. Ironically, the system imposed by New Deal liberals was, in part, a means of re-invigorating the more humanitarian aspects of Smith's invisible hand/impartial spectator dualism that had been lost in the evolution of the market-based economy.

To be fair, Friedman was writing at a time when Communism posed a serious threat to America. The major thrust of *Capitalism and Freedom* is that the mortal enemy of a liberal society is concentration of power. For Friedman and the neoliberals who would take up his then-revolutionary mission, true freedom was most threatened by a government that sought to control the economic life of its citizens, a government that believed in "taking from some to benefit others." Naturally this meant that any economic philosophy which sought to impose ethical standards on the business community was verboten; it smacked too vividly of the communist system. So, in translating the powerful vision that Adam Smith had prescribed for the first American capitalists, twentieth century free market economists kept the invisible hand but left his impartial spectator on the proverbial cutting room floor.

When *Capitalism and Freedom* was published in the early sixties it was considered a radical text. Shunned by the major liberal universities and intellectuals, no mainstream U.S. newspaper even bothered to review the book. But twenty years later, with many of the New Deal welfare state programs having proven to be ineffective as social reforms and the battle against Communism moving into its climactic nuclear phase, Friedman was celebrated as the new prophet of capitalism. His 1980 follow-up *Free To Choose* sold over 400,000 hardcover copies in its first year and was subsequently translated into twelve languages. When Ronald Reagan launched his attack on big government by announcing his candidacy for president, Friedman was right there as a top economic advisor to the campaign. The Chicago School economist could only have smiled from his seat at the 1981 Inauguration when Reagan declared "government is not the solution to our problem, government *is* the problem." [19] The welfare state was officially dead.*

Under Reagan, America became its own cultural cliché. Personified by Hollywood portrayals of greed merchants running wild on Wall Street (Michael Douglas's corporate tycoon Gordon Gecco in Oliver Stone's *Wall Street*) and coked-up Generation Xers strung out in Beverly Hills (Robert Downey Jr.'s Julian in *Less Than Zero*) the eighties were scored by a synthed-out soundtrack featuring Eurobands with bad hair and neon clothing. This was the advent of the "Me Generation" in which the former sixties Baby Boomers matured into a consumer society, leaving the radical liberalism of the last fifty years—derided by Reaganites as high-minded, elitist intellectualism—to dissolve in a vat of Polo cologne.

But for most Americans and, indeed, the world, Reagan's major legacy is rooted in the mythological. With CNN's worldwide broadcast of the 1989 fall of the Berlin Wall, Reagan was immortalized as the ultimate defender of the free world who vanquished the evil forces of Soviet Russia. Communism had failed and capitalism was firmly established as the victorious economic philosophy. Peter Whybrow argues that this ideological conquest had a transformative impact on the American psyche.

"We all know that story," he laughs, referring to the fall of the Wall. Then, quickly turning serious, he continues, "In fact, what I think happened to us is that we became prideful in a way: 'See? We've won. This is the best system in the world, all we have to do

---

* While Friedman's "monetarist" policies initially held sway over the new Reagan administration, they soon became a liability. Writing in the *Boston Globe*, Harvard's Richard Parker explains: "When Reagan reached the White House in 1981 he fully supported the Federal Reserve's adoption of Friedman's ideas. Yet monetarism's honeymoon proved short-lived. The Fed's application indeed choked inflation out of the economy—but in the process produced the worst recession since the 1930s. Reversing course by 1983, the Fed abandoned its newfound principles—and the economy took off, just in time for Reagan's re-election..." See "The pragmatist and the utopian," *Boston Globe*, February 6, 2005.

is let the market do its thing.' We moved increasingly towards the idea that we were best off as a nation, economically, if we allowed entrepreneurial activity to flourish and gave it no constraint whatsoever."

Despite Milton Friedman's protestations, political historians describe the Reagan-sponsored shift away from the welfare state as a move to the right. But, according to Peter Whybrow, this is a simplistic interpretation. Looking at it from a behavioral context, he explains, this reinvigorated emphasis on the individualistic, entrepreneurial model capitalism, without a balancing component of social reinvestment, represents a deviation to the instinctual.

"What those people didn't realize is," Whybrow scolds, "once you begin to take the brakes off, then instinctual behavior begins to drive. Instinctual behavior is self-interested behavior."

From a neurobiological perspective this distinction is important. Self-interest, or selfishness, is the most primitive form of human behavior. It is innate and reward-driven: hardwired into the neural mechanism of our survival instinct. By contrast, the empathy and self-restraint governed by Smith's impartial spectator are not instinctual. Rather, they are passed down from generation to generation and learned through imitation. And, without careful cultivation, they are easily lost. Just as we begin to forget our native language without constant practice and reinforcement, so too can a society lose touch with its learned behaviors, especially, as Darwin discovered, those that do not contribute directly to our (in this case, economic) survival.

For Peter Whybrow, this phenomenon has already begun to shape American social behavior. The shift away from self-restraint and toward instinctual selfishness has seeded a culture of immediate gratification that diverges radically from the original Protestant ethics of work and conservation upon which the original dream was founded. In their industrious quest to create a world in which anything is possible, Americans have created a society where every want or desire is within reach, just a phone call away. As a result, Peter Whybrow says, Americans have become a nation of anxious, over-crowded, debt-laden fast food junkies.

"If you look at it from a psychological standpoint, it's tied back to the fact that if you give human beings—or any animal for that matter—an extraordinarily rich environment, they will begin to become addicted to it," Whybrow explains in a concerned tone. "We have no way of constraining ourselves, except through intellectual thought." But for a majority of Americans, the intellectual has been permanently relegated to the back of the bus. Faced with the stark realization that the gap between have and have-not is only widening, average Americans have become desperate to grab a piece, or even a few crumbs, of the pie. And they've been stuffing themselves with it ever since.*

"What's happened is that you've got a whole group of people, some of whom have been misled and [continue] to go along with it—because the mythology of America is that if you work hard, and you're lucky, you will be rich and famous. Seventy to eighty percent of the population really believe that one day they're going to wake up and win the lottery, or happen to hit some extraordinary opportunity which will turn them into millionaires."

For Whybrow, this strike-it-rich mentality is the last vestige of the original American dream. Now rooted firmly in the instinctual mind, Americans cannot reconcile themselves with the sacrifices of ego and pleasure that were once a foundation of American capitalism. Instead of developing a rational plan for achieving their

* When Milton Friedman published *Capitalism and Freedom* in 1962, research statistics showed that thirteen percent of the American population was obese. By 2001 the World Health Organization pegged the number at 27 percent, with approximately 60 percent of Americans designated as overweight. More troubling is the stat on obesity in youth: 30 percent overweight and fifteen percent obese, with dramatic increases in diabetes, high blood pressure and psychological trauma associated with the social stigma of being fat.

wildest ambitions, most Americans have simply bridged the gap with a lien against their future. In order to finance the promised dream, today, Americans have incurred levels of personal debt unthinkable in the post-Depression era that inspired FDR's New Deal legislation. In 2004, the average American household held over nineteen bank cards—including credit, retail and debit cards—and carried over $9,300 in credit card debt, an increase of 116 percent since a decade earlier. Calculating personal debt payments as a percentage of after-tax income, in 2005 Americans left 13.6 percent on the table, the highest level since the Fed began tallying the stat in 1980.[*][20]

The United States has become a nation of Charlies, hoping to find their golden ticket in a Wonka Bar. To prove the level of irrationalism that has creeped into the national consciousness, Whybrow cites a survey conducted in the late 1990s that showed in order to fulfill what the average American categorized as their "dream," it would cost double the nation's median income. Whybrow tells me that this focus on financial wealth as a means of achieving individual success obscures the fact that the society has been stripped of the programs and resources that were once considered essential to realizing one's full potential.

"The true American dream, in my mind, is the opportunity to work hard, and be socially mobile. And yet social mobility in this country is now less than it is in Europe. Why? Because you can't be socially mobile by yourself unless you have resources. In

* Whybrow cites further evidence of America's debt crisis in *American Mania*: "By 1997 the combined indebtedness of the nation' households had reached an unparalleled 89 percent of total household income. Debt climbed from 95 percent of disposable household income early in the 1990s to 124 percent in the last quarter of the year 2000. The average rate of personal savings fell to zero over the same period and by 2001 was firmly in negative territory, at minus six percent—something not seen since the darkest days of the Great Depression when 25 percent of America's workforce was unemployed. The American dream is now heavily mortgaged." Quote from Peter C. Whybrow, *American Mania: When More Is Not Enough* (New York: W.W. Norton & Co., 2005).

most civilized countries, resources are provided so that the intelligent, resourceful person will find their way through the system. This means they need to get a reasonable education. And if you fall sick, you get reasonable healthcare. If you get old and haven't made it into the millionaire class, people will support you. This is the humanitarian side, the feedback loop of the social sentiment, which human beings, ever since inception, have realized is essential."

And just when I think Whybrow has digressed into a leftist rant against the capitalist system, he lands back to the firm ground behavioral science. "Human beings only became dominant because they realized they were stronger in a social context than they were in an individual context. Try killing a mammoth by yourself. It doesn't work. You have to have a group."

But Americans have been known, on occasion, to band together to kill a mammoth; especially one that threatens the status quo or the collective vision of American identity. Despite their romantic idealization of the individual who overcomes exceedingly difficult odds, Americans have always had very specific rules governing just who gets access to the dream. It is jealously guarded. And if ever a man should rise too far above his designated station, there has always been a mob ready to ensure the mistake was not repeated, even if that meant contravening every virtue that once inspired the migrants to come in the first place.

Documentary filmmaker Ken Burns captured the power of this phenomenon in *Unforgivable Blackness*, his PBS biography of America's first black heavyweight boxing champion, Jack Johnson. At a time when blacks made the papers only if they were lynched or caught stealing, Johnson became one of the most photographed sporting icons of the early twentieth century. Of Johnson's success at reaching the highest plateau for any black man of his generation, essayist and commentator Stanley Crouch remarked, "America, for whatever its problems, still has a certain elasticity and a certain latitude that allows the person to dream a big enough dream that can be achieved if the person is as big as the dream." Yet, for white America, Johnson had become too big for the dream, and thus, now represented its most potent threat.* 21

Because of Johnson's widely reputed love for prostitutes, the FBI opened a case against him for violating the Mann Act, a law that made it a crime to transport women across state lines "for the purpose of prostitution or debauchery, or for any other immoral purpose." Originally aimed at white slavery, or forced prostitution, the government was able to find a willing witness in one of Johnson's jilted lovers, a prostitute who claimed he had taken her from Pittsburgh to Chicago where they had sex. When the judge sentenced him to a year in federal prison, the champ fled to Europe.22

It was the beginning of a downward spiral that would eventually see him lose his title in Havana to an unknown American farm boy named Jess Willard. Broke and homesick, Johnson returned to America in 1920 to serve his sentence; he would never regain his belt. The object lesson provided by the legacy of Jack Johnson was so effective that when Joe Louis began his climb to the championship fifteen years later, his trainer Jack Blackburn, warned him:

"You know, boy, the heavyweight division for a Negro is hardly likely. The white man ain't too keen on it. You have to be something to go anywhere. If you really ain't gonna be another Jack Johnson, you got some hope. White man hasn't forgotten that fool nigger with his white women, acting like he owned the world."

* After Johnson won the world heavyweight title, white America went into shock. Almost immediately, the search began for a 'great white hope' to reclaim the belt. The black man could enjoy the spoils of the shining city, but he could not climb the steps to the throne; let alone become master. Even the socialist and author Jack London could not help but wish for a savior to come and "remove that golden smile from Jack Johnson's face," as he wrote in the *New York Herald*, "The White Man must be rescued."

Louis got the message, promising that he would never "disgrace the race," as Johnson did.[23]

In retrospect, these were not splendor-filled days in the shining city. With Johnson's victory in 1908, the twentieth century had begun with an ominous signal. For the first time Americans were forced to confront the reality of a society in which the potential of realizing the dream was open to *everyone*. And they didn't like it. Perhaps, deep within the nation's mass consciousness, there was also the realization that for most of them, too, the dream was never going to be reality. That in the social and economic hierarchy that is pyramid shaped, there was only ever enough room for a few at the top. Not all would become rich and famous, as the dream had promised. For a great majority of Americans, black and white, dreaming the dream was the closest they would get to touching it. Now, at the turn of the new century, the promise has become, to quote Peter Whybrow, "An illusion worthy of Charles Ponzi." *

What impact has this realization, even if subconscious, had on Americans? Did it make them more competitive, more ruthless, more individualistic as they began to fight against the remoteness of their chances? Did it change them at all? According to Peter Whybrow, we can learn much about the American people from how the world now looks on them and the dream the nation still promotes as its most valuable domestic product.

"I think we are selling a failed dream, and I think it's

---

* Through an elaborate scheme involving international postal coupons—which were bought in countries with weaker currencies—Charles Ponzi promised New England investors they could earn a 40 percent return in 90 days—compared to five percent for bank savings accounts. After paying off a few early investors to establish his credibility, word hit the street and a frenzy ensued, with people mortgaging their homes to get in on Ponzi's deal. One day he made over $1 million. But it was destined to crash because, in reality, he was giving birth to the "pyramid scheme" in which investors are paid off from the proceeds of a later investment instead of any actual business activity—robbing Peter to pay Paul, as it were.

becoming obvious to the rest of the world," he explains. "The fact is that Americans used to be an object of intrigue. America was a fascinating place—and Americans were generally liked. But now, it's completely the opposite. America is not liked. Americans are individually liked, to some degree, but they're considered brash, and belligerent, and loud. So there's been a definite shift."

Pausing, he adds, "They sense that America is not what it used to be."

We all know the myth of paradise lost, that things were better as children. It may be easier for us to imagine the world was once somehow greater than it is in the present, if only to release ourselves of the responsibility of becoming more than our ancestors were. But Peter Whybrow's analysis of the American psyche and corresponding decline of the population's physical and emotional health is rooted in scientific study. And it has parallels in the political domain, where some analysts have traced a marked degeneration in the democratic organs of the republic.

And few have done it more studiously than the man I would be seeing the following night in New York.

BY THE NUMBERS

Lewis Lapham is late.

I am ensconced at the bar of the Noho Star, downing olives and watching *Sideways* star Paul Giamatti play with his son in one of the booths.

Out of the corner of my eye, I catch Lapham strolling through the door. Smartly dressed in a pinstriped suit, crisp white shirt and matching blood red tie and handkerchief, he has more the presence of a dandified banker, than of a journalist. But after running *Harper's Magazine* for the last thirty years, I imagine he has had to be a little of both.

Spotting me, Lapham slides off his coat and pulls out a stool from the bar. "We've got to be quick. I have something at seven," he says and then, perhaps unconsciously triggered by the bearded Giamatti, orders a Pinot. I look down at his gold watch and realize this gives me 45 minutes. After spending the better part of five months to get this interview, I know there won't be a second chance. So I pull out my recorder and start taping.[24]

Founded in 1850 by two brothers in New York, *Harper's* was initially a monthly magazine publishing renowned authors like Charles Dickens and Walt Whitman. The venture was such a success that by the early 1860s it shifted to a weekly run that reached over 200,000 subscribers nationwide. But it wasn't until cartoonist Thomas Nast joined the magazine that *Harper's* became one of the most powerful political journals of its day,* ultimately securing the public's favor for presidential candidates like Rutherford Hayes and Grover Cleveland. Coming of age in the twentieth century, *Harper's* became a liberal outpost, featuring essays by the most brilliant minds in literature and politics, including Leon Trotsky, Henry James, Virginia Woolf, William Faulkner, James Baldwin and Tom Wolfe. It is, according to the website, the "oldest general interest monthly in America."[25]

Lapham, who was educated at Yale and Cambridge, came to the magazine in the sixties after working as a reporter for the *San Francisco Examiner* and *New York Herald Tribune*. By 1971, he was its managing editor, eventually taking over the corner office in 1976. In the early '80s, he redesigned the magazine, creating its textual format that juxtaposes short excerpts of everything from restaurant menus to business plans with fiction, political essays and, of

---

* Thomas Nast's unique and biting style of political caricature gave the Democrats their donkey, the Republicans their elephant and America its Uncle Sam. In the 1870s Nast waged a campaign to expose the crooked New York politician William Tweed. So viciously targeted were Nast's cartoons that Tweed offered him a $200,000 bribe to stop, but Nast refused and in 1876 Tweed was jailed for fraud.

course, Lapham's iconic brainchild, the "Harper's Index."

As a student, one of my favorite high school English teachers would start every week with the Index. What he loved about it most wasn't its replication of arcane statistics, but the way they were juxtaposed to create a narrative of their own. It was journalism, he told us, through numbers. I don't have any of those handouts left in my files, so I went into *Harper's* online archive and found a couple that capture the incisive commentary the magazine is able to convey through its weekly list of bullet point one-liners.

Ratio of the average amount a U.S. family spent on food, clothing, and shelter [in 1997] to what it spent on taxes: 3:4

Number of CIA laptops containing top-secret information sold inadvertently at a government-surplus auction in 1995: 25

Then there is this couplet and triplet from January and October 2005, respectively.

Total U.S. spending on poppy eradication and other anti-drug efforts in Afghanistan last year: $780,000,000
Amount it would have cost to purchase the country's entire 2004 poppy crop: $600,000,000

Number of House members in 1979 who voted against making Martin Luther King Jr.'s birthday a national holiday: 133
Number who are still in the House : 9
Number who are vice president: 1

Perhaps needing a break from the tumult of running one of the last of America's political journals in a highly competitive, and greatly diluted, industry, or sickened by the neoconservative spirit of the country, in November 2005 Lapham announced he would step down as editor. I have caught him right at the moment before his transition, before a successor has been named, and can sense a mixed air of melancholy and relief. At first his mood is salty, and he asks me to remind him what we are talking about.

"The promise," I answer, suddenly nervous and forgetting my words, "that if you came to the United States, there would be a new world waiting. One borne from Enlightenment era liberal values."

He sips his wine, waiting for a question.

"When you were growing up, was that promise still alive?" I ask, still flustered. "One in which the republic was sanctified by the competition of two parties, each representing a distinct half of the national character and interest, and in which each individual had an opportunity to reach their full potential. Or has it been destroyed? Has that liberalism that was once the promise of the shining city of John Winthrop's time been forgotten?"

Lapham looks at me quizzically. "Well, that's a lot of questions."

I blush.

"But, okay." Putting down his glass, Lapham slips into a quiet voice, recounting the legacy of the American liberal project since World War II. Not wanting to interrupt him and realizing I've probably blown a quarter of my time asking such an unfocused, open-ended question, I sit tightlipped, listening. My worry quickly transforms into keen attentiveness as Lapham runs through the decades of his life, providing a snap recap of everything I have taken in so far on my journey. But in his own distinctive seventy-year-old big 'L' liberal voice.

"I'm ten years old in San Francisco in 1945. My grandfather has been mayor in San Francisco during WWII and I'm used to seeing aircraft carriers in the bay and American navy pilots stunting under the Bay Bridge. My grandfather is still mayor in 1945 and he presides over the United Nations charter and I'm excused from school under his direction to go to all the plenary sessions. I'm very much caught up in Roosevelt's notion of the Four Freedoms, the liberal stance of the New Deal demonstrated by America's willingness to come to the rescue of the world in World War II.

"So I am very geared to the liberal idea—which at that point in time is the American idea. We are received by people all over the world, just as we are when U.S. soldiers come to shore in Normandy, as the sons of liberty. We stand for freedom from fear, freedom from want, freedom of expression, freedom of religious worship—those are the Four Freedoms. Throughout the end of the '40s and '50s, we have John F. Kennedy and the idealism he brings to the presidency ("ask not what your country can do for you, but what you can do for your country"), the Peace Corps. The liberal consensus holds with Lyndon Johnson's Great Society. It begins to come apart in the '70s because the early optimism and idealism that's embodied in the '60s: the flower children, the music of the Beatles, the Summer of Love, civil rights movement—that begins to turn bad in the early winter of '68.

"In the early winter of '68 you have the Tet Offensive in Vietnam; that war is clearly pointless. Johnson withdraws from the presidential election that year because the anti-war movement becomes so strong that he knows he cannot be re-elected. Martin Luther King is shot. Bobby Kennedy is shot in the spring. Then you have the Chicago convention in the summer of '68. And then in the fall, Nixon is elected. And within a matter of years, another 37,000 Americans are killed in Vietnam to no purpose. Then you have the Watergate story, and the COINTELPRO investigation. Suddenly, America is a very different place... begins to become a very different place. A lot of the idealism is gone from the atmosphere.

"The '70s are a period of withdrawal; small is beautiful, we can't afford the general's gesture, we go off the gold standard and suddenly find ourselves indebted and under the thumb of the Arabs. Reagan is elected in '80; the promise is that it's morning again in America. But it's morning again only for only some of us in America. Because now what begins to happen is what we now know as the neoconservative reactionary Republican doctrine that money matters more than people, and the legislation that has been working its way through the Congress over the last twenty odd years—no matter what the proposition is, whether it's medical care, tax cuts, bankruptcy laws, the absence of a minimum wage—we have had the constant cutting back on the freedom of the individual while expanding the freedom of property. And with it, the liberal ethos has lost conviction and intensity."

Lapham stops for a moment and reaches out for his wine glass. Lifting it slightly, he gestures at me, concluding, "The embodiment of the liberal idea of freedom, of extending the reach of the individual—which is the stature of the zenith of American power, let us say, in 1945—the light has gradually been going out over the last fifty years."

Truly, it would be impossible to imagine an American politician addressing the nation as Roosevelt did in 1944 when he laid out his now forgotten second, or Economic, Bill of Rights. With the Second World War coming to a close, Roosevelt delivered his State of the Union, declaring, "We have come to a clear realization of the fact that true individual freedom cannot exist without economic security and independence." With this, FDR invoked the concept of positive liberty that had originated with John Stuart Mill in the nineteenth century. This was the notion of liberalism as a political philosophy that went beyond the mere protection of individual rights, ultimately proposing that no person could be free unless they were provided with the opportunity to reach their fullest potential. Roosevelt's post-Depression New Deal legislation had established the basis for this interpretation, ultimately expanding role of government through the Social Security and National Labor Relations Acts. But the 1944 speech, which had so inspired the ten-year-old Lewis Lapham, took this idea of economic rights a step further. Using the language of Thomas Jefferson and the founders, Roosevelt outlined a series of rights that he determined to be "self-evident." Among them were: The right to earn enough to provide adequate food and clothing and recreation; The right of every family to a decent home; The right to adequate medical care and the opportunity to achieve and enjoy good health; The right to adequate protection from the economic fears of old age, sickness, accident, and unemployment; the right to a good education.

Lapham is too much of a realist to bemoan the loss of this political idealism. But he is alarmed by the level of social stratification that has come to define new millennial America. Although the United States, from its very beginning, was marked by extremes of individual poverty and wealth, the great promise of the twentieth century was that liberal society would not tolerate such vast discrepancies between its citizens. After all, it could only lead to the kind of hardened class animosities—jealousy and fear—that had inspired the original pioneers of liberal thought to dream of a new world. And so, for many in Lapham's generation, the myth of an American dream was reinvigorated by the kind of federal interventionism espoused by FDR, and which became the antithesis of neoliberal economics heralded by Milton Friedman and Ronald Reagan. I wonder if his sense of nostalgia for those days has also affected his view of history.

"But you don't believe that the American dream of universal social mobility was real for everyone," I ask.

"No," he answers gruffly. "It was never possible for everyone to move up. It never was, never will be. But it was plausible. It was something you could believe in. You could think that your child could climb further up than you could. You might have to be a wage slave but your son or daughter could own his or her own business. It didn't happen to everybody by any means, but it happened to enough people. But now, we are not as upwardly mobile a society as is France, believe it or not."

The beginning of George Bush's second term inspired a trend of *Harper's*-esque, statistic-driven editorializing, and from the least probable places. In its final issue of 2004, the *Economist* exposed the myth of an American meritocracy, in which anyone with enough will and talent could rise to the top. Indeed, the magazine reported, while 68 percent of Americans still believe they held the key to their personal success, a study by Indiana University of fathers and sons over a twenty-year span showed that in 1998, 70 percent of the sons "had remained either at the same level [of income] or were doing worse than their fathers in 1979."[26]

More damning, perhaps, is evidence that class entrenchment is only getting harder to overcome. The *Economist* report quoted another study from the Economic Policy Institute (EPI) which showed that between 1979 and 2000 the household income of the bottom twenty percent of Americans grew by 6.4 percent compared to that of the top fifth, which grew by 70 percent. In the Clinton-era boom years of the 1990s, less than eleven percent of those starting in the bottom twenty percent of wage earners were ever able to make it to the top 40 percent; a steadily declining percentage from previous decades.*

The *New York Times*'s ten-part series, "Class Matters," provided interactive graphics and focused on a series of characters from

---

* And, further dispelling the rags-to-riches myth of Horatio Alger, the *Economist* dusted off a study by American University economist Thomas Hertz which tracked 6,273 families, black and white, over two generations—a 32-year period. Like the EPI study mentioned above, only 6 percent of Hertz's families in the poorest fifth of America made it to the top 20 percent. But more interesting is that 42 percent stayed exactly where they started, while 24 percent moved up a notch to the next-to-bottom group. Unsurprisingly, between black and white families the former were pointedly less upwardly mobile and with little chance of escaping their lot. In 2005, 33 percent of black American children were living below the poverty line.

varying socioeconomic tiers struggling with, to list a few: unequal access to quality health care, inter-class marriage, failure to finish college, and being an immigrant in post-dream America. The *Times* reported the same solemn reality, that despite cultivating "the appearance of classlessness... Americans are arguably more likely than they were 30 years ago to end up in the same class into which they were born." [27]

The *Times* also introduced a new designation on the social ladder, the hyper-rich, profiling a battle on Nantucket, an east coast island haven, between the new money and "old aristocratic families." Again, echoing the *Economist* report, the *Times* wrote that the hyper-rich "resemble the arrivistes of the Gilded Age, which began in the 1880s when industrial capitalists amassed staggering fortunes." Buying up waterfront lots at $1 million an acre to build houses for their servants, the hyper-rich have so inflated the cost of living on Nantucket that its own indigenous class of whaling families can barely afford to live there any longer. But, according to the *Times*, the hyper-rich don't care, because "like their precursors, they tend to be brash, confident and unapologetic... and they seem unconcerned about being accepted by the old money." * [28]

For Lewis Lapham, the stratospheric financial surge of the hyper-rich is less of a concern than the ethos of greed and individualism that has triumphed in the corporate culture from which they emerge. One of the major impacts of the transition from FDR's welfare state economy to Friedman's neoliberal model, was the

---

* Writing in the *Boston Phoenix*, Chris Lehman compared the *Times* lecturing about class to parents explaining sex to their children, "there are simply far too many conflicts that run far too deep to result in any reliable account of how the thing works." Dismissing the work as an "anxious series of Tourette's-style asides," Lehman mercilessly deconstructed the series and the inherent biases of the journalists. Most telling perhaps was the installment on the working class habit of not finishing college. The cover photograph featured one of the story's subjects lying on the couch watching football while feeding a bottle his three-year-old son. Observes Lehman: "This, the casual reader is urged to conclude, is just the sort of layabout behavioral pathology that keeps working-class families from achieving serious upward mobility."

gradual depreciation of the working class upon whose shoulders the nation's economic supremacy was built. Lapham remembers a time when the fabric of society reached past the factory doors, ensuring the contribution of laborers would be rewarded long after they had retired.

"It could be seen in statistics," Lapham explains, "it could be seen in the kinds of wages that were being paid to automobile workers and the pensions that they could expect. And now what you're seeing is 15,000 fired by this company, 20,000 by another—you just saw United Airlines say it was going to stop paying all its pensions, and GM indicated they're going to do the same."

Lapham laughs and stabs an olive with a toothpick. "It's not the same place."

His words have a gravity that I did not feel when Peter Whybrow uttered a similar sentiment. For Lewis Lapham, this is more than just a critical observation, it is a point of great disappointment. A failure of American society as a whole and one that is, as ever, backed up by the numbers.

"Wages for the common man have declined over the past 25 years, when adjusted for inflation. In the 1970s the ratio between what an assembly line worker made as a wage and what a CEO of the same company made was about twelve to one. Today, it's 431 to one."

"That from the Index?" I laugh.

"That's a real number—I may not be right on the exact number," he replies, earnestly, "but I'm right on the proportion. That's outrageous." *

Now, Lapham explains, America has been compartmentalized

* In fact, income discrepancies between top executives and the average worker have now reached pre-Depression levels. In it's study of corporate wages, the Washington-based Economic Policy Institute found that the top 100 American CEOs had an average income of $37.5 million: over 1,000 times that of the average worker, who makes around $38,000. Thirty years ago it was $1.3 million, just 39 times what their boys in the shop were taking home.

into polar worlds. Separate universes. Ones in which the rich and poor only commingle via the impersonal interdependence of labor relations: boss to worker, golfer to greenskeeper, homeowner to maid. In new millennial America, these two worlds are defined in very simple terms, public and private, with the former being reserved for the poorest of society. But when he was a child in 1945, Lapham explains, these words had very different meanings. "The word 'public' carried with it the connotation of the good. That was the overtone. Public school, public health, public service, public transportation, public square—the common wealth, the 'we.' 'Private' carried with it the connotation of selfish greed—enlightened selfishness. Private was associated with the greedy banker figure of the late nineteenth century. And now those meanings have been reversed. Public connotes slum, incompetence, black people, housing projects, inefficiency, corruption. And private connotes all things good and beautiful—private trout stream, private school, private plane, private golf course, and so on. The country is dividing along the frontiers of class and race—but more class than race. The blacks don't get a fair shot at it at all, but it's because they're poor. Of course, it's also because they're black. I'm not trying to gloss over the racism, but..."

Lapham turns to me and shrugs; we have fifteen minutes left. There really is only one place left to go and that is Hurricane Katrina. In a discussion about race and class stratification, it is the 100-pound gorilla. No single historical moment has done more to desecrate the image of America and its hallowed dream than the aftermath of Katrina and the much-discussed neglect from federal agencies in bringing help to the stranded "refugees." Who can forget the photograph of that elderly woman's dead body, slouched over in a wheelchair and covered with blankets to reduce the stench of her rotting skin; or the early report of the man who shot his sister in the head over a bag of ice; or the news footage of filthy New Orleans streets, crowded with mostly black, newly homeless people waiting for water, food or some form of transportation to take them from that hell? For anyone who still held onto the myth of America as the shining city, Katrina relieved them of their illusions. Once the storm had passed and search and rescue operations had begun for survivors, two realities came to dominate the popular narrative. First, that the great majority of those who had been most affected were poor and black. Second, despite years of successive warnings about the potential for the levees to break, the government had done little or nothing to prepare for the disaster it would cause. It wasn't long before much of the world began to connect the two. Damning verdicts stained the pages of journals at both ends of the socioeconomic spectrum. Looking out from the *Economist*'s cover on newsstands in airports and five star hotels around the world, an exhausted, tear-drenched New Orleans woman justified the headline, "The shaming of America." Meantime, writing in the *Nation,* Robert Scheer called New Orleans a spectacle "of poverty and social disarray that tears away the affluent mask of the United States."

Within 24 hours of Katrina's August 29 strike, the unprecedented disaster began to fuel a frenzied marathon of ratings grabbing news reportage. Dispatched with greater agility and responsiveness than the national emergency apparatus, camera crews from all the major networks touched down at 'ground zero' and began sending images back to base. Watching the footage from CNN headquarters in Washington, Wolf Blitzer remarked, "You simply get chills every time you see these poor individuals... many of these people, almost all of them that we see, are so poor, and they are so black, and this is gonna raise lots of questions for people who are watching this story unfold." But if the questions Blitzer was hoping his viewers would ask were in any way reflected in those articulated by the news media, then they fell far short of the kind of national soul-searching Katrina should have inspired.

The commentary at the major networks was never more than skin-deep. Forgoing a more rigorous and demanding socioeconomic analysis of the images coming out of the Bayou, reports focused on looters, running gun battles between gangs and New Orleans police SWAT teams, and unconfirmed stories of rape and murder in the New Orleans Convention Center. But in the print media, the Hobbesian quality of Katrina's aftermath inspired a new wave of statistical analysis. And here, the mood shifted from the summer's diffident meditation on class to more hysterical revelations of America's slide into Third Worldom. "If it's shameful that we have bloated corpses on New Orleans streets, it's even more disgraceful that the infant mortality rate in America's capital is twice as high as in China's capital," lectured Nicolas Kristof from the back pages of the *New York Times*, telling us that in 2002, Washington, DC had double the number of babies who died before their first birthday than did Beijing.[29] And returning the focus to federal relief efforts, truthout.org's Marjorie Cohn told of a Force 5 hurricane that had hit Cuba in September 2004. "More than 1.5 million Cubans were evacuated to higher ground ahead of the storm," she wrote, "Although the hurricane destroyed 20,000 houses, no one died."[30]

On September 2, Grammy Award-winning rapper Kanye West appeared on NBC's live Katrina benefit. Paired with comedian Mike Myers, West looked bleary-eyed and dangerous right from the start. But as soon as Myers finished reading his two sentences, West cleared his throat and made telethon history.

"I hate the way they portray us in the media." West blurted, nervously. "You see a black family, it says, 'They're looting.' You see a white family, it says, 'They're looking for food.' And, you know, it's been five days [waiting for federal help] because most of the people are black. And even for me to complain about it, I would be a hypocrite because I've tried to turn away from the TV because it's too hard to watch."

Unsure of how to react, Myers stared forward, palooka-faced, nodding slightly as West continued. "I've even been shopping before even giving a donation," he confessed. "So now I'm calling my business manager right now to see what is the biggest amount I can give, and just to imagine if I was down there, and those are my people down there. So anybody out there that wants to do anything that we can help—with the way America is set up to help the poor, the black people, the less well-off, as slow as possible. I mean, the Red Cross is doing everything they can. We already realize a lot of people that could help are at war right now, fighting another way—and," he stammered, "they've given them permission to go down and shoot us!"

Realizing he had finished, Myers looked back at the camera and read from his card as if nothing had happened. The effect was surreal.

"And subtle, but in many ways even more profoundly devastating, is the lasting damage to the survivors' will to rebuild and remain in the area." Myers recited, "The destruction of the spirit of the people of southern Louisiana and Mississippi may end up being the most tragic loss of all."

Then West, whose eyes had not veered from the camera, stated: "George Bush doesn't care about black people!" And that was it. The shot cut to a startled, wide-eyed Chris Tucker who urged Americans to support the victims, the majority of whom, still stuck in the Convention Center, would have greeted West's comments with a mighty cheer had they been broadcast over the JumboTron.

For the next few days, West's outburst dominated headlines. More controversial and titillating than Janet Jackson's Super Bowl costume malfunction, video clips of Kanye West's unscripted rant raced through the internet. The speech was cut and remixed into beat-driven MP3s and downloaded onto iPods around the world. It was ironic because the most poignant political message of the NBC broadcast was far more subtle and had been pre-approved by the network. It came from New Orleans legend Aaron Neville who performed Randy Newman's classic song, "Louisiana 1927." With its chorus, "They're trying to wash us away, they're trying to wash us away," Neville was invoking the spirits of his Creole ancestors who endured the other great Mississippi flood in 1927. Rounded up and put into work camps, that generation of New Orleans blacks was held under armed guard and prevented from leaving the city—for fear they would not return to work the crops—as the waters rose. Legend has it the abandoned people could hear strains of "Bye Bye Blackbird" bouncing off the water as their white tormentors, safely stowed aboard a steamer, sailed off from the harbor.[*]

With Arkansas, Mississippi, and Louisiana submerged, President Calvin Coolidge appointed Herbert Hoover to head the flood relief effort. Hoover traveled to the region and used his influence in Washington to draw down federal funds for the victims. In response, the national press lionized him, emboldening Hoover to make a run for president. But soon Northern papers began publishing reports of National Guard troops, sent to Mississippi and Louisiana to patrol the work camps, robbing, beating, raping and killing blacks. Worried this would hurt his image as the flood saviour, Hoover brought in Booker T. Washington protégé Robert Moton to head an investigative commission. Moton was conservative and extremely popular with the white establishment, who generously gave to his Tuskegee Institute. And so, when his commission confirmed the abuse, Moton agreed to squash the report in exchange for a powerful role in Hoover's Republican

---

[*] In an effort to reduce the water's pressure on the city, civic leaders broke the levees, flooding the poor and middle class areas of New Orleans. After the waters receded, they refused to compensate those whose homes were destroyed.

administration. Hoover won the 1928 election and swiftly betrayed all of his promises to Moton and his black constituency. Outraged and vengeful, Moton pulled his support from the GOP and led an historic shift of the black vote from Abraham Lincoln's Republican Party to the Democrats of Franklin Delano Roosevelt, who handily won the 1932 election taking 472 electoral votes to Hoover's 59.

Back down South, the floodwaters came in and swept out a corrupt and viciously racist feudalistic system that was the last holdout to the liberal project of the shining city. Taking on the federal government that had reneged on its promise to rebuild the state, Huey Long rode a wave of populist idealism to become governor of Louisiana in 1928. Once in office, Long launched one of the most ambitious public works projects in U.S. history. He swore to take on big business and stamped a tax on Rockefeller's Standard Oil to pay for children's schoolbooks. When Rockefeller refused to pay, Long ordered the National Guard to seize Standard's oil fields in the Delta. In his grandstanding, fist-wagging style, Long chastised the rich, calling them parasites and used his unprecedented—some called it dictatorial—power over the state legislature to raise taxes on the state's highest income bracket.

But Louisiana was too small to contain Long's wild ambition. In 1930 he was elected to the Senate and two years later, vigorously backed FDR's run for the presidency. When Roosevelt rebuffed him, refusing to give him a federal post, Long turned against the president and his New Deal, advocating a rival "Share The Wealth" program that he claimed would do more to redistribute wealth to America's poor.* The first American politician to understand the power of radio, Long galvanized a national following that drew

* Huey Long was also a fan of the stat. He once claimed that in America, "Two percent of the people owned 60 percent of the wealth." During one radio broadcast he declared: "God called: 'Come to my feast.' But what had happened? Rockefeller, Morgan, and their crowd stepped up and took enough for 120,000,000 people and left only enough for 5,000,000 for all the other 125,000,000 to eat. And so many millions must go hungry."

7 million people into his "Share The Wealth" societies that were to be the support base for his presidential campaign in 1936. He would never get the chance to run. In September 1935, one month after announcing his candidacy, Long was shot in Louisiana by the son-in-law of a political rival. Theories spread through the poor communities that their champion had been assassinated by a conspiracy of interests that were threatened by his vast grassroots popular support. But Huey Long had made so many enemies in both the state and federal bureaucracies that no investigation was ever held. Roosevelt, who had privately called Long one of the "most dangerous men in America," won the election on his New Deal platform, ushering in the era of political idealism that would eventually close out in 1944 with the very speech that had once so inspired the ten-year-old Lewis Lapham.

Though none in the Washington establishment would admit it, Huey Long had tapped into the deep national hunger for liberal-minded reform. Like Hurricane Katrina, the flood of 1927 had exposed deep class and racial stratification in the American south. Long had built his entire political career on the foundation of public outrage that was the product of that tragedy. But in 2005, there was no political momentum to be derived from the disaster. America is gripped by the idea that it has solved its race and class issues. Even with the dazzling outlay of statistical data that had framed the summer media diet, there was still the sense that life would carry on and people would make the best of what they had. It has always been the way, until tragedy strikes and we are forced, even if for one moment, to see what our liberal project has become.

Katrina's aftermath showed Americans the social cost of a system based on rugged individualism and a laissez-faire approach to government. When the Louisiana politicians ordered the city to be evacuated, they had no understanding that thousands of poor

Louisianans had neither means of escaping nor any place else to go. Left to their own devices, the people simply held on to what little they had in the world. And then, when the federal government proved unable, or unwilling, to make their plight a major priority, the people of New Orleans fended for themselves. It was an ugly scene, but while some less socioeconomically sensitive commentators ridiculed the thousands of homeless victims for being too bullheaded to leave, and the rest just pointed out the obvious race/color parallels, very few in the American media asked the deeper questions about what Katrina would mean to the larger issue of American identity. David Brooks, "house-conservative" at the *New York Times*, came close: "The first rule of the social fabric—that in times of crisis you protect the vulnerable—was trampled. Leaving the poor in New Orleans was the moral equivalent of leaving the injured on the battlefield." [31] But it never occurred to him that the social fabric has been frayed to the point of disintegration by a social ethos of dog-eat-dog individualistic self-interest.

"So," I ask Lewis Lapham, "how do you look at what Katrina means and what it exemplifies about American society and where it's going. Does the fallout of that tell us anything?"

"It will tell us something," Lapham replies, "I think it will tell us where we place our hope of the future—do we place our hope of the future in the strength, intelligence and health of the American people or do we place our hope in the army and our technology and our bank accounts.

"It will be very interesting to see what gets built in New Orleans. They lost a lot of libraries. So do you put the money there... are we actually going to spend the money on strengthening the levees, trying to organize lower-class, middle-class housing, trying to get more public infrastructure: hospitals, schools, better salaries for teachers? Or do you put the money into a lot of flashy real estate, high-end condos, golf courses, Disneyland gambling casinos?"

He sounds almost hopeful. "People might say they want to strengthen the levees, improve the roads, improve the public transportation system, protect the water, or let the marshlands in the offshore islands grow back—and in return for that we're willing to accept not so many toys in the stores. And we'd like to arrange matters so we don't have the enormous disparities between rich and poor. We'll see that over the course of the next two or three years, we'll see where our priorities are."

If the initial stages of reconstruction were any indication, the government's priorities haven't changed.* Revisiting the blueprint that plagued the Iraqi reconstruction project with charges of cronyism and over-billing by contractors, the same small group of companies were given high dollar contracts in what were often "limited competition" bidding procedures. Instead of giving work to local companies that could have hired some of the region's unemployed workers, FEMA and the U.S. Army Corps of Engineers consistently brought in outsiders, and at considerably higher prices. A $40 million contract to provide mobile classrooms was given to Akima Site Operations, an Alaskan company, for $88,000/ unit when a local manufacturer, Adams Home Center, offered them at $58,000 a piece. But since it was a no-bid contract, Adams never got the chance to compete. Meanwhile, two companies who employ former FEMA head Joe Allbaugh as their Washington lobbyist were awarded plum jobs in the ravaged Gulf. Shaw Group Inc. took two $100 million orders related to water drainage and housing management while Halliburton's KBR division was given a $30 million contract to repair naval facilities hit by Katrina. Never

* As far as engineering a community-based rebuilding effort, UC Berkeley economist Steven Pitts observed it was only as victims that the people of New Orleans were able to participate in flood relief. "Dispersed residents got no help in returning to rebuild their homes and lives. When they tried to go back, they were treated as threats to law and order—impediments to potential gentrification." Quote from David Bacon, "Looking for Common Ground," *Colorlines*, Spring 2006.

far from the action, Bechtel was given $100 million to provide emergency housing for victims.[32]

Yet, even with the high level awards going to a small clique of insider firms, the few remaining unemployed residents of New Orleans could see some respite in the form of income in the rebuilding of the city. Those hopes were dashed quickly. On September 8, President Bush suspended application of the Davis-Bacon Act, a Depression-era law that enforces a minimum pay scale on government contractors. After a bipartisan revolt against the decision, the law was reinstated on November 8. But it was too late. The influx of migrant labor to cover bottom scale jobs placed the poor, jobless, mostly black Louisiana workers in direct competition with Latinos. Tempers flared at the city's first town hall meeting in November. "I'm working for $6 an hour!" yelled one African-American man at Mayor Ray Nagin. "They're bringing in Mexicans and expecting us to work for the same money. Is slavery over, or what?" With New Orleans's 500,000 residents scattered over 44 states, many of whom will probably never return, the very demographic complexion of New Orleans may be forever altered. "This," one Hispanic community representative told MSNBC, "is a future San Antonio, Texas."[33]

For anyone with a sense of history, the scenes that played out in the aftermath of Hurricane Katrina evoked painful and long-forgotten memories of a distant era. Government cronyism and indifference to the needs of the weak, corporate graft and monopoly, inescapable poverty, and the pitting of one minority against the other for the most basic of economic rewards; we could just as well be living in the era of Huey Long. Of course, the times are different and so the past is nothing more than a palimpsest, upon which we write our new stories. But the grooves of the old narrative are still intact and history repeats itself, in a fashion.

I ask Lewis Lapham if he believes the liberalism that FDR advocated at the end of his life, which were part of the political legacy that was borne from the 1927 flood, can ever return. Or, are we now in a more finite historical paradigm, where the competition for resources and wealth is so fierce, that American society can only support the leanest and most selfish of liberal philosophies?

"What happens when you do that," he replies, "if you follow the policy of enlightened selfishness to its logical end, what you end up with is a stupid and rancid oligarchy. And that in turn provokes either a revolution or a despotism. And then you start the circle back. The thing is, the United States has come to the end of the Enlightenment idea which has lasted roughly 200 years. And we don't have a new idea. We're groping around. Clearly the American political discourse is, to my mind, bankrupt."

Lapham stands at the bar and reaches for his jacket. Feeling, perhaps, that is too solemn a note to end with, he adds, "The world will come up with something. The question is, how much grief do we have to sustain before we begin to learn the lesson? I don't know the answer."

6

The Last Party

A false friend is more dangerous than an open enemy.
— Francis Bacon

THE LEOPARD

"I've made some important political discoveries," explains Prince
Salina to his troubled priest. "You know what is happening in our
country? Nothing. Simply an imperceptible replacement of one
class for another."

The seats are plush red velvet. Six rows of them, in the basement
of a modern Hollywood mansion, sequestered in the hills above
Los Angeles. A small group of us sit in rapt silence watching the
twelve foot hi-def screen as Burt Lancaster, speaking in perfectly
dubbed Italian, plays the titular role in Luchino Visconti's, *The
Leopard*. Set in the mid-nineteenth century, Visconti's classic film
tells the story of Lancaster's Prince Salina, facing the upheaval and
social revolution brought on by Giuseppe Garibaldi's conquest of
Sicily. Sitting in his ornate study, Salina deconstructs the political
situation. He is not troubled by the revolutionary Garibaldi, who
has landed with his red-shirted fighters to reclaim southern Italy
from the French Bourbon king Francis II. Even if noble families
like the Salinas are the king's beneficiaries in Italy, he assures the

nervous priest, there will be no true change in their standard of living.[1]

"The middle class doesn't want to destroy us," continues Salina, "it simply wants to take our place, and very gently, giving us a few thousand ducats in the process. Then everything can go on as it is. Understand Father? Ours is a country of arrangements."

Since its re-release in 2004—in the original Italian language version—Visconti's 180 minute film has been a favorite in the art house and film club circuit. It's the first time I have seen *The Leopard* and am struck by the timelessness and relevancy of its themes of class and political power. The audience is permitted to watch through Prince Salina's dispassionate eyes as the less refined capitalist class takes control of the country. In one local election, a wealthy businessman nominates himself mayor and rigs an election that delivers favorable results to the new order. Later, Salina sits atop a beautiful Sicilian panorama with an old friend, Ciccio, who is upset at the corruption and lack of respect for the nobles, who had been kind masters. But Salina calms him, explaining that the election was merely a ruse to "cure" the passions of the people who had become "overexcited by this Garibaldi's victories." He understands that the elite will always hold true power, as long as the masses are focused on the battles waged at the political level, where the results are superficial and without any true impact.

"Something had to change," Salina tells Ciccio, "for everything to stay as it was. The hour of revolution is past."[2]

After the screening, I stand on a patio that overlooks the shimmering constellation of lights that is Los Angeles. Watching the currents of energy sift through the city's electrical grid, I listen distractedly as my friend David discusses the film with a young broker named Jeremy. David sees the film as emblematic of all that is wrong with the two-party system in America. "It's a containment policy for the economic and social elites. Democrats and Republicans, the ones who have any real power in government, are representatives of the corporate sector. They just create the illusion of being antagonists so that people will think they are actually fighting over critical social issues."

It's an argument I have heard often. Obviously, so has Jeremy. He looks up at the sky and takes a deep breath, feigning incredulity. "That's just left-wing conspiracy theory. Did you even watch the debates during the last presidential election? Did you see the number of winning electoral votes? You think the public is that bitterly divided over non-issues?"

"They're divided over abortion and stem cell research, hot-button moral issues that have nothing to do with governing the country," David interjects.

"They're divided over Iraq. They're divided over tax breaks. Kerry's a bleeding heart socialist. Are you kidding? Michael Moore was behind him all the way. You're saying he was fooled too?"

David glances over at me for support. I shrug and look back at the city, preoccupied with thoughts of the interview I have scheduled with Gore Vidal the next day. No American thinker has given more energy to the idea of America as a nation in decline than Vidal, who was one of the first establishment writers to call it an empire, and then simultaneously declare its end. With a kind of ferocious honesty that established him as the nation's worthiest apostate, Vidal described the perversion of democracy that foists the lie of a competitive two-party system on its citizens to keep them dumb, blind and complicit. A few weeks ago, hearing that he has returned from Italy in order to sell his Los Angeles house, I made use of the private number given to me by a friend. After a few rings, a grave and delicate voice answered. I offered a brief introduction of the book and was gifted with an invitation for tea.

THE HAUNTING OF AMERICA

The roads that lead up into the Hollywood hills are steep and winding. Turning onto Outpost Drive, I imagine that it must have been beautiful once, this Hollywood Hills hideaway; but now it is pockmarked and crumbling. At one time or another, Outpost has been the address for a random assortment of celebrities like Billy Idol, Ben Affleck and Bob Barker, the imperishable host of *The Price is Right*. It has also been the American residence of Gore Vidal, who has now returned to sell the property. Lucky to catch him in between trips to his Italian estate, which he is also selling, and wary of his impatience with guests, I hurry to park the car.

I feel a tinge of gloom as I walk up to the door of Vidal's Spanish-style white stucco and red tile-roof house. Obscured by hanging foliage and tree branches, the house has a funereal quality. It is as if I am entering the lonely castle which now preserves one of the last remaining members of the true American nobility.

I knock on the thick wooden door. Nervous from expectation of the meeting, I don't feel impatient for the ten minutes that he keeps me waiting. But a sense of relief washes through me when, finally, Gore Vidal pokes his head out of a second story window. He doesn't say anything, which makes me feel like an intruder. I wonder if I should leave or, at least, ask him if this is still a good time. But, when he appears at the door a few minutes later, I do neither. Instead, I smile and thank him for seeing me.[3]

Once inside the house, I have to adjust my eyes to the darkness of the interior. But I can immediately make out the exquisite furniture, the giant mirrors, the paintings and sculptures, fine carpets, antique banister and pictures of people too famous to be asked about. It was in this house that Howard Austen, Vidal's lifelong partner, died just two years ago.

To say Vidal seems sad would be an understatement. Rather, he carries himself with the slow fatigue of melancholy. An agent of the old aristocratic class, he drapes himself in a long, cream colored manteau and guides me through the house toward the garden.

He points up at a very tall, pine tree that comes, he tells me, from the Canary Islands. "This crazy guy bought the house 80 years ago. He didn't think much of the fauna of Southern California, so he imported all kinds of exotic trees. Occasionally I get mad people with staring eyes who come here, just to look at the trees."

I ask him if he is working on anything. He sighs and admits that he is writing his second memoir (*Point to Point Navigation*). "Aside from the fact that I've lost all interest in myself, it should be riveting."

As one of America's most prolific authors, playwrights and essayists, Gore Vidal has never been afraid to infiltrate his literary works with themes that could excite and agitate the American mass consciousness. His third novel, *The City and The Pillar*, was published in 1948—when Vidal was just 23 years old—and became the first major literary work in U.S. history to feature a homosexual protagonist.[4] As Vidal would say, "No good deed goes unpunished," and the book received scathing reviews. The *New York Times* retaliated by refusing to cover his next five novels* in the paper.

Turning to Hollywood, Vidal began a long career as a screenwriter for film and television, the most famous of which are the Academy Award-winning *Ben-Hur* and the ultra-erotic Penthouse production of *Caligula*. In the late fifties, he began to assert himself as one of America's most important political and social commentators, writing a series of polemical essays for magazines, some of

---

* Despite these obstacles, Gore Vidal would go on to publish over a dozen best-selling novels including *Washington, D.C., 1876, Lincoln, Myra Breckinridge*, and *Creation*. The *Boston Globe*, among others, have celebrated Vidal as "our greatest living man of letters."

which were eventually published in the 1962 collection, *Rocking the Boat*. But it was not until Vidal unleashed his bestselling novel *Myra Breckinridge*—featuring a transsexual man-hating heroine—that he reclaimed his status as the country's most controversial author.[5]

Naturally, Vidal became a target for conservatives and, ever quick with a witty retort, was a favorite on nightly talk show where he became the Left's unofficial standard-bearer. Perhaps his most infamous moment came during the last days of the riotous 1968 Democratic National Convention, when ABC went live with Vidal squaring off against right-wing icon William F. Buckley. Earlier that day, Chicago police had rushed a group of protestors, one of whom had defiantly raised the Vietcong flag. Vidal had taken the side of the protesters, citing their constitutional right to assembly. Buckley argued for the police. With tempers flaring, ABC's Howard Smith asked, "Mr. Vidal, was it not a provocative act to try to raise the Vietcong flag in the park... Would that not invite... raising a Nazi flag in World War II would have had similar consequences."

Vidal responded: "You must realize what some of the political issues are here. There are many people in the United States who happen to believe the United States's policy is wrong in Vietnam and the Vietcong are correct in wanting to organize their country in their own way politically. This happens to be pretty much the opinion in Western Europe and in other parts of the world. If it's a novelty in Chicago that is too bad, but I assume that the point of American democracy is that you can express any point of view you want."

Frustrated, Buckley interrupted him, only to be dismissed by Vidal with a flick of his hand. "Shut up a minute."

"No I won't," Buckley continued indignantly, "Some people *were* pro-Nazi and the answer is they were well treated by people who ostracized them. And I'm for ostracizing people who egg on other people to shoot American marines and American soldiers. I know you don't care—"

Speaking over him, Vidal countered, "As far as I'm concerned, the only sort of proto- or crypto-Nazi I can think of is yourself. Failing that, I'll only say that we can't have—"

Smith, the moderator, was able to interject briefly, asking the two men to resist "name-calling," before Buckley struck back.

"Now listen, you queer, stop calling me a crypto-Nazi or I'll sock you in the goddamn face and you'll stay plastered," he sneered viciously.

"Gentlemen..." Smith pleaded.

"Let's go," smirked Vidal.

Clearly angered, Buckley stuttered incomprehensibly, mangling the title of Vidal's *Myra Breckinridge*, and then blurted: "Let him go back to his pornography and stop making any allusions to Nazis to someone who served in the infantry in the last war."

But it was Vidal who got the last word, correcting Buckley: "You were not in the infantry as a matter of fact, now you're distorting your own military record."[6]

While Vidal spent most of his political life associated with the Democratic Party—even running unsuccessfully for Congress in 1960 and, again, in 1982—in later years he grew more cynical about the two-party system and the rise of America's "national security state." These convictions were most powerfully articulated in his 1989 collection, *The Decline and Fall of the American Empire*, which portrayed America as a debtor nation now controlled by its war-mongering private sector and manipulated by a complicit corporate media.[7]

Over the years, his apostasy has moved toward a marginalizing advocacy of conspiratorial theses. In 1998, he began corresponding with Oklahoma City bomber Timothy McVeigh. Vidal became his friend and quasi-apologist, condemning the act of violence but sympathizing with the revolt against the trampling of American civil liberties. Two months after McVeigh died from lethal injection in June 2001, Vidal told an audience at the Edinburgh book festival that the one-time Special Forces aspirant had not in fact carried out the bombing but, after realizing he had been set up as the patsy, decided to play the hero to avenge the government's attack on the Branch Davidian camp at Waco, Texas. Vidal also claimed the FBI had infiltrated the right-wing militia group behind the bombing, but then allowed the plan to go forward in order to bolster the case for anti-terrorist legislation—the Anti-Terrorism and Effective Death Penalty Act, a prequel to the USA Patriot Act—that Bill Clinton was reluctant to sign.[8]

"Within a week of the bombing," Vidal informed his listeners, "Clinton signed it for 'the protection of the state and of persons', using the exact language that Adolf Hitler used after the Reichstag fire of 1933."[9]

After 9/11, Vidal took another leap away from the firm soil of conventional wisdom, publishing two collections of essays; the titles are sufficiently descriptive of the thematic content: *Perpetual War for Perpetual Peace: How We Got To Be So Hated* and *Dreaming War: Blood for Oil and the Cheney-Bush Junta*. In the former, Vidal compares Osama bin Laden to Timothy McVeigh and endeavors to describe "the various provocations on our side that drove them to such terrible acts." In the latter, he takes on the events of September 11, detailing the failures of intelligence, military and political leadership, ultimately raising the possibility that the administration allowed the attacks to occur.[10]

In this final incarnation, Gore Vidal can hardly provide an objective evaluation of the shining city on the hill. But his perception is invaluable because his life represents a singular journey from the womb of the American political and economic establishment to the cold frontier of anti-establishmentarian radicalism. Unlike many of those outsiders who are the most vehement critics of the American imperium, Gore Vidal is one of its children. American history, he reminds me, is in his blood.

"The Gores go back to the beginning of the republic. They were burnt down when the Yankees came through. My great-grandfather was wounded at Shiloh* and taken captive. We were not slave owners and we were pro-Union, but we were from Mississippi, and you fought with your family and friends, even if you didn't like the war. And out of that came this great political vitality, with which my great-grandfather and my grandfather, and some other members of the Gore family, started the People's Party."

The Populist, or People's, Party, was an agrarian-based third party movement formed in 1892 as a reaction to the Eastern business elites, whom they believed had caused a collapse in the price of crops. Distrustful of the big city Democrats and Republicans, Populists appealed to the farmers of the West and South as well as the disenfranchised industrial workers of the East. Their platform championed income tax reform, abolition of national banks, an increase in the money supply, pensions and an eight hour working day. But in 1896, the Democratic presidential candidate William Jennings Bryan made an alliance with the Populists, creating in the Democratic Party what Vidal calls, "the first left-wing party we ever had."

Gesturing at the cloudless sky, he continues, "It was a real labor

---

* One of the bloodiest battles of the U.S. Civil War, the battle of Shiloh (in southwestern Tennessee) was fought over two days, ultimately killing 3,400 and wounding 16,000. Union Commander Ulysses S. Grant was among the injured, but his side eventually prevailed, driving the Confederate army back into Mississippi on April 7, 1862. Of the battle, Grant later wrote that the field was so covered with dead bodies, it would have been impossible to walk through it without stepping on them. Ironically, Shiloh is a Hebrew name for "Place of Peace."

party. It represented working people, rural farmers from the south; it was racist, naturally, as everything was at the time. But on social issues other than race, it was something new under the sun."

Into this political legacy Gore Vidal was born. Growing up in Washington, DC under the roof of his maternal grandfather, the blind Democratic Senator Thomas P. Gore, the young Vidal was quickly indoctrinated.

"I wanted to be a politician, and was brought up to be one. My grandfather was blind so by seven or eight I was reading to him, and I would lead him onto the floor of the Senate, and I would sit beside him listening to the Senate debates. I was marinated in the politics of the republic and the Senate was the great engine room of power. So I had a crash course in government, firsthand."

It was in this environment that Vidal formed his views on political power. The notion of a two-party system that provides democratic society with a balance between 'conservative' and 'liberal' political values, he argues, is "simplistic." I wonder if that isn't the jaded view of an insider, one who was too entrenched in the political culture of Washington to appreciate the mechanics of the local and state party system, where the basic issues of American life were fought. A far as Vidal is concerned, politics on every level are about one thing: power. All other pretensions are merely symbolic and ideological, to maintain the illusions held by the citizenry.

"You're not going to find me believing any of this stuff that is taught in junior high school. I know it's not true, I know how they operate, and I remember every time I heard hot-eyed people arguing politics—'I'm a conservative, I'm a liberal'—well yes, specifically, we're all one thing or the other on a given issue. But the idea that there is a party line to follow, an overarching ideology..."

Vidal lets his words hang for a moment and then shrugs with mock resignation, "Senators didn't think in such terms. There is absolutely no connection between the real political world and the theoretical one which you learn about in books or in schools, and which is by and large propaganda of one kind or another. When you see real power at work, real power is maneuvering, trading. So it's a bazaar, a marketplace. There are good guys and bad guys."

Taking a sip of Diet Coke, he sits back in his chair and utters one of his favorite and most quoted analogies.

"The two-party system was never anything, just two political factions fighting over jobs, money, influence and power. We have only one political party, the Party of Property, which has two right wings: Republican and Democrat, and that's it. There are no great differences."

I ask if there was ever an "ah-ha" moment when he concluded definitively that politicians were merely collaborators in sustaining the illusion of partisanship, actors who played up the battles from their respective sides of the aisle.

"I knew that from the beginning. My grandfather, after all, was a leading Democrat. He had a lot of seniority. And he got along with everybody. I can't think of anyone that I can recall in the Senate that would have been his enemy, or that he would have been dumb enough to think was his enemy, or act as if he was his enemy. You don't do that. In those days, there were 96 senators, 48 states. He knew them all, got along with them. They all got along with each other. There would be great rows, territorial wars, but the power—who's going to be the head of Ways and Means—that's the real fight, that's where the money goes." *

I play devil's advocate, citing the hotly contested and widely

---

* Writing in *Decline and Fall*, Vidal lamented: "Every four years the naïve half who vote are encouraged to believe that if we can elect a really nice man or woman president everything will be all right. But it won't be. Any individual who is able to raise $25 million to be considered presidential is not going to be much use to the people at large. He will represent oil, or aerospace, or banking, or whatever moneyed entities are paying for him. Certainly he will never represent the people of the country..." Quote from Gore Vidal, *The Decline and Fall of the American Empire* (Berkeley: Odonian Press, 1992).

disputed 2000 election. If nothing else, that proves that there is a bona fide ideological split between the two parties. Not so, claims Vidal.

To prove his convictions about the burlesque fakery of the two-party system, Vidal doesn't need to look any farther than his own namesake—2000 Democratic presidential candidate Al Gore. For much of the population, both on the left and right, Gore epitomizes the kind of liberal politics that are the ideological cornerstone of the Democratic Party. But to hear Vidal tell it, Gore's liberalism is merely a prop developed to bring him to the head of the Democratic Party.

"Well, although I was a friend of his father's, I've always thought he was absolutely pointless as a politician. He's just another conservative southerner."

In fact, Al Gore's voting record as a senator was overwhelmingly conservative until he rolled his eye toward the White House. Throughout most of his career, he was pro-life and had an 84 percent anti-abortion rating from the National Right to Life Committee. From 1979–81, he voted five times on the side of a Republican sponsored rider that granted a tax exemption for schools like Bob Jones University that discriminate on the basis of race. He was openly anti-gay, calling homosexuality "abnormal" and "wrong," and telling the *Tennessean* in 1984 that he did "not believe it is simply an acceptable alternative that society should affirm." Gore was such a strong supporter of the gun lobby—ultimately voting against the critical 1985 legislation for a mandatory fourteen day waiting period for handgun purchases—that National Rifle Association leader Wayne LaPierre once said, "We could have made Al Gore NRA Man of the Year—every single vote." Finally, when it came time to vote on conservative Supreme Court nominees, Gore publicly praised but voted against the scandal-ridden Clarence Thomas. He voted in Antonin Scalia. If the wider public had been more aware of his legacy, few would have recognized the Al Gore of 1988 who ran for the Democratic presidential nomination.[11]

Pulling his hat down so that his eyes are shadowed from the sun, Vidal continues his effortless assault on Al Gore: "Another border state, southern lover of the Pentagon… there was never anything the Pentagon asked for that Cousin Albert wasn't down there giving it to them; he voted for the first war in the Gulf."

Indeed, Al Gore was one of only ten Democrats to break with the party and vote for President Bush Sr.'s Gulf War in 1991. But while Vidal sees this as a facet of Gore's eager-to-please statism, others have attributed his dissenting vote to self-interest. Former Republican Senator Alan Simpson accused Gore of peddling his vote on the Iraq War in exchange for high-visibility, headline-grabbing speech time on the floor. According to Simpson, the night before the vote Gore stopped by the GOP cloakroom and asked, "How much time will you give me if I support the president?" Taking him at his word, Simpson and Senator Bob Dole offered Gore twenty minutes, thirteen more than his own party would grant. In Simpson's account, over the course of the night Gore jockeyed to have the floor during prime time to ensure that he would get coverage in the next day's news cycle. The negotiations went right up to the last minute, leaving Simpson to conclude that Gore "arrived on the Senate floor with… two speeches in hand. [He] was still waiting to see which side—Republicans or Democrats—would offer him the most and the best speaking time."[12]

For Vidal, stories like this just prove the moral bankruptcy of American politicians who serve no master other than their own ambition and their corporate backers. In Gore's case, this meant Russian-born oil tycoon Armand Hammer, owner of Occidental Petroleum. Though it was Gore's father, Senator Al Gore Sr. who was the primary beneficiary of Hammer's support—in exchange for political and diplomatic favors to further his international business interests—Gore Jr. slipped quietly into his father's shoes.

Occidental is one of the worst corporate polluters in the world. In its most scandalous case, an Occidental subsidiary dumped thousands of tons of toxic chemical waste near the residential area of Love Canal, New York, causing birth defects, miscarriages, and incidents of cancer in the nearby community. But Gore remained a friend of the company. And the company, a good friend to Al Gore.

Despite being a predominantly Republican supporter, Occidental funneled hundreds of thousands of dollars in campaign contributions to the Clinton/Gore Democrats over the course of their two term administration.* In return, Gore maneuvered to facilitate Occidental's acquisition of oil drilling rights in the Elk Hills National Petroleum Reserve outside Bakersfield, California. Long held as a federal oil resource, Elk Hills represented the largest turnover of public lands to a private corporation in American history. It tripled Occidental's U.S. petroleum reserves, increasing the company's stock value by ten percent. Gore later admitted to controlling between $250,000—$500,000 worth of shares through a family held trust.[13]

Gore's vaunted record as an environmental populist clashed harshly with the 1996 Elk Hills-Occidental deal. Democratic fundraiser (and former Gore campaign manager) Tony Coelho sat on the board of the private company hired to provide an environmental impact report for the Energy Department. After the deal was approved, Peter Eisner of the DC-based Center for Public Integrity remarked, "I can't say that I've ever seen an environmental assessment prepared so quickly." Perhaps even more

---

* While Gore's beautifully produced film *An Inconvenient Truth*, heroically raised the profile of global warming, the fact that he made no passing references, nor remorseful confessions about his own past dealings with the oil industry was disheartening. Perhaps he has had a change of heart on the issue. But it also smacks of the opportunism that can return faded political actors to center stage. And in that case, can we truly depend on Gore to take on the oil lobby?

damning, Elk Hills is part of the Kitanemuk people's traditional lands. Despite protests from the tribe, it took less than five years for Occidental's massive operations to wipe out any trace of the 100 native archaeological sites, including ancient burial grounds, that were left in Elk Hills.[14]

Throughout Al Gore's campaign for the 2000 Democratic presidential candidacy, environmentalists protested his relationship to Occidental. This time the issue was Gore's defense of the company's plan to drill near the sacred grounds of the Colombian U'wa tribespeople. During Clinton's second term, Occidental spent millions lobbying for American military aide to Colombia in order to bolster the country's ability to defend its pipelines from rebel armies. The close links between the company and national security forces surfaced when U'wa leaders sued Occidental, claiming the Colombian army used the company's planes in an operation that ultimately resulted in the murder of eighteen innocent peasants. As a measure of last resort, the 5,000 remaining U'wa threatened collective suicide if Occidental refused to alter their drilling plans. But, in February 2000, when U'wa representative Robert Perez traveled to Washington in order to make his people's case against the company, Gore refused to meet him.* In 2002, after a protracted public battle over the U'wa drill site, Occidental pulled out, saying that U'wa protests had "no effect at all" on Occidental's withdrawal decision. Apparently, neither did Al Gore.[15]

But, for Vidal, the act that most proves Gore's contempt for

---

* In a letter to Gore dated February 22, 2000, Democratic Representative Cynthia McKinney pleaded with the vice president to meet Perez and put his support behind the suspension of the drilling project in northeastern Colombia. "I am concerned that the operations of oil companies, and in particular Occidental Petroleum, are exacerbating an already explosive situation, with disastrous consequences for the local indigenous people," she wrote. "I am contacting you because you have remained silent on this issue despite your strong financial interests and family ties with Occidental." In a brief note, Gore explained that he was too busy to meet Perez. See Ken Silverstein, "Gore's Oil Money," *The Nation*, May 3, 2000.

representative politics was his total acquiescence in the face of the contested 2000 presidential election result in Florida. The image of Gore presiding over the certification of Bush's victory was a moving, if tragic, scene in Michael Moore's *Fahrenheit 9/11*. There he stood, banging his gavel as each successive member of the Congressional Black Caucus rose to challenge the assignment of Florida's 25 electoral votes to Bush.[16] "There was a hell of a lot of people ready to march," Vidal says defiantly. But Al Gore wasn't one of them.

"He is of above average intelligence on issues that people didn't really care about, like the environment. But if there's a hot issue, he runs the mile," Vidal concludes firmly and then, looking up at the clouds that have moved over the sun, rises. I follow him back into the house, watching as he carefully lowers himself down into a soft armchair in his living room. On the table are a few books. One catches my eye; on its cover a thick, black circle is drawn on pristine white background. It is an Italian translation of Vidal's bestselling historical novel, *Creation*. Next to it is John Dean's political exposé of the Bush administration, *Worse than Watergate*. In the book, Dean, who was Nixon's White House counsel, charges that Bush has committed impeachable offenses.[17] I linger over it for a moment, looking at the blurry image of a tightlipped Cheney standing behind Bush. Vidal waves me onto the seat next to his.

I want to return Vidal to his charge that the two-party system is a dictatorship in disguise; an "oligarchy" of the propertied elite. Implicit in this is a hefty degree of contempt for the electorate, who have bought into, and helped perpetuate, the illusion. Of these doltish masses, Vidal once quipped: "fifty percent of people won't vote, and fifty percent don't read newspapers. I hope it's the same fifty percent."

But all hope is not lost. There is always the chance that an authentic populist leader will break through the spectacle of political mud wrestling and excite the passions of the people. In Gore Vidal's estimation, this phenomena was last seen with "the unexpected arrival of Howard Dean."

In Dean, Vidal sees a politician who was not afraid to challenge the national security state by reaching deep into the American mass consciousness.

"He tapped into the strongest political tide in American history," declares Vidal, "which is isolationism. The word has been so demonized, we now think of an isolationist as a racist who believes in flying saucers and so forth. Dean has the confidence of the aristocrat, but also at the same time a rather thick skin, an inability to see the effect his words are having on people. But in the search for money—knowing the internet was a place that no one had figured out how to tap—Dean finds that people don't want the war. He says 'I don't want the war either.' People say, 'Good, I'm giving you ten dollars.' And suddenly there's a whole movement propelling him for the nomination."

Vidal raises his chin. "Well, suddenly, he was talking to the interests of the average American; the average Americans that started to blog. And suddenly he had a following and then of course they were smart enough to start registering them, wherever they could be. And suddenly, he is a leader of an anti-war movement. This terrified everybody,* and this is where you see that there is only one political party, the party of Property. The rulers of the Democratic Party have the same set of lobbyists that are running the Republican Party. They live in the same town, they have offices

---

* Ironically, it was Al Gore who jumpstarted the Dean campaign when he endorsed the Vermont governor in early December, 2003. But even that was met with a skepticism by insiders who saw it as yet another act of political opportunism. As political commentator Adam Nagourney explained on PBS's *Newshour*: "One [theory] is that what is going on here is a proxy war between the Clintons and the Gores over the future of the Democratic Party. I think there is an element of truth to that."

on K Street."

But it was not just the Democratic lobbyists who were concerned about Dean's energizing brand of town hall politics. When he stood up and announced, "I'm Howard Dean, and I represent the Democratic wing of the Democratic Party!" Dean pulled in an entire generation of would-be political operatives who had been waiting for something they could believe in. They were "Generation Dean" or "Dean 2.0" and granted the "Dean Machine" a youthful, idealistic aura that no other Democratic candidate could muster. He was waging war on the Democratic Old Guard.

Going on the offensive, Dean attacked John Kerry as a DC insider, charging that he "had accepted more special interest and lobbyist money than any other senator in the last 15 years."[18] The Vermont governor could truthfully contrast that legacy to his campaign, which was primarily financed through small personal donations. "If you make me president," Dean stumped, "I'll go to Washington, and I won't owe anybody anything, except for you."[19]

It was statements like this that sent a collective shiver down the spine of the party establishment. And the establishment struck back. Leading the charge was the Democratic Leadership Council (DLC), the centrist organization devoted to keeping left-of-center, anti-corporate liberalism out of the Democratic Party. Reacting to Howard Dean's unexpected dominance of the early primary race, DLC leaders Al From and Bruce Reed moved to pull mainstream support out of the governor's grassroots campaign. In a memo titled *The Real Soul of the Democratic Party*, From and Reed declared "the great myth of the current [Howard Dean] cycle is the misguided notion that the hopes and dreams of activists represent the heart and soul of the Democratic Party." The report continued, "What activists like Dean call the Democratic wing of the Democratic Party is an aberration..."[20]

As far as Vidal is concerned, this was business as usual. "He frightened the regular Democrats." With Dean on the ropes after losing key primaries in Iowa, New Hampshire and South Carolina, Rep. Ron Obey (D-Wis.) articulated the establishment view when he praised Dean for energizing the party but put his full support behind the torpid candidacy of John Kerry. "We need to close ranks, and get about the task of putting into the White House a president with a sense of history, and a sense of justice," said Obey.[21]

"Dean didn't have any counter to that because he was too busy screaming," Vidal explains. "There were a lot of ways he could have gotten out of it, but he didn't find one of them. So that was the end of him."

Vidal looks down at the geometric pattern on his carpet. I wonder if he is spent.

"But Dean could be interesting," Vidal says quietly, looking up at me without raising his head, "because he has grasped the fact that this is an isolationist country that doesn't want to go abroad..." Vidal pauses and now, in the voice of a nineteenth century Federalist, hisses, "to *slay dragons*. Nor does she enlist banners other than her own, no matter how noble their sentiment, because if she did she could become mistress dictatress of the world, and she would lose her soul." *

Pronouncing the last three words with a slow staggered inten-

---

* At 80, Vidal's memory is still better than most college students. His recital of John Quincy Adams's legendary warning (1821) came close to the original: "[America] goes not abroad, in search of monsters to destroy... She well knows that by once enlisting under other banners than her own, were they even the banners of foreign independence, she would involve herself beyond the power of extrication, in all the wars of interest and intrigue, of individual avarice, envy, and ambition, which assume the colors and usurp the standard of freedom. The fundamental maxims of her policy would insensibly change from liberty to force... She might become the dictatress of the world. She would be no longer the ruler of her own spirit..."

sity, he then leans back into his chair and looks off into the void. "And that is the greatest advice given us by any president since Washington."

I want to ask him to what advice from Washington he is referring but before I can speak, Vidal mounts another diatribe. "Now we're in every war that we can get our hands on. Plans are afoot to go into Iran, probably a sideswipe at Syria. In the long run we'll be headed to North Korea. In between, China will give us some problems, and we're apt to be destroyed, I mean totally destroyed totally by a country like China, which has more people, they're just as clever at atomic weapons as we are, they can blow up the reservoirs and so forth.

"It's the sissies that want the wars. It's the weak little boys, like George W. Bush, or the really disturbed and twisted boys like Cheney, who like wars, and see to it that they themselves are never at risk. You don't know the contempt my generation had for people like that," Vidal shakes his head, "and now everyone agrees that Vietnam was a mistake, so they were smart, that they stayed out. They twisted it all around... they were totally in favor of Vietnam, for other people to fight.

"So, we're heading towards the last roundup, with a gang of thugs the likes of which we've never seen in American politics. I've observed American politics for practically all of the twentieth century and this much of the twenty-first. There's never been anything as viciously low and as dangerous. Everything is confrontational; it's in your face. 'Don't like the French? Fuck the French.' 'Don't like this? Tell them to go fuck themselves.' We're snarling orders at everybody, and everybody hates us. And then we wonder why, because," Vidal raises his voice an octave, mocking, " 'we're so nice and fat and pink. They should love us.' But they don't. Because we are repellent, we are a repellent people to the rest of the world. But we'll never find that; we live in a bubble. It's like living in Samoa without a radio."

And here it was; the root of Gore Vidal's anger and disappointment with America. The country had been stained and blistered and corrupted by the very arrogance and exceptionalism that was the antithesis of the blind senator's populist message. It had meddled too much in the affairs and fortunes of others. And now it was hated.

Hoping to raise him out of his mood, I ask what Washington's advice was. He nods at me appreciatively—"you're listening"—and replies:

"George Washington said nations do not have friends and enemies and passions. Nations have interests and nothing but interests. And, he said, to demonize another country, or to worship another country, is to enslave yourself to the idea, negatively or affirmatively, of that other country. That was very wise advice he was giving at the end."

In Vidal's citation lay a powerful admission. For all his precision bombing of the injustices and hypocrisies of the American Republic, he was still powerless over it. In demonizing it, he has become enslaved by the idea of it. I can only imagine that he loathes a part of himself for that ironic misfortune.

Sitting on the plane on my way back to New York, I type the transcript of our conversation. Meditating on his assertion that America's two parties are merely a containment strategy to protect the elite from any true populist upsurge, I realize that he hasn't provided any further insight than the blanket allusions to aristocratic power channeled through Visconti's portrayal of the nineteenth century Salina family. Vidal's exposure to the Senate is almost as ancient. If the two-party system has truly crumbled into a well-played spectacle for the masses, then I would need to find an insider who could make me believe.

A POLITICAL TOURIST

Gore Vidal's indictment of the American political system does not exist in a vacuum of conspiratorial anti-establishmentarianism. In fact, it is exactly because of the way that Democrats and Republicans have ganged up on third party candidates that "bipartidism," the academic term used to describe a two-party system, has evolved into a pejorative.

The bipartidism critique focuses on the control of the two-party system by a myth in which Democrats are supposedly the party of the people, while Republicans are the agents of establishment power. The parties, critics assert, use hot button or wedge issues like abortion or health care reform to compartmentalize the political discourse, while ultimately supporting economic policies that favor their true constituents, the wealthy and corporate elites in the country. Writing in his book *Contours of Descent*, economist Robert Pollin noted dryly, "the general requirement of product differentiation in an electoral market entails that, at the margin, any Democratic president will offer more social concessions than a Republican of the same cohort. But we should be careful not to make too much of such differences in the public stance of these two figures, as against the outcomes that prevail during their terms of office." Pollin's book targets the supposed '90s "boom" under Bill Clinton, explaining that, even while Clinton was seen as a friend of the poor, his policies actually did more to harm average workers whose wages stagnated as they faced more job insecurity than under his Republican predecessor, Bush Sr.[22] So, the theory goes, while modern day political leaders trade off their party's conservative or liberal legacy to keep voters entranced, in reality, as country music legend Waylon Jennings once said, "There ain't a dime's worth of difference between them."

That wouldn't have surprised American historian and political economist Walter Karp, who analyzed a century of collusive political scheming in his hard-to-find volume *Indispensable Enemies*. Karp's book exposes a political system run at both state and federal levels by "party bosses" whose sole mission is to maintain control of their party organization. With their power and wealth dependent on the measure of influence these bosses exert on their parties, Karp explains "every elected official is a potential menace." Thus, American political history can be viewed through a radically different lens, especially in those instances when, as Karp alleges, bosses have purposely lost elections in order to protect themselves from internal threats in the form of "insurgent" candidates. Citing examples that span from the late 1800s right through to the early 1970s, Karp argues that once reformist candidates win office, they often turn their attention to the corrupt party machine itself.[*] With the support of the electorate, there is nothing to stop them from "attempting to oust local party leaders, from bringing new men into the party ranks, from passing reforms that weaken the party organization, from winning public support so strong that the organization cannot deny him renomination... There are times, therefore, when losing an election becomes an absolute necessity."[23]

Extrapolating these Machiavellian tactics to the broader state and national political scenes, where Republicans and Democrats portray themselves as ideological enemies, Karp is no less thorough in his deconstruction. Looking back over seventy years of political action, he points to the fact that in most states the relative power— ie. minority or majority status—of each party had remained virtually unchanged. How can this be, he asks, if the sole purpose of each party organization is presumably to do all they can to win elections? Can the party organizations in their respective districts

---

[*] Karp begins by citing the cases of a dozen Republican governors (including Robert La Follette of Wisconsin and Hiram Johnson of California) who "overthrew Republican organizations in the Western states in the years before the First World War."

simply fail that consistently to field winning candidates without a major overhaul? According to Karp, it's common sense. For party bosses whose real concern is not winning, but maintaining power, it is far more important to strike alliances with their supposed opposition so that they can collaborate in maintaining and protecting each other's base of power.[24]

Karp uses the failed insurgency of Democratic Senator Eugene McCarthy to illustrate this dynamic. After the assassination of Robert Kennedy, the Democratic Party bosses had a problem. McCarthy stepped into the campaign and channeled the energy of the Kennedy delegates into his own reformist campaign. Young students and hippies traveled across the country, cutting their hair and going door-to-door for their candidate under the slogan "Get clean for Gene." Worried about the destabilizing influx of new party activists, Karp contends, the bosses decided to push "party hack" Senator George McGovern, who would put forward his own reformist agenda to splinter McCarthy's rank and file. Then, using their power at the party convention to engineer the Democratic presidential nomination for Hubert Humphrey, despite the fact he had not won a single primary, the bosses threw the election to stem the tide of reformist idealism that was sweeping through the party. As Karp explains, a victory "could only make genuine insurgency more promising to many and encourage yet more newcomers to enter active politics. On the other hand, a defeat… would strengthen the party oligarchy considerably. Newcomers to active politics would be crushed with disappointment, branded as losers and quickly returned to private life."[25]

Beyond their mutual need to protect each other's control of the party organization, the party bosses must ensure that the economic support base—namely, their wealthy and corporate donors, many of whom spread their charity to both parties—is not harmed by a reformist candidate. Karp even goes as far as saying that since the authority for policing elections and operating election machinery is left to the state parties—who are assumed to be rivals—the opportunity for colluding in vote fraud, in the case of an upstart victory, is very real.*[26]

While much of Karp's analysis involves specific examples of skullduggery and planned outcomes of various state and federal campaigns, he also posits a larger, more far-reaching assertion about the intent of these collusive political tactics. Karp was an anthropologist and, in applying a macro lens to the phenomenon he was exposing, discovered that, in order to protect its power, the fundamental mission of the party machine was "to eliminate the political condition that breeds independent ambition." In other words, to engineer in the electorate a sense of apathy or, as he puts it, a "gratitude for small favors and a deep general sense of the futility of politics."[27] While this claim is the most difficult to prove, it is interesting to note that around the same time that Karp was writing *Indispensable Enemies*, Harvard intellectual and foreign policy analyst Samuel Huntington generated a report for the Trilateral Commission which warned that the rise in radical consciousness and civil unrest during the 1960s would have long-term effects on the governability of American society. More, he warned, it had endangered the establishment authority, which was "based on hierarchy, expertise and wealth." Aptly titled *The Crisis of Democracy*, Huntington's report reminded its readers that "the effective operation of a democratic political system usually requires some measure of apathy and noninvolvement on the part of some individuals and groups."[28]

---

* Of course, many of America's best-loved presidents have campaigned and won on a tide of populist hope. But Karp spills a good flow of ink to show how programs like FDR's New Deal and LBJ's Great Society were powerful rhetorical vehicles that, upon reaching Congress, were subjected to a scheme of self-sabotage in which one wing of the victorious party—the obstructionists—would play the role of bad cop to the reformist wing's good cop, thus shutting down much of the original value of the platform.

We don't need to look much farther than the statistics on American voter turnout to see that, whether inculcated by elites or from a widespread sense of boredom, political apathy has always been a fact of nature in U.S. politics. Addressing the media one week before the 2004 presidential election, Curtis Gans, the director of the Committee for the Study of the American Electorate, told reporters that Americans are "now 139th out of 172 democracies in the world in our level of voter turnout..." In fact, the highly contentious 2000 election inspired a turnout of approximately 106 million people, representing 54 percent of the eligible voters. Comparing the turnout of voters to that of the sixties era, he cited a long list of factors including "a lower level of trust in our leadership than perhaps at any time" in American history. Yet, while professing a general sense of pessimism about the future of voting patterns, he did predict that the 2004 election would yield a marked surge in people 30 and under.[29] As it turned out, he was right.*

Few media campaigns have been as successful at bridging the gap between a candidate and the young electorate than Alexandra Pelosi's 2001 film, *Journeys with George.* Shot on the press junket following George W. Bush's 2000 campaign for the presidency, Pelosi's startlingly informal "home video" achieved for its subject what Karl Rove's wily media strategy could not: it humanized him.[30]

Considering that Pelosi is the daughter of Congresswoman Nancy Pelosi, Republican archenemy (and now the Speaker of the House of Representatives), Bush is incredibly candid with her,

---

* According to the Census Bureau, nearly half of all eligible voters 18–24 came out in 2004; up from 36 percent in 2000. With an increase of over five percentage points, the youth were the biggest gainers of all age groups. It's no surprise, considering the heavy pressure on the rap fans to "Vote or Die," as a high profile national billboard campaign featuring Hip Hop gangsters and divas warned. At election time, it was the Democrats who ruled Generation Y with Kerry taking 56 percent of votes cast by people aged 18–24, while Bush earned 43 percent.

at one point even mocking his own dyslexia and simultaneously giving the film its title.

"Now is this movie going to be called, George and Alexandra?" Bush asks, standing on the campaign bus.

"I don't know," Pelosi responds from behind her Handicam, "What do you think it should be called?"

"How about Journeys With George?" Bush suggests. "Pretty good one, huh?" then adding, "Do you think you could spell it with a G?"

Despite her political lineage, Pelosi established a rare level of intimacy with the candidate. In one scene, Bush calls her "baby" and gives her advice on a burgeoning romance between she and another reporter. In another, shot on the campaign plane, Bush comes back to mediate between a drunken, rowdy group of reporters and those who are trying to sleep. Clasping a nonalcoholic beer, Bush puts his lot in with the partiers whom, he sympathizes, "only wanted to have a good solid margarita and get hopping at 45,000 over Nebraska… These are my people. It takes an animal to know an animal." But Bush also proves to be as slippery as he is jovial. When Pelosi pushes him on his welfare agenda, asking, "Are you going to look out for the little guy?" Bush easily slides out from the trap, "I'm a little guy," he says. "Have you noticed? I'm about five eleven. My brother is six foot three."[31]

It is these jocular, uncontrived moments that made *Journeys* a must-see film and guaranteed Pelosi more than her fifteen minutes of prime time real estate. Calling it "fascinating," "casually astonishing" and "entertaining as hell," reviewers gave an enthusiastic thumbs-up for its November 2002 HBO premiere. And while some White House staffers feigned indignation at its crossed boundaries, the timing could not have been better for Bush who, though still basking in the heat of post-9/11 patriotic fever, was starting to beat the war drums and benefited from the disarming, collegial vibe the film presented. Yet, perhaps the most profound impact of the film's success was on Alexandra Pelosi herself. The child of a hardcore Democratic politician who had been raised to believe that George Bush was sub-human, suddenly found herself in the strange position of defending the president, in one instance telling a group of Oxford University students, "He's a lot smarter than people give him credit for... The people around him, the Ashcrofts and the Cheneys and the real evil Republicans of the world. They scare me. But Bush I think he's just this nice guy who believes his own compassionate conservatism. I didn't think of him as that evil guy... I think of him as a person." [32]

But it was not until 2004 when Pelosi finished shooting her less acclaimed follow up, *Diary of a Political Tourist*—following Democratic hopefuls Dean, Gephardt, Lieberman, Kucinich et al from the early primaries to the presidential election—that she really came to understand just how overdramatic was her mother's demonization of the Republican Party. [33] Drinking a chai latté at a busy café in lower Manhattan, Pelosi tells me that, when she got up close to Kerry and Bush, "I didn't think there was much difference between them." [34]

For readers of Vidal and Karp, this might be obvious, naïve stuff. But for a large part of the American population the two political parties are as authentically antipodean as the New York Yankees and Boston Red Sox. These people live or die by the elephant or the donkey, no matter what some ivory tower intellectual says. And Alexandra Pelosi knows the cultish aspect of party politics. She was born into the kind of family for which politics is the most powerful force in the universe.

"It was like a religion," she says. "You're indoctrinated, you don't know any better. I'd love to say I'm so intelligent that I became a Democrat. But it's not the case."

Growing up in a family of devout big 'L' liberals, Pelosi had little choice but to become a Democrat. Her grandfather, Thomas D'Alesandro, Jr. was one of Maryland's favorite sons, serving as a Democratic congressman from 1939–47 and then as Baltimore's mayor from 1947–59. His son Tommy Jr. followed in his shoes with a stint as the city's mayor in the 1970s. But it was his daughter Nancy who seized the torch and carried it into American history as the first woman ever to lead a major party in the U.S. Congress. As the representative of California's Eighth District, which includes San Francisco and is considered one of the most liberal districts in the country, Nancy Pelosi is also the standard-bearer for the party's leftist agenda.[*]

"My mom has spent her life doing what Democrats do," Pelosi says.

"What kind of things?" I ask.

"Taking care of other people." Pelosi says, "You know, like having people over for dinner who had nowhere else to go. It's that idea that you don't have to be poor to protect the rights of the poor," she smiles warmly, adding, "It's sort of a bleeding heart thing."

Pelosi leans up on the small coffee table and touches the rim of her cup on her bottom lip, pensively. "My mom grew up being able to tell other people how to get a hospital bed. I remember from when I was five or six years old, she used to tell us stories like, 'When I was your age I was running a homeless shelter that was in my house.'"

Throughout her own childhood, Pelosi was instilled with a very strict delineation between liberal and conservative values, one that

* The 8th district is a hardcore liberal stronghold. In 2004, John Kerry won San Francisco country with 83 percent of the vote with Pelosi taking the same share of the votes in her district. As former leader of the House Progressive Caucus, Pelosi's voting record has consistently put her on the far left of the party: She's *against* tax cuts, increases in military spending and the invasion of Iraq; and *for* abortion, gay and lesbian rights, and expanding social programs, including federally subsidized needle-exchange programs for drug addicts and expanded welfare benefits for immigrants.

assigned all the New Deal mythology to the Democratic Party.

"Somehow at a very early age I got the impression that what Republicans do is spend their money on bombs and they go to war and Democrats spend money on building shelters for people to sleep. I know these are just clichés but this has always been my impression. My sister's kids are five and seven years old and are Democrats—"

I cut her off: "They're Democrats?"

She nods her head, smiling. "Full fledged Democrats. They've been brainwashed. I mean, I have three sisters that moved to the suburbs and had kids. One married a Republican, which is like a mixed marriage."

"A mixed marriage?"

"Yeah. He's a Texas Republican. He's like a Tom DeLay/George Bush Republican."

"Does he hang out with your mom?"

"No," she laughs, "I remember when he said he was ashamed to be her son-in-law because she said Bush was doing a terrible job."

Pelosi speaks of her family with doting affection, the kind that she expresses with an implicit wink: *I love them, but they're crazy.* But she also plays the half-serious role of one who has wriggled out of an ideological straightjacket.

"I was indoctrinated into the Democratic Party and I was taught that Bush was pure, concentrated evil, because his father was. So, I always believed that Bush was going to be a really bad guy. But when I met him he was nothing like what I expected."

This irrational suspicion and hatred of the *other* is not reserved for the children of politicians alone. The phenomenal success of Michael Moore's *Fahrenheit 9/11* helped fuel a mass movement that had its own acronym, ABB (Anyone But Bush), and used all the fear tactics traditionally associated with their Republican opponents to drive voters into the Democratic Party. "It wasn't just the politicians, Pelosi remembers, "but the pundits too... that were saying 'Oh, Bush is going to destroy America.' I mean, remember all those people who were like 'I'm moving to Canada if Bush wins!' They're still buying into this whole left/right thing, you know. My point is that I realized that none of it is that simple. It's all very nuanced."

But there was no nuance in 2004. The mainstream liberal mindset, once celebrated for its ability to handle a multiplicity of political allegiances, collapsed around a binary, "either you're with us or against us" militancy. In their manic drive to "un-elect" George Bush, the ABB cult made an enemy of anyone who threatened the Democratic Party. The doctrinaire fervency of the left became so pitched that, during an appearance on Bill Maher's show, Michael Moore got down on his knees and begged the pro-jobs, anti-war independent candidate Ralph Nader not to run for president; this from a former Michigan union organizer who made the plight of an abandoned working class, who were being forced by economic need into military service, one of the most powerful themes of *Fahrenheit 9/11*.

In this all or nothing, Kerry or bust paradigm, Pelosi found herself distanced even further from the hardcore liberal base who are her mother's key constituents. "I care about the things that Democrats care about," she explains. "I'm not happy about the idea that Bush is—I mean I'm afraid about what he's doing to the country. But at the same time..."

Pelosi looks off for a moment and then delivers a line that must be the closest thing to heresy in the church of the Democratic Party.

"I don't know how the country would be any different if John Kerry were now president."

She smiles, almost defiantly. This is outsider territory, usually roamed by socialists or libertarian cowboys who, like Gore Vidal, see presidential elections as a choice between the lesser of two evils.* But for a woman who grew up watching her mother become one of the most successful fundraisers in the Democratic Party, the cynicism doesn't come so easy. Nancy Pelosi taught her daughter that "You don't have to be sick to be a doctor," meaning that to be a good liberal Democrat, one didn't have to be poor. And so even if there was very little in the socioeconomic legacy of John Forbes Kerry to distinguish him from George Walker Bush, one could still believe. Or could they?

In the prolonged autopsy of the 2004 Democratic campaign, much was made about the remarkably unexceptional nature of Kerry's platform. With so much fervent hope and, even, fear, propelling his supporters, he never seemed to break a sweat. Which only added to the off-putting magisterial posture that turned out to be his biggest weakness, polarizing conservatives and failing to convince the treasured swing voters that he was really anything but the same shit in a different package. Claiming to be "against powerful interests" and distancing himself, at least rhetorically, from "the privileged," Kerry fronted as a populist. But it all came off as a pose. By the time he took the stage after upsetting Howard Dean to win the New Hampshire primary, most people knew Kerry was married to a heiress, Teresa Heinz, whose fortune would have made him the third richest president in U.S. history; one notch below his hero, JFK. Then there were the pictures of him skiing, snowboarding and windsurfing, the Botox rumors, his French connection. Kerry provided the perfect target for what Thomas Frank referred to as the "backlash conservative… [who] approaches politics not as a

---

* Even the *New York Times*'s David Brooks joined the chorus of cynics. Describing an encounter he had with the spirit of Karl Marx, Brooks itemizes a laundry list of philosopher's complaints, some of which, he admits good points, including: "Periodically members of this oppressor class hold mock elections. The Yale-educated scion of the Bush family may face the Yale-educated scion of the Winthrop family. They divide into Republicans and Democrats and argue over everything except the source of their power…" Quote from David Brooks, "Karl's New Manifesto," *New York Times*, May 29, 2005.

defender of the existing order or as a genteel aristocrat but as an average working person offended by the arrogance of the [liberal] upper class."[35] Even when he beat George Bush in the presidential debates, Kerry managed to promote the president's image as an authentic, boots-on-the-ground commoner. Instead of rallying the economically dispossessed and politically disenfranchised, the Democratic challenger just came off as a wannabe, a pretender; Tweedledee to Bush's Tweedledum.

But then who is, or was, John Kerry after all? The story of his Swift boat heroics in Vietnam, three Purple Hearts and subsequent high profile anti-war stance were flogged shamelessly by the Democratic Party in an election year that was defined by America's descent into a new military quagmire. Kerry was sold to us as a war hero who understood the great cost Americans pay for their intervention in foreign conflicts. But the brand never took hold of the electorate's imagination.

"That's what the campaign taught us," Pelosi says. "He didn't know who he was and he didn't know what the public thought of him. I think he thought we all thought he was a war hero."

When the Democratic presidential candidates finally hit the campaign trail for the 2004 primaries, it wasn't a surprise that John Kerry got off to a slow start. Establishment Democrats were still aching from Al Gore's loss and, galvanized by Bush's radical conservatism, a new generation of insurgents poured into the machine. But they weren't looking for an old school candidate to lead America back from the edge. They wanted a genuine iconoclast and Howard Dean initially took masterful advantage of his opponents' ties to special interests and backing of the Iraq war. Dean could truthfully claim to be an outsider, and the Democratic base loved him for it. Money flooded in from internet contributions as young activists flocked to his campaign. All the while, from the background, the party elite was watching.

In this case, it was the Democratic Leadership Council (DLC) which was most threatened by Dean's insurgent campaign. Formed in 1985 after the Democrats were steamrolled by Ronald Reagan's Republican juggernaut two elections in a row, the goal was to reform the Democratic Party by moving it away from its "liberal" stigma. But it wasn't until 1988, when George Bush Sr. humiliated Michael Dukakis for being wasteful economically, soft on crime, and inexperienced in matters of national security that the DLC really got activated. It's co-founder, Al From, positioned the DLC as GOP-lite, advocating a tougher free market liberalism and moving closer to big business. In 1990, From convinced Bill Clinton to become the Council's chairman. When Clinton and Gore won the 1992 presidential election, the DLC could proudly claim two of its founding members had taken over the Democratic leadership. Their prosperous two-term run established the DLC's hold on the party and successfully suppressed the traditional liberal activist base that had become out of touch with the new political paradigm.

But after Al Gore's loss in the 2000 election, those disenfranchised Democrats spoke up. Many blamed the close results on the fact that his platform was fundamentally indistinguishable from that of George W. Bush. So when Howard Dean stood up and said, "I'm Howard Dean, and I represent the Democratic wing of the Democratic Party!" Dean was not just asserting his populism, he was reclaiming the party platform from the big business, establishment liberals who dominated it for the last ten years. And the base responded by giving the Dean campaign an unprecedented level of small, personal donations. When the media seized on the story and made Dean the cover boy for the Democratic presidential campaign, the DLC was forced to defend their turf.

"What activists like Dean call the Democratic wing of the Democratic Party is an aberration; the McGovern-Mondale wing, defined principally by weakness abroad and elitist, interest group liberalism at home," read a May 2003 memo titled *The Real Soul of the Democratic Party*.[36] In response, top Democrat donors began to fund anti-Dean attack ads in key regions while John Kerry and Dick Gephardt began conspiring to take down the populist insurgent. In October 2003, the *New York Times* reported that officials from both campaigns admitted "They are sharing information about Dr. Dean that helps fuel each another's attacks."[37]

One of the disappointments of *Diary of a Political Tourist*, Alexandra Pelosi's follow-up to *Journeys With George*, was that she did not apply any of her insider knowledge to the analysis of the Democratic primaries. Instead of looking at the power struggle that was emerging between the reformers and the elite, she stuck to superficial and comically mundane observations. So while Howard Dean is first shown carrying his own bag, John Kerry takes time off from a bowling game to warn, "I do not believe this administration is making America safer with its blustering arrogant foreign policy." Meanwhile, John Edwards is seen eating chocolate chip ice cream and being fawned over by young would-be voters who call him "Mr. Hottie."[38]

When Dean surges ahead of the others in the Iowa and New Hampshire, Pelosi rejoices, "Dean's in the lead and we're eating brie." Soon the Dean Machine is in full force, with the candidate speaking to packed halls, while Kerry is seen talking to ten people beside a lake in Exeter. But when Dean surprisingly finishes third in the Iowa primary and then loses his cool during his nationally televised response, Pelosi focuses on the network coverage of "the scream," analyzing it as "death by a thousand edits." In reality, Dean's self-destruction act was only the final act in a fairly adversarial media assault on the candidate.[39] A study by the nonpartisan Center for Media and Public Affairs revealed that through 2003, 49 percent of Dean's television interviews were deemed positive compared to 78 percent for his competitors.[40] Now, of course, this could simply be the natural result of journalists' placing tougher emphasis on the frontrunner. When NBC's Tim Russert grilled Dean on the number of American troops in Iraq and found the candidate's estimate lacking, he scolded, "As commander in chief, you should know that." It's hard to imagine him treating John Kerry that way.

Summing up her experience on the Democratic campaign trail, Alexandra Pelosi admitted, "The truth is after a year on the road, I know why the other guys lost. But I still don't know why John Kerry was the winner."

Maybe she wasn't looking hard enough. After all, for the Democratic establishment who had just fought off the grassroots insurgency of Howard Dean, John Kerry was safe harbor. He could be trusted to articulate the neoliberal business agenda of the party's corporate backers while appealing to the crucial independent voters with a safe social platform. Launching his campaign for the White House, Kerry shrugged off the Democratic base, distancing himself from labor, opposing gay marriage, and signing on to Bush's tax breaks proposal. But on the most decisive issue of all, the future of America's involvement in Iraq, Kerry showed no sign that he would offer an alternative to the Republican strategy. Instead, it would be a matter of fine-tuning the details so that America was able to maintain her status as the unchallenged world superpower. Both advocated the right for America to exercise unilateral military intervention without international sanction. In May 2004, former Kerry legal counsel and a foreign policy adviser Jonathan Winer told the *Christian Science Monitor* that Kerry's goals in Iraq were "the same goals the Bush administration has. It's how you achieve the goals that would be very different." And how? "John Kerry would be less authoritarian than the Bush administration," explained Winer.[41] He'd be a wolf,

Winer seemed to be saying, but in sheep's clothing.

Kerry's foreign policy platform was modeled on the theme of "muscular internationalism" that emerges from the Progressive Policy Institute (PPI), a DLC think tank. Think of it as the mirror image of the neoconservatives' controversial Project for the New American Century. Where that group, which includes Dick Cheney, Donald Rumsfeld and Paul Wolfowitz, stated their vision for a militarized American foreign policy in their 2000 manifesto, *Rebuilding America's Defenses*, the PPI white paper similarly calls for "the bold exercise of American power" at the heart of "a new Democratic strategy, grounded in the party's tradition of muscular internationalism that would keep Americans safer than the Republican's go-it-alone policy." [42]

And here was the key difference between the neoconservatives and the neoliberals. Under Kerry, there would be a return to the multilateralism of the Clinton administration, precisely what the international business community had demanded in the run-up to Iraq. Or so it seemed. But just in case the liberal hawks worried that Kerry be constrained by a overly "liberal" desire to please the world, in February 2004 he told a packed audience at UCLA that while he would work on rebuilding alliances, "no president would ever let them tie our hands and prevent us from doing what must be done." In other words, the neocons "go-it-alone" policy was still in play, but only if the country's safety was compromised. And if Kerry's words blurred the lines between his liberal ideology and Bush's conservative one, then it became even harder to distinguish when he declared that "working with other countries in the War on Terror is something we do for our sake—not theirs," implying that allies were only useful as long as they supported the U.S. mission. [43]

A few months later, as Kerry prepared to start the long summer of campaigning, PPI president Will Marshall articulated the neoliberals' own vision for Iraq, which he called "the grand strategic prize." Despite his candidate's professed desire to increase troop levels in Iraq, Marshall explained that the true battle between Islam and liberal democracy was ideological. "More than death in battle," Marshall reassured the Democrats, "our enemies fear the subversive pull of liberal ideas." And in the list of "economic and political reforms" to be implemented in the region, the first on his list was "a strategy of gradual liberalization would entail opening markets and expanding trade." [44]

But in the end, Kerry succumbed to the same fate as Al Gore before him. He lost by two percent of the popular vote in an election that came down to a hotly contested state where hundreds of thousands of African-Americans were kept from voting through the dubious machinations of the Republican secretary of state. And while many were outraged by the apparent evidence of another stolen election, the fact that it was even that close presents a more troubling reality than the potential corruption of the electoral process: That at the highest, most influential levels, there simply is no major difference between the two political parties. In a contest against one of the most inarticulate presidents in U.S. history, Kerry failed to provide any distinctly alternative vision to that of the Republicans. Despite all the blunders and missteps of the Bush administration, Kerry could offer nothing new to the American public.* As Thomas Frank wrote in the *New York Review*

---

* When Kerry reportedly hinted at another run, telling his dispirited campaign staff, "There's always another four years," the party faithful at DemocraticUnderground.com channeled their frustration into the on-line forum. "The Dem party leadership has become so much a part of the wealthy elite that there ain't a nickel's worth of difference between them and the repugs in who they identify with," wrote one member named *reprobate*, "It's sure not the working people of this country." And *LibDemAlways* lamented, "I sent money that could have gone to pay bills. What do I and millions of other have to show for their efforts on your behalf? Four more years of the worst nightmare in American history." A dejected George Soros could obviously relate. Soros, who reportedly poured $25 million into the Democratic campaign, shrugged it off saying, "Kerry did not, actually, offer a credible and coherent alternative. That had a lot to do with Bush being re-elected."

of Books, "Kerry moved to the center, following the well-worn path of the corporate Democrats before him, downplaying any 'liberal' economic positions that might cost him among the funders and affirming his support for the Iraq invasion even after the official justifications for that exercise had been utterly discredited." [45]

None of this is news to libertarian muckraker and *Nation* columnist Alexander Cockburn, who has built a small literary franchise out of the contention that Democrats and Republicans have fused into a single ruling oligarchy. In *Dime's Worth of Difference: Beyond the Lesser of Two Evils,* a 2004 compendium of essays dealing with the vanishing two-party spectrum, Cockburn wrote, "Amid the defilements of our political system, and the collapse of all serious political debate among the liberals and most of the left, the Democratic candidate becomes a kind of Hegelian Anybody, as in Anybody But…" [46]

Where once the Democrats picked candidates beholden to a legacy of liberal values and policies, now all that mattered was that they could beat Bush, hence the Anyone But Bush (ABB) movement that became the rallying cry of the 2004 election. According to Cockburn, it is precisely this kind of fear-driven, one dimensionality that creates the conditions for establishment interests to control the election. Protected by the manic Michael Moore-led ABB campaign, few Democrats would hold Kerry accountable to the party's leftist planks. No one would dare weaken the only chance Democrats had of rescuing the country from another Bush term. So Kerry's unapologetic middle-of-the-road stance became his biggest asset; all the better in the critical mission to woo swing voters. For the average liberal, it no longer mattered that he'd voted for the Patriot Act, Bush's tax cuts, and the invasion of Iraq. One-time radicals looked past his declared opposition to same-sex marriages, his pledge to send 40,000 more troops and extend the Iraqi occupation by a minimum of four years. There was barely a noise when when Kerry professed his openness to appointing anti-abortion judges, with the meaningless caveat, "as long as it doesn't lead to the Supreme Court overturning *Roe v. Wade.*" The "ghost senator" as one DC insider called him, had become the hope chest for a legion of voters who, under any other circumstances, would have been ashamed to wear his pin.

Writing in his *Nation* column two months before the election, Cockburn describes a discussion he had with one ABB-er.

"I asked him," Cockburn writes, "about his long-term political perspective. Here he was beating the drum for a man who stands for everything he opposes: war in Iraq, war in Colombia, war on drugs, war on the deficit, war on teen morals. 'Oh,' he said, 'the day after we elect John Kerry we'll go to war on him.' "[47]

But they never got the chance. The nation was spared the spectacle of a grassroots Democratic revolt against their Trojan horse candidate. Instead, despite a contested electoral result in Ohio, Kerry conceded defeat and literally disappeared into the Congressional woodwork from which he had emerged. Meanwhile, the Republican victory was characterized as a signal from "mainstream" America, who did not see their "values" reflected in the "liberal" program offered by the Kerry campaign. Almost immediately, the Democratic Party machine began scrubbing barnacles from their sinking ship and repositioning it for the next voyage. As the AP's Tom Raum reported just days after the election, "Democratic leaders are trying to figure out how to make the party more relevant to mainstream Americans and keep it from slipping into perpetual minority-party status."[48] Crystallizing the impact of her party's stunning loss, Nancy Pelosi said, "We have lost just about everything that we can lose."[49] Pelosi understood more than most how profoundly the election would shift Democratic political values to the center right, away from her long-cherished liberal code.

But for another group of political operatives, who are seeking to transform the American electoral system, this is exactly what they have been waiting for.

BACK TO THE FUTURE

One of the more complex phenomena of the modern American political scene is that while the ideological divide between presidential candidates seems to be ever diminishing, the partisan mudslinging and animosity between the two parties is increasingly hateful. It's a weird paradox. But it's not uncommon to hear critics of the two-party system decry a choice between Tweedledum and Tweedledee just as the highest rated television news programs are driven by raucous debate between right and left.

For *Daily Show* host Jon Stewart, it isn't a paradox at all. There is no disconnect between the professional politicians and the activists that drive those debates. In fact, it's exactly the way they want it. Because a polarized public, focused on hot-button issues like abortion, tax cuts and school prayer, keeps their focus off the fact that the two parties have essentially become the servants of one very important class of voters, the corporations.

So when we see representatives of the Left and Right go at it on *Hardball* or *Hannity and Colmes*, it's just a big act to sustain the illusion that there is authentic debate between the two parties. These shows, Stewart has said, "are emblematic of the decay of the American political system." They provide uncritical platforms for the politicians to manipulate and divide the nation, rendering the American public impotent in the face of the great problems confronting their country.

This was precisely the message that Stewart brought to CNN's *Crossfire* in October 2004. Ostensibly there to promote his new book, *America: A Citizen's Guide to Democracy Inaction*, Stewart had bigger things in mind. He came to make a direct criticism of the faux debate genre and to take *Crossfire*'s two hosts—liberal Paul Begala and conservative Tucker Carlson—to task for perpetuating it. The result, as we all know, was one of the most memorable bitch slaps in television history. Three months after Stewart reduced Carlson to a sniveling brat whose last stab at self-respect was to call his opponent an anally-receptive liberal partisan, CNN announced that it would cancel *Crossfire* and drop Carlson from its roster. When Klein was asked why he axed one of CNN's oldest and most successful programs, he said, "I guess I come down more firmly in the Jon Stewart camp."

He wasn't alone. Over three million people tuned in to watch the Jon Stewart/*Crossfire* appearance. Unfortunately for CNN and their advertisers, three quarters of them did it online. *Wired* reported that it was one of the most downloaded video clips ever.

Whether people were more drawn by the spectacle of such a high-profile bitch-slapping or the inherent message of Stewart's critique, we'll never know. But clearly, his words had a resonance that captured an element of the political zeitgeist: people are fed up with the manipulative and divisive tactics of the two parties and the media that serves them. Instead of engaging in rational debate that brings the nation to a consensus on critical issues, party leaders have allowed the political process to degenerate into bitter partisan rivalries. And just as that has driven the ratings of news shows that let them go at each other, it has also served to activate the electorate into funneling money into their respective party machines.

For journalist and political strategist John Avlon, these tactics are not only cynical and disingenuous, they also pose a very real threat to American civil society. Because while the small, interchangeable group of partisan agitators cynically program the national discussion from Washington, DC, they have no control over what can be unleashed in the small towns of red and blue state America.

Sitting in a quiet bar in Manhattan's trendy West Village, Avlon explains, "One of the dangers I see in American politics today is that we're courting a season of violence. Using hate as a recruiting tool increases the polarization of American politics. And I think that is the root of our problems." [50]

Fast-talking and wildly articulate, Avlon speaks the language of a political insider without any of the DC Beltway attitude.* Perhaps that's because he has no interest in being mistaken for a member of the establishment. Instead, Avlon's mission is to reform the American political system by engineering a realignment of the two-party system. This can only happen, he argues, through the earnest pursuit of a centrist political philosophy.

In his book, *Independent Nation: How the Vital Center is Changing American Politics*, Avlon writes, "Centrism is the most effective means for achieving the classic mission of politics: the peaceful reconciliation of competing interests." He describes the nation's left and right extremes as an "illusion." Far from being representative of the country's political spectrum, he writes, "they are ultimately the same thing." [51]

But this doesn't quite square with the vicious antipathy we saw during the George W. Bush's two controversial electoral victories. "The people were deeply divided," I say.

"No," Avlon shakes his head. "The American people, in both foreign and domestic policy, are not *deeply* divided, they are *closely*

* Avlon talks about politics the way ESPN anchors wrap up weekend sports highlights: "FDR gets elected in 1932, he's the first Democrat since Woodrow Wilson, and before that the Republicans have been running the White House since Lincoln. Democrats ran the table from '32 to '68 with the interim period of Eisenhower. Since Nixon in '68, Republicans have basically owned the federal government except for the Clinton gap and the Carter hiccup, which was a post-Watergate reaction which was still a squeaky election."

divided. And the two parties profit when they exacerbate differences. They profit when they play to their extremes. It's a divide-and-conquer strategy which employs wedge issues quite intentionally to give people false choices that they have to choose between."

Just like *Crossfire*. Jon Stewart is a big fan of Avlon's *Independent Nation* and centrist philosophy. So, a few months after Bush's 2004 victory over John Kerry, Avlon appeared on the *Daily Show*. The two hit it off like old college buddies.

Holding up the book, Stewart beamed, "This is my *raison d'etre*," and then asked why centrists have not had more impact on the political process.

"Well, you know, we're living in an incredibly polarized time," Avlon responded. "But the thing is, this isn't normal. The center is under attack right now which is why it's important that we fight back, which is what I think your show is doing."

"We're for the center, baby," Stewart clowned. "The problem with the center is, the center doesn't give as much of a shit as the crazies."

Watching Avlon on the *Daily Show* felt like I was seeing the future of American politics. Clean-cut without the geek factor, he exudes an aura of confidence and idealism that is rarely seen today. More, his earnest indictment of the partisan system and call for moderation and compromise is woefully lacking in the older political set. Jon Stewart was so impressed that he asked if Avlon was "reading from cards or something, because you're very good at this."

But I was suspicious. Here he was on national television, talking about centrists like a rare and endangered species of bureaucratic wildlife. What about Bill Clinton? John Kerry? Al Gore? They're hardly extremist Democrats. Neither, for that matter, was George Bush running too far from the center when he took the presidency in 2000. Sure, we have seen some really ugly political battles in recent years—the humiliating drama of the comatose Terri Schiavo comes to mind—but, if anything, centrists are the status quo in American politics.

"Aren't they?" I ask him.

"No," Avlon answers firmly. "What I'm arguing is absolutely the opposite of the *status quo*. What I'm arguing—the centrist position—is rebellious. It's a direct contradiction of what passes as conventional wisdom in politics today."

"Which is what?"

"You go behind closed doors of any party, it's all about ideological conformity. It's all about playing to the base. It's all about fealty to special interests. I mean, Grover Norquist* says 'bipartisanship in another word for date rape.' That is an ethos you hear both parties articulate in different proportions."

The bar is starting to fill up and Avlon has to speak over the din of the crowd. He leans in and continues his defense.

"After [the 2004] election I had a Republican strategist say to me, only half in sadness, 'this election proves there's no such thing as too divisive.' That's the ethos of American politics that's accepted as conventional wisdom. Don't mistake that, that's the establishment here. What we're articulating is a principled rebellion against the status quo. It's not an articulation of the status quo, at all."

With that, Avlon looks down at the martini sitting in front of him and takes a sip. It's the first time he's touched the drink since the waitress brought it twenty minutes ago. He scans for the room for a moment, taking in the beautiful crowd. If I didn't know him, I would think he was one of them, another smart young thing in an expensive suit. But to hear him speak, it's clear that John Avlon

---

* In his prime, Grover Norquist was one of DC's leading conservative strategists. An anti-tax activist—he once compared the estate tax to the Holocaust—Norquist's ties to disgraced lobbyist Jack Abramoff were the source of a federal investigation.

wants me to know he's on the outside looking in. And that it's all going to change.

His goal in *Independent Nation,* he tells me, is to show centrists that "they don't have to feel politically homeless." So, beginning with the 1901–1909 presidency of progressive Republican Teddy Roosevelt, Avlon traces the legacy of America's "vital center" over the course of a century, right up to the New York City mayoralty of Rudy Giuliani. It's a natural place for him to end since he served as a Giuliani's chief speechwriter during the height of his political dynasty in 2000–2001.

Writing for Giuliani, Avlon learned how to fuse conservative values of social order and fiscal restraint with the liberal maxims of freedom of expression and civil rights. This alchemy of two seemingly antithetical platforms was critical to Giuliani's two-term Republican mayoralty in a city that is 87 percent registered Democrats. According to Avlon, Giuliani had to represent a political vision that transcended partisan ideology. But he also had to address the serious crisis that had enveloped the city. Between 1990 and 1993, New Yorkers lost 330,000 jobs. Racial tensions were driving an explosion of violent crime that, combined with an average of 2,000 murders a year, made New York the crime capital of America.

"People had given up on New York," Avlon remembers, "They called it the ungovernable city. That was a given: 'the best you can do is manage the decline.' But when you employ solutions that aren't simply liberal or conservative in a doctrinaire way, there is room for evolution." Rudy Giuliani may have been elected a Republican, but he governed, Avlon tells me, as a New Yorker.

He places Giuliani in a category of "Third Way" mayors— including LA's Republican Richard Riordan and Cleveland's Democratic Michael White—who emerged in the 1990s. These politicians were successful, Avlon argues, because they shrugged off the "ideological straightjacket" placed on them by their parties and focused on practical solutions to the desperate problems faced by their cities.

"One way of understanding these mayors who brought urban America back from the brink is they were not doctrinaire liberals and they were certainly not doctrinaire conservatives. They were something different. They weren't beholden to special interests on either side, therefore they were free to choose the best solutions. It's about what works."

And make it work he did. Rudy Giuliani became the first Republican re-elected mayor of New York in sixty years. Looking back at the eight-year span (1994–2001) of his two terms, it was a remarkable feat. At the peak of Newt Gingrich and Pat Buchanan's far right conservative domination of the national Republican Party, Giuliani was establishing a liberal record on social issues such as gun control, gay marriage, immigration and abortion. And, in what might have been his most daring act of independence, during New York's 1994 gubernatorial race, he backed the Democratic incumbent Mario Cuomo over his own party's candidate, George Pataki. When Pataki won, Giuliani was essentially excommunicated by rank-and-file Republicans.

But that is not to say he was any more popular with liberals. Faced with a $2.3 billion budget deficit Giuliani slashed public spending, enacted "workfare" programs that forced welfare recipients to clean streets and parks, and beefed up the police force to 40,000 officers, its highest level ever. Advocating a program of "zero tolerance" for crime, Giuliani gave carte blanche support to the NYPD, which aggressively pursued its mandate and became embroiled in a series of controversial cases including shooting unarmed suspects and harassing minorities for everything from jaywalking to turnstile jumping in the subways. Finally, in an effort to clean up Times Square, Giuliani passed urban redevelopment laws which favored large corporations like Viacom and Disney while pushing low income residents out of the city.

And this was the key to Giuliani: he understood that being a successful mayor meant establishing an environment in which corporations could thrive. He had to make New York a magnet for investment. So while he was tolerant of gays and progressive on abortion, Giuliani's true legacy was built on clearing out all of the unsightly and ill-mannered constituents of the nation's biggest metropolis. As crime went down, businesses moved in and property values went up, benefiting that key electoral contingent of landowners—conservative and liberal. But for those homeless, ghetto-dwelling minorities who slipped through the ever-widening gaps of the social safety net, New York became an impossible city and they were forced to seek refuge elsewhere. And herein lies the real danger of a centrist reform movement.

Giuliani won by adopting the liberal values of individual freedom and social tolerance in combination with the conservative tactics for dealing with crime and poverty. In other words, it was an alchemy of those components of liberalism and conservatism which ultimately served and satisfied the middle and upper classes of the society. More importantly, it was just the kind of practical thinking that made New York a haven for corporate investment. By depoliticizing the public sphere, Giuliani was able to focus his government's energies on solutions to a particular set of problems. Those of the wealthiest tiers of his city. And while no one can argue that New York is not a cleaner, safer and better managed city as a result of the Giuliani's mayoralty, we must cannot forget those who were forced out to accommodate the dream.*

---

* For Avlon, Giuliani's non-partisan balancing act is crystallized in a statement his boss made one night at a Broadway charity function. Standing onstage dressed as a transvestite named "Rudia," Giuliani was asked by *Victor/Victoria* star Julie Andrews if he could now sympathize with the difficulty of her role, which demanded she play "a woman pretending to be a man pretending to be a woman." Giuliani replied that he did, explaining that he was "a Democrat pretending to be a Republican pretending to be a Democrat."

And this is what most worries me about the kind of centrism that strategists like John Avlon are advocating. Just like the corporate-driven neoliberalism of Thomas Friedman that has become the *de facto* program for American economic foreign policy, centrism provides the American elite with a vehicle that will create sanitized environments for business to thrive. And this will be achieved by effectively cutting out the dissenting wings of both the Republican and Democratic Party. While I can't say I'll shed too many tears for the marginalizing of right-wing Christians like Ralph Reed and Pat Robertson, we should all be concerned about the silencing of those Democrats—whom centrists call 'extreme'—who have traditionally championed America's poor and politically disenfranchised. If political strategists like John Avlon have their way, the two-party system will be dominated by moderates who have agreed to disagree on their fundamental social differences in order to focus their priorities on fixing the problems as identified by their most influential patrons. Undoubtedly, they will fix one problem by defanging partisans who make a living on finding the cracks and fissures that divide the American people. But they could also create a situation in which the two parties finally, openly, turn into one.

When I imply that he may be championing a system that resembles Gore Vidal's model of a one-party system—"the party of property"—with two right wings, Avlon shrugs it off.*

"I think that's too simple. I don't think the old classism analysis, the class warfare argument of American politics has much future. I think there's a bit of a Radiohead analysis of American politics

---

* To be fair, even if most centrists are advocates of a business-friendly brand of centrism, Avlon's vision is rooted in the "non-ideological" tradition of Teddy Roosevelt. In an email exchange before *Wolves* went to print, Avlon reminded me that while Roosevelt was no socialist, he realized that "to save the integrity of capitalism he would need to moderate its excesses, and while the Republican Party was then—as now—considered the party of big business, Teddy Roosevelt was the first one to specifically take on what he described as 'the malefactors of great wealth' by busting the Trusts of his day."

here," he smirks, referring to the British band who have made attacks on American politics a major theme of their songwriting.

But I'm not so sure. Looking back at the 2004 presidential election, John Kerry presented the perfect example of a Tweedledee playing to Bush's Tweedledum. Forget the symbolism of their shared membership in Yale's secretive Skull and Bones society, Kerry's marriage to Teresa Heinz made him wealthier than Bush, the son of an American dynasty.

"For many people," I argue, "Kerry didn't ever seem like a true option. He may have tried to articulate a competitive political platform, but he came across as another professional politician who really offered very few substantive alternatives to Bush."

Avlon nods and leans in closer to make sure I can hear him over the crowd. "The criticism of the Kerry campaign provides an interesting Rorschach to the criticism of American politics," he says, referring to the Swedish psychologist who asked patients to identify amorphous inkblots in order to evaluate and diagnose their personality characteristics.

"There's a group of people who say Kerry was too centrist. There's another group of people, probably a higher number, who said he was too liberal. It shows the way we've entered a hall of mirrors era in American politics where people project their own biases onto the candidates and people haven't figured out how to cut through the spin cycle."

The spin cycle he is referring to was that of Karl Rove, who Avlon sees as one of the major forces behind the partisan tribalism that is wreaking such havoc in American politics. During the 2004 election, Avlon tells me, Rove pushed every conservative button available to him, casting Kerry as the ultimate East Coast political insider: weak on defense, wrong on abortion and out of touch with the American heartland. But this is nothing new. Avlon explains that Rove was only simulating the tactics of Republican strategists under Ronald Reagan and George Bush Sr. who successfully branded Democrats as shallow, unpatriotic imposters. They were able to engineer this attack by capitalizing on two fundamental crises in the identity of the Democratic Party.

First, with the tragic failure of the Vietnam War—which, Avlon reminds me, had been launched and strategically conceived under a succession of Democratic presidents—the party lost confidence in terms of foreign policy. Secondly, the violent, drug-induced excesses of the anti-war movement, which were perceived as anti-American, became identified with liberals and, hence, the Democrats.

"Neither the Democratic Party, nor the word 'liberal', ever fully recovered," Avlon shrugs.

But up until the end of Cold War, this negative association originated in the minds of the electorate. It was not until George Bush Sr.'s 1988 presidential campaign against Michael Dukakis that Avlon pinpoints the beginning of an overt, targeted assault on the "liberal" brand. When Dukakis surged ahead in the polls, Bush responded with ads that attacked the Democrat as a "frost belt, big spending, big taxing liberal who comes from the state that brings you Ted Kennedy." The architect of these ads was Lee Atwater, a man Avlon describes as "a fairly dark political genius." Atwater understood the stigma of anti-Americanism that had carried over from the Cold War and decided to exploit it in another ad that described Dukakis as "a card-carrying member of the ACLU." [52]

Avlon sips quickly from his drink and continues. "Now that intentionally borrows language from Joe McCarthy who says: 'a card carrying member of the Communist Party.' And the construction is not an accident," he shakes his head. "So there's a conscious effort, at this time, to make the word 'liberal' a negative association that people try to wash off their hands. And conservatives, all of a sudden, appear common sense, by attacking the far left but stigmatizing half the American people in the process."

Bush won and the Republican Party, due in large part to the ideological attacks on liberals, was flooded with extremists from the conservative right. It was what Avlon terms a "season of political violence" that brought racist, homophobic and rabidly Christian, pro-life players like Pat Buchanan to the head of the party. This was epitomized in Buchanan's keynote speech at the 1992 Republican National Convention, when he called for a culture war against liberal Democrats like Bill Clinton.* But it could not last. Frightened off by the radical platform of the far right, Americans began looking back to the center, and Clinton was there to greet them.

Avlon tells me this shift away from the extremes is a "self-correcting mechanism in American politics." So that whenever one party becomes possessed by its fanatical wing, the American political pendulum will naturally begin its cyclical return to the center. And the leader who seizes on the overreach and marks their platform in the rational center will reclaim the high ground and steer the nation back into safe water.

"You know, one of the real insights Bill Clinton had with his centrist strategy is he was able to say, 'You know what? The religious right represents the Republican Party. And they claim to love America but too often they hate Americans. They don't hate you, but they may hate your sister, your neighbor, your best friend.' And by painting the Republicans as the party of the far right, which he effectively did by seeding the center, he was able to

---

* From flag-draped stage of the Astrodome, Buchanan boomed: "The agenda Clinton & Clinton would impose on America—abortion on demand, a litmus test for the Supreme Court, homosexual rights, discrimination against religious schools, women in combat—that's change, all right. But it is not the kind of change America wants. It is not the kind of change America needs. And it is not the kind of change we can tolerate in a nation that we still call God's country."

win the Presidency. Whichever party is able to associate the other party with the extremists, tends to win."

Avlon reminds me that in each of the three presidential elections leading up to Clinton's 1992 victory, the Democrats had lost by more than forty states. And while many in the party had called for a return to the grassroots liberal activism that once defined it, it was Clinton's uncompromising adherence to the middle way that won it for them.

"Not coincidentally," Avlon nods, "he was the first Democrat re-elected president since FDR."

Meanwhile, watching from the sidelines was Karl Rove, who saw the potential for a centrist Republican candidate to steal the White House from an increasingly placid and overfed Democratic Party machine.

"Now look what happens in 2000," Avlon taps his finger on the table. "People tend to forget that after the Clinton run, the Republican Party was on the ropes. And George Bush was not the conservative Christian right's first choice. But they understood the nation still saw them as the extremist party of Pat Robertson and Pat Buchanan, so they went for the pragmatic choice. They went for the center."

Avlon explains it was Clinton's successful brand of southern centrism that inspired Karl Rove to initially cast George W. Bush in the quintessentially centrist mold of an inclusive, "compassionate conservative" who worried about education and health care while expertly keeping the party's fickle base onside by talking up abortion, tax cuts and even isolationism.* When David Horowitz interviewed the would-be presidential candidate for *Salon* in May

* Many will forget Bush's highly visible nod to the traditional conservative plank of isolationism. In the first presidential debate he scolded Al Gore over the Clinton administration's adventures in Somalia and Yugoslavia, saying, "The vice president and I have a disagreement about the use of troops. He believes in nation building. I would be very careful about using our troops as nation builders."

1999, Bush staked his claim to the center, saying "I'm a uniter, not a divider." [53]

However, when the nation was left bitterly divided after the contentious Florida recount and subsequent Supreme Court decision to give him the White House, Bush did little to repair the rift. His presidency sputtered under a cloud of illegitimacy as he focused his energy on shoring up support within his own splintered party, and paying back his corporate sponsors. In the first six months he pressed ahead with his plans to privatize social security, opened federal land to oil drilling, moved to restrict patients' right to sue their HMO, and passed an enormous tax cut for the rich.

Then came September 11, and with it what John Avlon calls an "historic" opportunity to lead by moving beyond the partisan donnybrook. At first, Bush seemed willing to play the part. Speaking at the National Cathedral three days after the attacks, he quoted the beloved Democrat FDR, reminding Americans they could find comfort in the "warm courage of national unity." And it worked. Bush had the nation, and much of the world, behind him throughout the invasion of Afghanistan. But when the administration began its campaign for regime change in Iraq, demonstrating its willingness to act unilaterally, at any cost, all hope of truly uniting the country was lost.

"Democrats saw an elective war, with a larger to-do list than simply dealing with al Qaeda," Avlon shrugs. "It devolved quickly."

As Bush waged his War on Terror, liberals were forced into a defensive posture. They could only watch as the Republican-controlled Congress attacked the Constitution and backed the invasion of Iraq, making America a pariah in the global political arena. But conservatives have never cared much for world opinion. And with the 2004 election fast approaching, Karl Rove focused his president's message directly at the party's base of Christian evangelicals. It was a heretical defiance of the prevailing wisdom that elections can only be won by focusing on undecided voters. Yet Rove had tracked the stats and seen the number of declared "swing" voters decrease sharply from 32 to 21 percent since the 2000 election. And with both parties sharing approximately the same number (50 million) of reliable votes, Rove bet the presidency on a massive ground campaign to rally the Republican base. His first priority was the 4 million evangelicals who had not voted in 2000.

Gone were the centrist slogans and flirtation with moderates. Instead, Bush ridiculed John Kerry's liberal credentials and Hollywood connections, shooting straight for the hearts and minds of conservatives. "We're strong because of the institutions that help give us direction and purpose: our families, our schools, our religious congregations," he told an adoring crowd in Wisconsin in the summer of 2004.[54]

After Bush squeaked through another hotly contested election—which was decided in the battleground state of Ohio under remarkably similar conditions to the 2000 Florida debacle[*]—it looked as if Rove's strategy had paid off. And while most observers framed the election as Kerry's loss, blaming it on a weak-kneed campaign that failed to offer a tangible political alternative, Avlon sees it through different eyes. Instead, he places emphasis on Bush's marginal victory as a failure of Rove's extremist campaign.

"The American people don't like to vote against a Commander-in-Chief who sent our troops to war. I think, especially after the Vietnam experience, it goes against our sense of fairness. And

---

* In Ohio, thousands of African-American voters were disenfranchised because of numerous irregularities including names being scrubbed from the voter lists and the misallocation of voting machines that caused long lines at the polls. Moreover, the state's electoral process was overseen by Republican Secretary of State Kenneth Blackwell, an evangelical Christian.

even with all that, Bush was re-elected with the lowest percentage of any Republican incumbent in American history. That is not a mark of electoral success! A Republican president during wartime should walk. It should be Reagan and Nixon—49 state victories. The fact that Bush, after our nation is attacked, objectively failed to unify the country and squeaked by in a re-elect is a sign of weakness, not strength."

Avlon attributes Bush's marginal victory to the public's widespread acknowledgment of his broken promise to unite the country through a centrist doctrine.

"I think he listened to those people whispering in his ear," Avlon explains, "who said it didn't matter that he was betraying his mandate. He made an explicitly centrist appeal to the electorate and then governed as a conservative."

When Bush turned his back on the center in 2004, voters realized his "compassion" had been more a campaign strategy than core philosophy. So they punished him. And yet, Avlon says with disbelief, Karl Rove was celebrated as a genius for playing to the conservative base in the 2004 election.

"Well, that's nuts," he says, finishing his drink. "That's self-evidently wrong, it's against the laws of history and politics generally. It is, effectively, very short-term."

Clearly, Avlon is right. Six months before the 2006 midterm elections, Bush's job approval ratings hit an historic low. Then came the "thumpin," to use Bush's own word, at the polls that saw the Republicans lose control of both the House and Senate. Of course, this was largely due to the widely held view of Iraq as a poorly executed failure. But for moderate Republicans like former New Jersey Governor Christine Todd Whitman, it is Rove's strategy, not the war, that sabotaged the GOP.

"My fear is at what cost to governance and what cost to the future of the party, because by hardening the base, by everything

being aimed at that base of the evangelicals and the social fundamentalists, there was no effort to reach out to the middle," she
told PBS.[55]

For Avlon, it is not just a matter of pragmatism. He places
a deeper social responsibility in the hands of political strategists
who he blames for America's fractured political society.

"I think there is a more moral way to go—which is to reach
out and try to win over the reasonable edge of the opposition."

As both parties prepare to elect leaders for the 2008 election,
America finds itself in the charged climate of a political turf war.
And while it may have been ignited by the fear-baiting tactics of
Republican strategists, their Democratic counterparts haven't
exactly taken the high road. Since Howard Dean took over the
Democratic National Committee, he has emulated Rove's play-to-
the-base strategy, riling his party's grassroots members by calling
Republicans "a white Christian party" who have "never made an
honest living in their lives." *

Seemingly unconscious of his own polarizing influence, Dean
declared America "is about as divided as it has been probably since
the Civil War" to a group of religious leaders in June 2006.

Needless to say, John Avlon agrees. In the final minutes of
his appearance on the *Daily Show*, Avlon warned that if moderates
do not take back the political dialogue, it could lead to a severe
national crisis that would rival the Vietnam War era.

"There's a cost to this stuff because hate ultimately leads
to violence and we're not immune to that. That's why we've got
to step in and say, 'hey, stop, enough. Let's have some reasoned

---

* Dean's confrontational fund-raising tactics horrified moderate Democrats like Joseph
Biden. But Republicans were energized by the controversy. Republican operative Jon
Fleischmann, told the *San Francisco Chronicle*, "He's the best thing to happen to the GOP
in ages." Tom Del Becarro, chairman of the Contra Costa County Republican Party, added
"Howard Dean is scaring away the middle. People don't like angry people. They like
hopeful people." Quotes from "In S.F., Dean calls GOP 'a White Christian party'" *San
Francisco Chronicle*, June 7, 2005.

balance.' It shouldn't be a revolutionary idea that neither party has a monopoly on virtue."

Walking out into the warm evening air, I feel a mixture of respect and revulsion for Avlon's centrist ideal. No one wants to see America torn apart by political violence, especially since the Patriot Act endows the government with such wide reaching power to punish dissidents. But at the same time, the street fighting protest culture of the '60s and '70s that Avlon blames for tainting and stigmatizing the liberal brand represents the last great American bottom-up insurgency. Far from unpatriotic, their national pride inspired them to fight a war that, had it continued, could have replaced Hiroshima as the blackest mark on the nation's historical record. Yet the driving force of the movement was not simply anti-militarist, it was pro-human. It sought to impregnate America's domestic and foreign policy with a compassionate sensitivity to the suffering and injustice being experienced by the world's people—both within and outside the United States. Yes, there were bad elements. But reducing the entire movement, as most centrists do, to the authoritarian radicalism and drug-induced antics of the manic fringe is just the perpetuation of an historical lie, one promoted by those who understand how powerful and transformative that kind of a groundswell can be. The great majority of these young activists were acting out of a desire to protect their country from the same political and economic forces that have driven the U.S. into a succession of costly expansionist military adventures. And now that it is embroiled in a guerrilla war that could inflame the Middle East and draw in a broader Muslim front, America has never been more in need of a dynamic, independent political movement that can pull support across party lines and win back the trust of the world.

If the results of the midterm elections are any indication, this is not soon going to happen. Though the Democratic victory, and the ascendance of Nancy Pelosi to the Speaker of the House of Representatives, ends 12 years of Republican dominance, the sea change looks mostly skin deep. As Joe Klein reported in *Time* Magazine's post-election cover story "Why The Center is the New Place To Be," Democratic strategists who picked the various challenger candidates chose them "on pragmatism, not principle... The common denominator wasn't liberalism or moderation but the ability to win."

Indeed, as one of the rising stars of the Democratic Party, Illinois Senator Barack Obama was a magnet for campaign cash during the 2006 midterms. Using the Hopefund, his own Political Action Committee (PAC), Obama was able to funnel that money into the coffers of candidates he believed had the best chance of taking seats from Republicans. As Ken Silverstein reported in *Harper's Magazine,* "In several primaries, Obama's PAC has given to candidates that have been carefully culled and selected by the Democratic establishment on the basis of their marketability as palatable 'moderates'—even when they are facing more progressive and equally viable challengers." Among those backed by Obama's fund was the hawkish one-time Gore vice presidential running mate and self-declared centrist, Joe Lieberman. Lieberman is a valuable watermark for conservative Democrats who want to protect the party from its more progressive elements. In May 2006 the Democratic Leadership Council's Marshall Wittman, told the *Los Angeles Times* that Lieberman's Connecticut primary "is a fight for the soul of the Democratic Party"* because "it will have reper-

---

* One of the biggest stories in the Democrat sweep of 2006 was the rise of the Blue Dog Coalition, which is even more conservative than the DLC. There are now 37 Blue Dogs in Congress and, as Joshua Frank reported on *CounterPunch,* "not one had opposed the invasion of Iraq. All supported the Bush tax cuts as well as the wall along the border of Mexico. None support impeachment. All support Israel unequivocally, and if Bush moves ahead with a military intervention in Iran, they'll all be on board." Speaking to the *LA Times* before the elections, Blue Dog Rep. Mike Ross (D-Ark.) put it all in perspective: "The Democrats are going to retake the House of Representatives by electing conservative and moderate Democrats. We're going to move our party back to the middle."

cussions for the 2008 presidential campaign and whether centrists will feel comfortable within the Democratic Party."

Writing in *Independent Nation*, John Avlon explains that the symbol for centrism is the American eagle. "Independent, patriotic, eagles don't fly in flocks; they soar over the American landscape possessing, above all, a sense of perspective." [56] When I read that passage, I couldn't help but shudder at the irony. While the eagle is beautiful and majestic, it is also a bird of prey. How fitting an emblem for a political philosophy that would strip American politics down to its barest essentials—the interests of a plundering corporate sector—and confirm what much of the world already sees. I ask Avlon if he is worried that the neoliberal foreign policy of centrists like Clinton and Kerry has contributed to the widespread anti-American sentiment, he jokes that he's never understood the meaning of the word.* For him the word is just another political brand used by politicians to divide and conquer the electorate. But to the rest of the world, it has great meaning. Namely that American liberalism is a euphemism for economic plunder. They believe, as Sergeant Hollis does, that "when Americans say freedom, we mean capitalism." The virtues of liberty and justice have become doormats for corporate expansion and military conquest.

Avlon doesn't buy it. "America is an international symbol of freedom. Are we perfect? No. But should we feel guilty about standing up for individualism and equality in the world? Absolutely not. We cannot allow ourselves to retreat. And whatever party starts apologizing for what makes America great, that always-imperfect, but still-evolving tension between freedom and equality, they will lose."

---

* Avlon's feigned ignorance about the term neoliberalism hints at a wider truth. Most Americans have no idea what it means either. They use the word globalization instead. As Mark Engler told me, "Anyone who travels outside the country will hear that discussion all the time; about American neoliberalism. Here what does that mean? It means nothing. There's no common usage of the term and people just don't understand it."

Which is precisely the problem. The single political act that could actually re-establish some level of harmony between America and the ever-growing movement against it would be the election of a leader who could take the unprecedented step of apologizing for the mess that has been created in the wake of 9/11. If Americans could find a way to demonstrate at least a symbolic gesture of a collective self-questioning, it could literally change the world. Would it deter the Islamist fighters? No. But it would most certainly reverse the unspoken sympathy that many moderate Muslims and Third Worlders feel for the mission, if not the actions, of al Qaeda. Otherwise, America will be doomed to live in a perpetual state of conflict with the rest of the world, one sustained by a purposeful ignorance that Bill Maher captured perfectly when he joked, "They hate us because we don't know why they hate us."

There's little hope for that to change if left to A-list centrists like John McCain, Rudy Giuliani and Hillary Clinton. All three voted for the Iraq war and none hold much hope for a revitalized social liberalism. Of the three, perhaps the most significant is Senator Clinton, who provides an object lesson in how the centrist platform strips candidates of their humanist ambitions. While her husband was ignoring Rwanda, bombing Kosovo and smilingly untying the last threads of America's social safety net, the former First Lady was able to project the veneer of a compassionate liberal who would stand up for the poor and disenfranchised. When she ran for office, Clinton gave die-hard Hollywood liberals like Susan Sarandon and George Clooney confidence that this was a politician who would challenge the kind of corporate militarism that drove the invasion of Iraq. But once elected, Senator Clinton had no choice but to vote for the war. To oppose it would have destroyed any hope she had of reaching the White House for a second time. As Clinton began her public flirtation with a presidential run in '08—grabbing photo ops with Newt Gingrich and making nuanced statements against abortion and illegal immigration—Sarandon spoke out. "What America is looking for is authentic people who want to go into public service because they believe strongly in something, not people who are trying to get elected."

The problem of course is that in order to get elected, politicians must appease the corporate interests that are driving American domestic and foreign policy. Hillary Clinton spent over $30 million on her 2006 re-election campaign, the most of all Senatorial candidates. Bush and Kerry raised $274.7 million and $253 million respectively for their 2004 presidential campaigns and analysts are estimating the cost of running will double for the 2008 election. So what's to be done?

Ironically, it is John Avlon who provides me with the most durable hope for the birth of a new humanity-centered liberalism in America. Avlon believes the traditional brands of the two-party system are losing value. Where once voters wore party pins as "badges of honor," today they are rejecting party identification outright. In *Independent Nation*, Avlon points to a University of Michigan study showing the number of independents rose from 23 percent to 40 percent between 1950 and 2000. Even more encouraging is that "the number of independents in the country has increased an average of 300 percent in the fourteen years since Ross Perot won 19 percent of the vote as an independent candidate in 1992."

This mass defection, he explains, is being driven by the nasty ideological battle that has made membership in either of the two major parties untenable for many Americans. Avlon sees these alienated independents as the critical mass that could pull the political pendulum back from the extremes and drive a centrist leader into the White House. But these voters aren't just the best chance for the centrist movement, they're also the greatest hope for a return to the kind of humanitarian radicalism that made the Boomer generation of Christopher Hitchens, Paul Berman and Todd Gitlin the most formidable global front in the twentieth century.

The fact that young America has not responded to the American establishment's bipartisan support for the Iraq war by uniting in a broad-based, counter-cultural revolt is not, as their parents would like to believe, proof of their ambivalence. It is because they lack the kind of leadership their parents had when it was their time to change the world. Granted, the challenge is far more complex this time around. It is no longer a distant enemy on a foreign land. Today the threat is local and ever-present. The terrorists can and will attack without warning. In this environment, dissenting voices—let alone actions—are easily stigmatized. To challenge the government, we are told, is to weaken our defenses and create opportunities for our enemies who want to destroy America.

But what's left to destroy? I know this sounds like a cynical question, but if I have learned anything on this journey to the end of American liberalism, it is that the United States exists more now as a holograph than an embodiment of its original intent. It seems destined to go down as the world's only bottle-rocket empire; shooting into history with spectacular promise before fizzling into the death throes of a grabby and decadent global cop.

In the new millennium Americans have a choice to make. They can continue to elect leaders who view the rest of the world as hostile combatants, and thus push us ever-closer to apocalyptic conflict, or they can turn inward and trace a finger back to those aspirations, values, policies that once made them great, which made them the lodestar and safe harbor for the world. If they choose the latter, they can start building a globalization movement that is compassionate, fair and inclusive. They can use their vast technological resources to construct a platform that unites cities, countries and continents around the vision of a truly global identity, one that finally makes the conservation and equitable distribution of our limited planetary resources the primary goal of our species. This is both a conservative and liberal idea. It's an authentically centrist idea for it makes our collective survival and harmony, not that of just the United States, the center of an ideology.

In the short time that I have traveled around the world, visiting close to ninety countries, the one recurring message I have heard from people is that despite all its negatives, America is still regarded as the unrivaled source of innovation and new ideas. It's time for a new idea. And it's not one for me to outline here in the final pages of this short diary. Rather, it's one for you to begin mapping in the blank pages that follow. We don't have much time.

As Jon Stewart was wrapping up his interview with John Avlon, he asked, "Will something more dire and desperate need to happen for the moderate majority that you speak of to actually take control?" The truth is, the dire and desperate event Stewart is talking about has already happened. Though it may take some time for the political anthropologists to catalogue it, I think the trauma of 9/11 will be seen as the force that uprooted the crucial ballast of social liberalism and shifted the axis of American politics, perhaps irrevocably. Unless Americans can find a leader from outside the professional political culture with enough wisdom and integrity to steal the hearts and minds of the moderate majority and convince them that the last best hope on Earth lies in an entirely new internationalist movement, then I'm with Avlon, who looked at Stewart confidently, "I think it's going to get a lot worse before it gets better, but I think it's going to break in 2008. We're going to see a realignment in American politics."

I hope he's right.

EPILOGUE

In Heat

Our ideas are our spectacles.

— Alain

"*Dandayamana janushirasana,* standing head to knee pose," sings the lithe, beautiful woman as she walks past me. I bend over, interlock my fingers and lift my right foot into the cup shape made by the flex in my hands. Beside me, a slightly overweight man in a Speedo arches his back and groans. Sweat pours off his head and arms, dripping into a puddle that has formed on the rubber mat below him.

"Lock the standing knee so it's rock hard, like a lamppost," commands the goddess.

I fix my gaze hard on the mirror in front of me, trying to ignore the fleshy tribe of bikini-clad women who fill the space around me. There are sixty of us, lined in three rows in front of a wall mirror, working in the room. The temperature is over 105 degrees; the humidity level is off the charts. It's unbearable, but it's yoga; and my chance to connect with the inner calm of the universal subconscious.

"Okay, drop your leg," the yogi instructs. "Now place your right hand beside your right hip and hold it out, just like you are holding a bag of money."

I lose my focus for a second and look up.

"Come on, hold it out there," she orders from the back of the room. "Imagine you've got a big bag of gold, you don't want to lose grip of it, do you? Good."

At first I am a little off-put by the sudden injection of materialism. But then, I shouldn't be. This isn't any regular yoga class. It's *Bikram* yoga, the proprietary creation of Bikram Choudhury who took a selection of poses he learned as a yoga student in Calcutta, put them in his own unique order and cranked up the heat. It's made him into a multi-millionaire.

When Bikram was featured on *60 Minutes* in June 2005, he told correspondent Mika Brzezinski, "I don't sell cheesecake. You come there to suffer. If you don't suffer you don't get anything. Nothing easy in life." [1]

Nothing is easy, but nor is it free. When independent studios began opening up and teaching Bikram's twenty-six poses, he sued them. Claiming his interpretation of the yogic poses was no different than a composer who arranges notes to create a song, Bikram won and today no one can teach his yoga without first attending a $5,000 training course offered by Bikram himself. With 1,200 franchises across the United States and classes all day, every day of the week, you do the math.

In the *60 Minutes* story, Bikram led the wary journalist out to his Beverly Hills garage and took her for a drive in one of his fleet of Rolls Royces. When she remarked that his life didn't seem "very yogi like," Bikram replied, "Depends what kind of yogi. I'm an American yogi."

And that he is. In the truest sense, Bikram has proven that even yoga, which has been practiced for hundreds of years without patents or proprietary clauses, can be infiltrated and transformed by American economic liberalism. That's the nature of the system: it remakes things in its image. So, it's not surprising to hear Bikram instructors tell their students to shape their bodies into a 'T' like Tom Cruise, or to squeeze their knees together as if they are holding an American Express 'Black' card.

Now I have nothing against Bikram's success. In fact, my afternoons in his so-called "torture chamber" were crucial to sustaining me through the writing of this book. But his story is an important example of how invasive the American brand of capitalism can be. We tend to regard it as an organic system that operates in harmony with the rough and tumble of the global marketplace, but that's just not true. America has risen to its great power in the world because its leaders have shaped their society into a republic of competitors who must chase a slowly vanishing carrot while fleeing an increasingly larger stick. In fact, the harshly individualistic pursuit of wealth has become as fundamental to the American character as the founding principle of democracy itself. And while American capitalists have used the banner of freedom to invade and exploit foreign markets since the Spanish-American War of 1898, the combining of democracy and capitalism into a clearly stated foreign policy objective did not happen until the beginning of the Cold War which was defined, as Peter Beinart wrote in the *New York Times*, "as a struggle not merely for democracy but for economic opportunity as well, in the belief that the former required the latter to survive." [2]

If democracy is dependent on "economic opportunity" to survive, then how has democracy been transformed by it? And how far has it come from the original design of the liberal humanists who envisioned a system that could ultimately honor and protect the rights, integrity, and mobility of each individual participant? If Bikram yoga is any indication, we've come a long way.

But we aren't naive idealists. In the modern world, we understand that systems are imperfect. Today's liberalism is a "lesser than" liberalism that, while not guaranteeing an authentic social and economic mobility, nor even the fullest promise of individual integrity, can ensure that each citizen will fulfill their own destiny without interference from the State. Just don't count on it for help, unless you are a large corporation. During my research and travels, perhaps the best encapsulation of the modern state of liberalism I encountered was Todd Gitlin's, who admitted, "Liberalism today is rickety."

And if that's true, then shouldn't we think twice before trying to impose it on foreign nations who are laboring under conditions that seem intolerable to us?

Flying back from Los Angeles in late November 2006, I watched footage from Iraq on the small TV set embedded in the seat in front of me. It was a landmark day for violence in Iraq. More than 200 people died in Shia-controlled Sadr City in a series of car bomb attacks. From his side of the split screen, GOP operative Reed Dickens tried to sound upbeat, reminding Americans that among other things Iraqis had a constitution and Baghdad was feeling the "buzz of capitalism."[3] I think at this point many Iraqis are quietly asking themselves if they wouldn't be happier with that statue of Saddam back up in Firdos Square.* But, most Americans will never know how they feel, these recipients of the liberal dream. In all the reports from Baghdad, how many times have we actually heard average Iraqis asked about how they feel about what has happened? And that's just the point.

I believe the planning and execution of the Iraqi invasion was so slipshod because its architects never really cared about the Iraqis themselves. When I was in Baghdad a few months after the war, it was already a widely held view among educated Iraqis that a violent sectarian civil war would be the major outcome of the invasion. One translator I worked with even hinted that this wouldn't neces-

---

* Firdos Square is the site of that infamous CNN shot just after the liberation of Baghdad, when U.S. Marines helped jubilant Iraqis knock down a large statue of Saddam Hussein.

sarily be bad for the Americans, as it would give them an excuse to remain in-country as peacekeepers. Conspiracy theories abound in post-Saddam Iraq, but one thing is clear: looking back at the manufactured evidence of Saddam's WMD, the vast amount of taxpayer money that has been spent and each precious American life that has been lost, it would seem as if there was a larger plan afoot. One that makes Iraq, as Sergeant Hollis explained to me at the beginning of my journey, the first stage in a sweeping political, social and economic transformation of the Middle East.

Americans want to be greeted as liberators, so that is what they call themselves. But the world is weary of self-identifying saviors. As Gore Vidal explained to me, "I never identified my self as anything. That is for others to do." And that's the way it should be. In the end, it's not important how Americans view the liberalism they want to gift to the world, it what the world thinks about American liberal values. In *The Liberal Virus*, Samir Amin writes that "in the eyes of the Washington establishment, we have all become 'redskins,' that is peoples that have a right to exist only in so far as we do not obstruct the expansion of the transnational capital of the United States."[4] This is the radical leftist view, but it is not too far from the common perception amongst street protestors across the planet, from Quito to Lahore to Jakarta. If the world believes America has sacrificed its ideal of liberty for a militarism that uses freedom as a veil to hide their expansionist whims, then how long can the United States maintain its hegemony without exhausting its already weakened military forces?

The health of any organism, whether the human body or a nation-state, depends on balance. But what we have seen in the wake of 9/11 is a hard rightward shift in the American political compass which brought many of the greatest '60s era liberal minds into supportive alignment with the Bush Administration's over-throw of Saddam Hussein. Of course, there are still many voices on the left who cried out against the action. But what about after the next attack comes? Or what if the American dollar continues to fall and the nation goes into a deep recession? How long will the liberalism that stands for social justice hold out against that neo-liberalism which seeks to expand the reach of U.S. economic hegemony under the free market system?

Writing in the *Towards a Social Ecology*, researchers F.E. Emery and E.L. Trist determined that "there can be an awareness of world changes without an awareness of that awareness."[5] In this way, people can begin to compromise their values and ideals, even voting against them, out of a reaction to a subconscious realization that they are imperiled. Once a nation—which has risen to such unrivaled greatness, with such unprecedented speed—is faced with the possibility of its own decline, then its citizens will make markedly different choices about the kind of political society they will tolerate in order to prevent the inevitable fall from occurring. Even the most liberal citizen will be moved to conserve their status, to prevent the loss of what they have become accustomed to. It's human nature... to become ferocious protectors of what defines you and to seek the annihilation of that which has come to take it.

Even with the 9/11 attacks, American society hasn't suffered that kind of deep trauma that propels it into an irreversible political and social decline. But it may not have to. Just as a loosely organized, international popular front has begun to align itself against American expansionism, it has also moved to the state level. Iran's Mahmoud Ahmadinejad is forging alliances with economic and military powers that could pit nuclear powers against each other in a replay of the Cold War that was once unimaginable. The victory of liberalism over communism was supposed to herald the end of history. But instead, it created a vacuum that brought us into an even more dangerous global conflict.

In the post-Cold War era, there is no parallel ideology to

compete against capitalism and liberal democracy. So, without anything to compare itself against, liberalism has fallen to a very low standard.

What are we to make, then, of the liberal project to spread American values around the world, even, if necessary, through the use of military force? I think it comes down to fear. Ours. As Corey Robin writes in the *Nation*, "liberals need fear: to justify their principles, to warn us of what happens when liberalism is abandoned. And so they are driven abroad to confront the tyrannies that make life miserable elsewhere, in order to derive confidence in their own, admittedly imperfect but infinitely better, regimes. A souped-up version of Churchill's adage that democracy is the worst possible government except for all the others." [6]

The pursuit of a global democratic order is not the cause célèbre of one political party or interest group. It's the driving force behind all U.S. foreign policy: a plug 'n' play killer app that guarantees immediate access to the global market. So don't be fooled by the sea change in Washington. American liberalism is being readied in newer shinier boxes for shipment to the rest of the world. As balloons fell onto the delegates at the 2004 Democratic Convention in the final moments of Alexandra Pelosi's *Diary of a Political Tourist* she remarked with perfect detachment: "So this is it. This is democracy. And we're exporting it all around the world." [7]

Ready or not, here we come. Again.

There is a tendency in books critical of American politics to offer solutions; a desire on the part of the author to give some hope to their readers, who have invested their time and intellect in the discovery of all that is wrong. But to be honest, I don't think there are any pat, bullet-point solutions that can be offered at this point. In my view, what needs to happen is a very profound shift in the consciousness of the American people themselves. Only then can the collective will be focused on their political and economic systems in a way that will change them for the better. Sadly, these kinds of evolutionary leaps do not usually occur on their own. More often than not, they are triggered by a crisis or cataclysmic event that forces the population to make very serious decisions about who they are and what systems they want to operate under in order to survive.

Is capitalism the poison pill buried within the social contract of liberal democracy? I don't know. But I do think that "democracy" and "capitalism" are due for an overhaul. And who better to do that deep, soul-searching kind of work than the new millennial Americans who are the inheritors of the legacy founded on these two systems? However it's going to happen, I think the first stage of any solution is self-awareness. And that is what I wanted to help contribute to when I started out on the journey that became *Wolves in Sheep's Clothing*.

Ironically, the most sage advice comes to me late one Friday night while I am back in the Bikram yoga studio. I am drenched in sweat, quiet in meditation before holing up for the weekend to finish work on the book. The 90-minute class has ended and we're all lying down with our eyes closed in what is called *Savasana*, or corpse pose. The teacher, one of my favorites (he never talks money) is about to close the class when he suddenly breaks his mantra and says:

"The world is a hectic place. It can be ruthlessly competitive and unfair. But in here, we're just with our breathing. It's just you and your self. So stay there for a moment. Try to remove all of your fears and wants and instincts to break out of your quiet peace. Just stay in the middle. For a moment. And breathe. And if you can't do that, then ask yourself why not."

It's a simple message. But as I lie here, eyes closed, listening to the sound of my chest rising and falling, I realize that it's big enough for all of us. If Americans are going to be authentic members of the so-called "global community," then they have to seriously ask themselves what it is that drives any action they take outside of their borders. Is it unconditional support of burgeoning democracies and evolving communities? Or is it self-interest masquerading as benevolence? Or is it somewhere in the middle?

Those of us who want to participate in the new century from a place other than in front of our television sets or computer monitors understand that we must challenge our own conventional wisdoms. We must unveil our own collective myths. We must be courageous enough to put down the blunt swords and broken shields of our half-truths and, even if for just one moment, consider the accusations of those who have become defined as our enemies. Because in that kind of open willingness to be challenged, there is a glimmer of the whole. And we mustn't be scared of it. It will not swallow our individualism. Rather, it will fortify it and make us more powerful, authentic proponents of the world itself... as a collection of individuals who understand their power as a worldwide family. We don't have to be sheep. And nor do we have to be wolves. I don't really know what animal lies between those two poles, but I'll risk a guess—and call it human.

PROLOGUE: CREATION THEORY

1. Choonghoon Lim and Douglas Michele Turco (Illinois State University).

2. Stephen Marshall ("Author"), Interview in Islamabad, Pakistan, April 14, 2006.

3. Jonah Goldberg, "Conservative Zoology 101," *National Review*, June 16, 2002, available at http://www.nationalreview.com/goldberg/goldberg061600.html.

4. Author, Interview with Chris Hedges, October 10, New York.

5. Author, Interview with Sgt. First Class Robert Hollis, October 26, 2003, Samarra, Iraq. Unless otherwise noted, all future information and quotations in this section derive from this interview.

6. "Charles E. Wilson, January 25, 1953–October 8, 1957, 5th Secretary of Defense, Eisenhower Administration," n.d., available at http://www.defenselink.mil/specials/secdef_histories/bios/wilson.htm.

7. Thomas L. Friedman, *The Lexus and the Olive Tree* (New York: Anchor Books, 2000), 464.

8. Paul Berman, *Terror and Liberalism* (New York: Norton, 2003), 60–101.

9. Ibid., 185.

10. Michael Ignatieff, "One Year Later," *San Francisco Chronicle*, September 10, 2002, available at http://www.sfgate.com/cgi–bin/article.cgi?f=/c/a/2002/09/10/MN100332. DTL.

11. Michael Ignatieff, "It's war—but it doesn't have to be dirty," *The Guardian*, October 1, 2001, available at http://www.guardian.co.uk/g2/story/0,,560891,00.html.

12. Ibid.

13. Michael Ignatieff, "The Divided West," *Financial Times*, August 31, 2002, available at http://www.ksg.harvard.edu/news/opeds/2002/ignatieff_divided_west_ft_083102. htm.

14. Michael Ignatieff, "The Year of Living Dangerously," *New York Times Magazine*, March 14, 2004, available at http://www.ksg.harvard.edu/news/opeds/2004/ignatieff_year_dangerously_nyt_031404.htm.

15. Michael Ignatieff, *The Lesser Evil: Political Ethics in the Age of Terror* (Princeton: Princeton University Press, 2004).

16. William Strauss and Neil Howe, *The Fourth Turning: An American Prophecy* (New York: Broadway Books, 1997), 3, 299.

17. John Gray, *Al Qaeda and What It Means to Be Modern* (New Press, April 20, 2005), 1.

18. Louis D. Brandeis quoted in American Judicature Society, "Preserving liberty when the nation is at war," available at http://www.ajs.org/ajs/ajs_editorial–template. asp?content_id=24.

CHAPTER 1: BIRDS OF A FEATHER

1. Author, Interview with Richard George William Pitt Booth, May 28, 2005, Hay–on–Wye, Wales. Unless otherwise noted, all future information and quotations in this section from derive from this interview.

2. John F. Kennedy, "In Praise of Robert Frost, Celebrates the Arts in America," October 27, 1963, available at http://www–static.cc.gatech.edu/people/home/idris/Speeches/kennedy_frost.htm.

3. Tariq Ali quoted in "In Enemy Territory? An Interview with Christopher Hitchens,"

September 23, 2004, available at http://www.johannhari.com/archive/article.
php?id=450.

4. Author, Interview with Joan Bakewell, May 27, 2005, Hay–on–Wye, Wales. Unless otherwise noted, all future information and quotations in this section derive from this interview.

5. For Joan Blackwell reading, see for example, http://www.dazereader.com/kirkupjesuspoem.htm; for James Kirkup's poem, see for example, http://www.annoy.com/history/doc.html?DocumentID=100045.

6. Adam Smith, *The Wealth of Nations* (Philadelphia: Printed for Thomas Dobson, [1789]; New York: Bantam Books, 2003).

7. Author, Interview with Alan Rusbridger, May 28, 2005, Hay–on–Wye, Wales. Unless otherwise noted, all future information and quotations in this section derive from this interview.

8. John Maynard Kenyes quoted in Michael Albert, *Briarpatch Magazine*, September–October 2005.

9. "About our History," *The Economist*, available at http://www.economist.com/help/DisplayHelp.cfm?folder=663377#About_The_Economist.

10. Author, Interview with John Micklethwait, May 28, 2005, Hay–on–Wye, Wales. Unless otherwise noted, all future information and quotations in this section derive from this interview.

11. "Showdown looms on Capitol Hill as Galloway talks tough," *The Times*, May 17, 2005, available at http://www.timesonline.co.uk/article/0,,7374–1615553,00.html.

12. "Galloway v the US Senate: transcript of statement," *The Times*, May 18, 2005, available at http://www.timesonline.co.uk/article/0,,3–1616578_1,00.html.

13. Christopher Hitchens, "Unmitigated Galloway," *The Weekly Standard*, May 30, 2005, available at http://www.weeklystandard.com/Content/Public/Articles/000/000/005/641kyjkk.asp.

14. Author, Interview with Ben Ramm, May 29, 2005, Hay–on–Wye. Unless otherwise noted, all future information and quotations in this section derive from this interview.

15. Christopher Hitchens, letter, *Commentary Magazine*, April 2003, available at http://www.commentarymagazine.com/archive/digitalarchive.aspx?panes=1&aid=11504005_1.

16. Christopher Hitchens, "O, Brother, Why Art Thou?" *Vanity Fair*, n.d., available at http://www.vanityfair.com/commentary/content/articles/050606roco01?page=2.

17. Author, Phone Interview with Peter Hitchens, June 4, 2005. Unless otherwise noted, all future information and quotations in this section derive from this interview.

18. Peter Hitchens, "Not in our name," March 29, 2003, *The Spectator*, available at http://www.lewrockwell.com/spectator/spec46.html.

19. "When Christopher Met Peter," Hay Literary Festival transcript, *The Guardian*, May 31, 2005, available at http://www.guardian.co.uk/g2/story/0,3604,1521751,00.html.

20. Author, Interview with Christopher Hitchens, May 28, 2005, Hay–on–Wye, Wales. Unless otherwise noted, all future information and quotations in this section derive from this interview.

21. Connor Cruise O'Brien, *Writers and Politics* (New York: Pantheon Books, 1965), xiv.

22. Martin Walker quoted in Meryl Gordon, "The Boy Can't Help It," *New York Magazine*, April 26, 1999, available: http://newyorkmetro.com/nymetro/news/media/features/868/.

23. "Hitchens: Journalists' British Bad Boy," *The Washington Post*, February 12, 1999, available: http://www.washingtonpost.com/wp–srv/politics/special/clinton/stories/hitchens021299.htm.

24. Christopher Hitchens, *The Trial of Henry Kissinger* (London, New York: Verso, 2001).

25. Christopher Hitchens, *Regime Change* (London: Penguin Books Ltd., 2003), vii.

26. Author, Interview with Sgt. Hollis.

27. O'Brien, *Writers and Politics*, xv.

CHAPTER 2: IMAGINARY FORCES

1. Thomas L. Friedman, *The World Is Flat: A Brief History of the Twenty–First Century* (New York: Farrar, Straus & Giroux, 2006).

2. Friedman quoted in "Thomas Friedman Throws in the Towel on Iraq," *The Progressive*, August 5, 2006, available at http://www.commondreams.org/views06/0805–22.htm.

3. Thomas Friedman and Robert Novak quoted in "Comment," *New Yorker*, August 21, 2006, available at http://www.newyorker.com/talk/content/articles/060821ta_talk_hertzberg.

4. Friedman, *The World Is Flat*, 7.

5. Ibid., 48.

6. Ibid., 280.

7. Ibid., 277.

8. Samir Amin, *The Liberal Virus: Permanent War and the Americanization of the World*, translated by James Membrez (New York: Monthly Review Press, 2004).

9. Ibid., 37–41.

10. Ibid., 20.

11. Ibid., 22.

12. Ibid., 24.

13. Friedman, *The World Is Flat*, 229.

14. Ibid., 8.

15. Thomas Friedman, "A Theory Of Everything," *The New York Times*, June 1, 2003, Sec. 4, 13.

16. Author, Phone Interview with Naseer Aruri, July 25, 2005. Unless otherwise noted, all future information and quotations in this section derive from this interview.

17. Woodrow Wilson, "First Inaugural Address," March 4, 1913, available at http://www.yale.edu/lawweb/avalon/presiden/inaug/wilson1.htm

18. Hans J. Morgenthau, *Politics Among Nations: The Struggle for Power and Peace*, 5th ed., rev. ed. (New York: Alfred A. Knopf, 1978), 4–15.

19. Michael Hirsh, "Death of a Founding Myth," *Newsweek*, January, 2002, 21.

20. Author, Interview with Aruri.

21. Friedman, *The World Is Flat*, 21.

22. Naseer Aruri, "The Rationale for US Intervention," n.d., aviailable: http://www.umassd.edu/specialprograms/mideastaffairs/rational.htm.

23. *Life and Debt*, directed by Stephanie Black (2001; Tuff Gong Pictures).

24. Ibid.

25. *Why We Fight*, directed by Eugene Jarecki, (2006; Charlotte Street Film).

26. Author, Phone Interview with Naomi Klein, November 10, 2003. Unless otherwise noted, all future information and quotations in this section derive from this interview.

27. John Kenneth Galbraith, *The Affluent Society* (New York: The New American Library, 1958), 6–17.

28. Author, Phone Interview with Mark Engler, August 29, 2005. Unless otherwise noted, all future information and quotations in this section derive from this interview.

29. Mark Engler, "The War and Globalization: Are They Really Connected?" *Foreign Policy In Focus* (Silver City, NM: Interhemispheric Resource Center, October 2004), available at http://www.fpif.org/papers/0410warglob.html.

30. Ibid.

31. The Blair Commission for Africa, Report, available at http://www.commissionforafrica.org/english/report/introduction.html.

32. Lesley Richardson, Charity Wristbands Made in 'Sweatshop' Factories, *The Scotsman*, May 29, 2005.

33. CNN, June 30, 2005.

34. George Dor, "G8, Tony Blair's Commission for Africa and Debt," Global Policy Forum, July 7, 2005, available at http://www.globalpolicy.org/socecon/bwi–wto/g7–8/2005/0707tony.htm.

35. Amin, *The Liberal Virus*, 30.

36. Ibid.

37. Jean–Claude Shanda Tonme, "All Rock, No Action," *The New York Times*, July 15, 2005, A19.

38. Ibid.

39. John Perkins, *Confessions of an Economic Hit Man* (San Francisco: Berrett–Koehler Publishers, 2004), xi.

40. Ibid., 18.

41. Ibid., 25.

42. Ibid., 119.

43. Author, Phone Interview with John Perkins, January 17, 2006. Unless otherwise noted, all future information and quotations in this section derive from this interview.

44. Emad Mekay, *Inter Press Service*, August 2, 2005.

45. Timms and spokesman quoted in "G8 Debt Relief Could Lead to New Borrowing," US Network for Global Economic Justice, August 2, 2005, available at http://www.50years.org/cms/updates/story/269.

46. WDM press release, 19 September 2005.

47. Reuters, October 26, 2005, available at http://lists.essential.org/pipermail/stop–imf/2005q4/001145.html.

48. *The Corporation*, produced by Mark Achbar et al., (2003; Zeitgeist Films).

49. Ibid.

50. World Bank, "Notes on the Philippines Country Program Review, July 28, 1972," prepared by H. Schulmann on August 15, 1972, quoted by D. Kapur, J. Lewis, R. Webb,

1997, Vol. 1., 303.

51. Jean Ziegler, "The World Bank of last resort," translated by Harry Forster, *Le Monde*, October 2002, available at http://mondediplo.com/2002/10/.

52. Alexander Cockburn, "Don't Say We Didn't Warn You," CounterPunch, February 7, 2004, available at http://www.counterpunch.org/cockburn11062004.html.

53. Perkins, *Confessions*, 150.

54. Ibid. 91.

55. Ibid., 232

56. Ibid.

57. Ibid., xi.

58. "Hugo Chávez Departs," *The New York Times*, A16.

59. State Deptartment Statement, April 12, 2002.

60. Perkins, *Confessions*, 234.

61. Ibid., 234.

CHAPTER 3: ONCE WERE RADICALS

1. Author, Interview with "J.Z.", July 13, 2005. Unless otherwise noted, all future information and quotations in this section derive from this interview.

2. Robert Cohen, "Student Activism in the 1930s," in *Encyclopedia of the American Left*, edited by Mari Jo Buhle, et al., (New York: Oxford University Press, 1998), available at http://newdeal.feri.org/students/move.htm.

3. Ibid.

4. Tomislav Sunic quoted in "Anduril's Seminal Anarchic Philosophy and the Schmittian Friend/Enemy Distinction," [c. 2005], available at http://www.attackthesystem.com/andurilschmitt.html.

5. Bob Dylan, *Chronicles* (New York: Simon & Shuster, 2004), cited in *The Economist*, September 29, 2005.

6. *The Wanderers*, directed by Philip Kaufman, (1979; Orion Pictures et al.); Students for a Democratic Society, Port Huron Statement, 1962, available at http://coursesa.matrix.msu.edu/~hst306/documents/huron.html.

7. Author, Phone Interview with Todd Gitlin, August 29, 2005. Unless otherwise noted, all future information and quotations in this section derive from this interview.

8. Port Huron Statement.

9. Ibid.

10. Todd Gitlin, *Letters to a Young Activist* (New York: Basic Books, 2003), 49.

11. Ibid., 49.

12. Ibid, 110.

13. Kari Kunst, "Letters to a Young Activist," AlterNet, July 28, 2003, available at http://www.alternet.org/wiretap/16481/.

14. Todd Chretien, "Gitlin: The Duke of Condescension," CounterPunch, June 21, 2003, available at http://www.counterpunch.org/chretien06212003.html.

15. Naomi Klein, "Naomi Klein Reviews Letters to a Young Activist," *Arts & Opinion*, Vol. 2, No. 4, 2003, available at http://www.artsandopinion.com/2003_v2_n4/klein.htm.

16. Carl Oglesby, "Let Us Shape the Future," speech delivered at the March on Washington,

November 27, 1965, available at http://www.studentsforademocraticsociety.org/docu-ments/oglesby_future.html.

17. Ibid.

18. Ibid.

19. Ibid.

20. Author, Interview with Alan Rusbridger.

21. U. S. Government, "Overview of America's International Strategy," 2002, available at http://www.whitehouse.gov/nsc/nss/2002/nss1.html.

22. The National Security Strategy of the United States, September 2002.

23. Paul Berman, A Tale of Two Utopias: The Political Journey of the Generation of 1968 (New York: W. W. Norton & Co., 1996), 63.

24. Corey Robin, "The Fear of the Liberals," The Nation, September 8, 2005, available at http://www.thenation.com/doc/20050926/robinl.

25. The New York Times, September 27, 1986, Sec. 1, 7.

26. Paul Berman, Mother Jones, December 1986.

27. Ibid.

28. Author, Phone Interview with Paul Berman, October 3, 2005. Unless otherwise noted, all future information and quotations in this section derive from this interview.

29. Richard Nixon, "Why," The New York Times, January 6, 1991, Sec. 4, 19.

30. Paul Berman, "Protestors Are Fighting the Last War," The New York Times, January 31, 1991, A23.

31. Paul Berman, Terror and Liberalism (New York: Norton, 2003).

32. Ibid., 183.

33. David Horowitz, Radical Son: A Journey Through Our Times (New York: The Free Press, 1998), 53.

34. Art Goldberg, "Art Goldberg and Stew Albert fire back at David Horowitz," Salon.com, December 13, 1999, available at http://www.salon.com/letters/1999/12/20/art_gold-berg/index.html.

35. Horowitz, Radical Son, parts 3 and 5.

36. Ibid., 224.

37. Ibid., 247.

38. David Horowitz, "Who killed Betty Van Patter?" Salon.com, December 13, 1999, avail-able at http://www.salon.com/news/col/horo/1999/12/13/betty/print.html.

39. Ibid.

40. Horowitz, Radical Son, 280.

41. Author, Phone Interview with David Horowitz, September 18. 2005. Unless otherwise noted, all future information and quotations in this section derive from this interview.

42. Horowitz, Radical Son, 349.

43. Ibid., 350–351.

44. Ibid., 357.

45. Peter Collier and David Horowitz, Destructive Generation: Second Thoughts about the Sixties (San Francisco: Summit Books, 1989), cited in Radical Son, 380.

46. Paul Berman, The New Republic, cited in Radical Son, 385.

CHAPTER 4: THE LIBERALS' WAR

1. Fukuyama, "The End of History?"

2. Ibid.

3. Norbert Walter, "German Unity—12 years on," August 27, 2002, available at http://www.aicgs.org/file_manager/streamfile.aspx?path=&name=walter12years.pdf.

4. Author, Interview with Manfred, June 17, 2005, Dietzhausen, Germany. Unless otherwise noted, all future information and quotations from Manfred in this section derive from this interview.

5. "Germany, 15 Years After the Wall," *The Christian Science Monitor*, November 9, 2004, available at http://www.csmonitor.com/2004/1109/p08s03–comv.html.

6. Author, Interview with Miki Milakovic, June 19, 2005, Belgrade, Serbia. Unless otherwise noted, all future information and quotations in this section derive from this interview.

7. Ibid.

8. Christopher Hitchens, "Port Huron Piffle," *The Nation*, May 27, 1999, available at http://www.thenation.com/doc/19990614/hitchens.

9. David Rieff quoted in Stephen Holmes, "The War of the Liberals," *The Nation*, October 26, 2005, available at http://www.thenation.com/doc/20051114/holmes/5.

10. Bill Clinton quoted in Mary Meiksins Wood, "Kosovo and the New Imperialism," *Monthly Review*, June 1999, available at http://www.monthlyreview.org/699wood.htm.

11. Bill Clinton and William Cohen quoted in Benjamin Schwarz and Christopher Layne, "The Case Against Intervention in Kosovo," *The Nation*, April 1, 1999, available at http://www.thenation.com/doc/19990419/schwarz/4.

12. Paul Berman, *Power and the Idealists* or, *The Passion of Joschka Fischer and its Aftermath* (Brooklyn, NY: Soft Skull Press, 2005), 308.

13. Berman, *Power and the Idealists*, 91.

14. Fareed Zakaria "The Balkans Keeping Kosovo: The costs of liberal imperialism," *National Review*, September 27, 1999, available at http://www.findarticles.com/p/articles/mi_m1282/is_1999_Sept_27/ai_55820849.

15. Freedom House, "About Us," http://www.freedomhouse.org/template.cfm?page=2; accessed September 19, 2006.

16. *Minimising Resistance to Reforms and the Integration of Serbia*, Centre for the Development of Civil Society, May 31, 2003, 1.

17. Ibid.

18. Ibid., 11.

19. Ibid., 28.

20. Ibid., 1.

21. Author, Interview with Srbijanka Turajlic, June 20, 2005, Belgrade, Serbia. Unless otherwise noted, all future information and quotations in this section derive from this interview.

22. "U. S. Advice Guided Milosevic Opposition," *The Washington Post*, December 11, 2000, available at http://www.washingtonpost.com/ac2/wp–dyn/A18395–2000Dec3?language=printer.

CHAPTER 5: THE SHINING CITY

1. H. W. Brands, *The Strange Death of American Liberalism* (New Haven: Yale University Press, 2001).

2. Ibid., 125.

3. Ibid., 159.

4. Ibid., 174.

5. William J. Clinton, "State of the Union Address," January 24, 1995, available at http://teachingamericanhistory.org/library/index.asp?document=1411.

6. John Winthrop, "A Model of Christian Charity," 1630, available at http://www.gilder-lehrman.org/teachers/seminar_docs/religious_doc3.html.

7. Ronald Reagan, "Farewell Address to the Nation," January 11, 1989, available at http://www.reaganlibrary.com/reagan/speeches/farewell.asp.

8. Peter C. Whybrow, *American Mania: When More Is Not Enough* (New York: W. W. Norton & Co., 2005), 53.

9. Whybrow, UCLA Neuropsychiatric Institute, "Director's Welcome," available at http://www.npi.ucla.edu/director.html.

10. Whybrow, *American Mania*, 4.

11. Author, Phone Interview with Peter Whybrow, July 16, 2005. Unless otherwise noted, all future information and quotations in this section derive from this interview.

12. Alexis de Tocqueville, *Democracy in America* (London: Longman, Green, Longman and Roberts, 1862).

13. Tocqueville quoted in Whybrow, *American Mania*, 58.

14. Adam Smith, *The Wealth of Nations* (Philadelphia: Printed for Thomas Dobson, [1789]; New York: Bantam Books, 2003).

15. Adam Smith quoted in Whybrow, 35.

16. Milton Friedman, *Capitalism and Freedom* (Chicago: University of Chicago Press, 1962), 39.

17. Ibid., 133.

18. Ibid., 109–110.

19. Ronald Reagan, "Inaugural Address," January 20, 1981, available at http://www.reaganfoundation.org/reagan/speeches/first.asp.

20. Center for American Progress, "Reduce Debt Burdens by Fighting Abusive Lending," available at http://www.americanprogress.org/site/pp.asp?c=biJRJ8OVF&b=1375357.

21. *Unforgivable Blackness: The Rise and Fall of Jack Johnson*, directed by Ken Burns (2005; Florentine Films).

22. Ibid.

23. Ibid.

24. Author, Interview with Lewis Lapham, October 28, 2005, New York. Unless otherwise noted, all future information and quotations in this section derive from this interview.

25. http://www.harpers.org/index.html.

26. "Ever higher society, ever harder to ascend," *The Economist*, December 29, 2004, available at http://www.economist.com/world/na/displayStory.cfm?story_id=3518560.

27. "Shadowy Lines that Still Divide," *The New York Times*, May 15, 2005, available at

http://www.nytimes.com/2005/05/15/national/class/OVERVIEW–FINAL.html?ex =1273809600&en=2fb756e388191419&ei=5088&partner=rssnyt&emc=rss.

28. "Old Nantucket Warily Meets the New," *The New York Times*, June 5, 2005, available: http://www.nytimes.com/2005/06/05/national/class/NANTUCKET–FINAL.html?e i=5090&en=4225cda3ce4bef53&ex=1275624000&partner=rssuserland&emc=rss&pa gewanted=all.

29. Nicolas Kristof, "The Larger Shame," *The New York Times*, September 6, 2005, available at http://www.nytimes.com/2005/09/06/opinion/06kristof.html?ex=1283659200& en=23e813b5e1061443&ei=5088&partner=rssnyt&emc=rss.

30. Marjorie Cohn, "The Two Americas," truthout.org, September 3, 2005, available at http://www.truthout.org/docs_2005/090305Y.shtml.

31. David Brooks, "The Bursting Point," *The New York Times*, September 4, 2005, available at http://www.nytimes.com/2005/09/04/opinion/04brooks.html?ex=1283486400& en=37eeb8918dbb6e2e&ei=5090&partner=rssuserland&emc=rss.

32. SourceWatch, available at http://www.sourcewatch.org.

33. Arian Campo–Flores, "A New Spice in the Gumbo," *Newsweek*, December 5.

CHAPTER 6: THE LAST PARTY

1. *The Leopard.*

2. Ibid.

3. Author, Interview with Gore Vidal, October, 26, 2005, Los Angeles, California. Unless otherwise noted, all future information and quotations from Vidal in this section derive from this interview.

4. Gore Vidal, *The City and The Pillar* (New York: New American Library, 1948).

5. Vidal, *Myra Breckinridge* (New York: Random House, 1986).

6. 1968 Buckley–Vidal Debate, ABC News, August 28, 1968.

7. Vidal, *The Decline and Fall of the American Empire* (Berkeley: Odonian Press, 1992).

8. Fiachra Gibbons Arts, "Vidal praises Oklahoma bomber for heroic aims," *The Guardian*, August 17, 2001, available at http://books.guardian.co.uk/edinburgh-bookfestival2001/story/0,,538191,00.html.

9. Ibid.

10. Vidal, *Perpetual War for Perpetual Peace: How We Got to be So Hated* (New York: Thunder's Mouth Press, 2002), xiii. See also *Dreaming War: Blood for Oil and the Cheney–Bush Junta* (Thunder's Mouth Press, 2002).

11. John J. Miller, "Through His Teeth—Quotations from Chairman Gore—Al Gore," *National Review*, May 22, 2000; "Gore's Gun Problem," Karen Tumulty, CNN, February 7, 2000.

12. "Al Gore's Gulf War Vote," *Rocky Mountain News*, September 3, 2000.

13. Bill Mesler, "Al Gore: The Other Oil Candidate," CorpWatch, August 29, 2000.

14. Ibid.

15. William Baue, "Occidental Returns Siriri Oil Block to Colombia," Amazon Watch, September 9, 2005, available at http://www.amazonwatch.org/newsroom/view_news. php?id=604.

16. *Fahrenheit 9/11*, written and directed by Michael Moore (2004; Miramax Films).

17. John W. Dean, *Worse Than Watergate: The Secret Presidency of George W. Bush* (New York; Little, Brown, and Co., 2004).

18. *CNN Sunday Morning*, February 1, 2004.

19. "Howard Dean's last stand?" Minnesota Public Radio, February 10, 2004, available at http://news.minnesota.publicradio.org/features/2004/02/10_kelleherb_deaniwisc/.

20. Al From and Bruce Reed, "The Real Soul of the Democratic Party," Democratic Leadership Council, May 15, 2003, available at http://www.ppionline.org/ndol/ndol_ci.cfm?kaid=127&subid=900056&contentid=251690.

21. Obey quoted in "Howard Dean's last stand?"

22. Robert Pollin, *Contours of Descent: U. S. Economic Fractures and the Landscape of Global Austerity* (London: Verso, 2003), 9.

23. Walter Karp, *Indispensable Enemies: the Politics of Misrule in America* (New York: Franklin Square Press, 1993), 23.

24. Ibid., 7–49.

25. Ibid., 79.

26. Ibid., 33.

27. Ibid., 110.

28. Noam Chomsky, *Radical Priorities* (AK Press, 1981).

29. Curtis Gans, "The Upsurge in Voter Registration and Expectations for Turnout in the 2004 Elections," October 25, 2004, available at http://fpc.state.gov/fpc/37382.htm.

30. *Journeys with George*, written and directed by Alexandra Pelosi (2002; HBO).

31. Ibid.

32. Pelosi quoted in "Getting High on George," *New York Observer*, November 3, 2002, available at http://www.journeyswithgeorge.com/news_body.htm.

33. *Diary of a Political Tourist*, written and directed by Alexandra Pelosi (2004; HBO).

34. Author, Interview with Alexandra Pelosi, May 16, 2005, New York. Unless otherwise noted, all future information and quotations in this section derive from this interview.

35. Thomas Frank, "What's the Matter with Liberals?" *The New York Review of Books*, May 12, 2005, available at http://www.nybooks.com/articles/17982.

36. From and Reed, "The Real Soul of the Democratic Party."

37. "Mutual Threat Unites 2 Rivals Opposing Dean," *The New York Times*, October 12, 2003, available at http://select.nytimes.com/gst/abstract.html?res=F3061FFA385B0 C718DDDA90994DB404482.

38. *Diary of a Political Tourist*.

39. Ibid.

40. John Nichols, "The Media and Howard Dean," *The Nation*, February 1, 2004.

41. "Kerry pitches his global view," *Christian Science Monitor*, May 24, 2004, available at http://www.csmonitor.com/2004/0528/p01s01–uspo.html.

42. "Progressive Internationalism: A Democratic National Security Strategy", (Washington, DC, October 30, 2003) ; "Rebuilding America's Defenses: Strategy, Forces, and Resources for a New Century" (Washington, DC: Project for the New American Century, September 2000).

43. "John Kerry in UCLA Address Promises More Effective War on Terrorism," February 27, 2004, available at http://www.international.ucla.edu/article.asp?parentid=8320.

44. Will Marshall, "Jihadist Virus," May 7, 2004, available at http://www.ppionline.org/ppi_ci.cfm?knlgAreaID=124&subsecID=307&contentID=252566.

45. Frank, "What's the Matter with Liberals?"

46. Jeffrey St. Clair and Alexander Cockburn, eds., *Dime's Worth of Difference: Beyond the Lesser of Two Evils* (New York: Counterpunch, 2004).

47. Alexander Cockburn, "Zombies for Kerry," *The Nation*, August 26, 2004, available at http://www.thenation.com/doc/20040913/cockburn.

48. Tom Raum quoted in "As I Please," available at http://tmg110.tripod.com/please/index.blog?start=1100834674&topic_id=85.

49. Pelosi quoted in "Dems Ponder How to Bounce Back," Foxnews.com, November 8, 2004, available at http://www.foxnews.com/story/0,2933,137763,00.html.

50. Author, Interview with John Avlon, May 21, 2005, New York. Unless otherwise noted, all future information and quotations in this section derive from this interview.

51. John P. Avlon, *Independent Nation: How the Vital Center is Changing American Politics* (New York: Harmony Books, 2004), 12.

52. Author, Interview with Avlon.

53. David Horowitz, Salon.com, May 6, 1999, available at http://www.salon.com/news/feature/1999/05/06/bush/.

54. George W. Bush, "President's remarks at Ashwaubenon, Wisconsin Rally," July 14, 2004, available at http://www.whitehouse.gov/news/releases/2004/07/20040714–15.html.

55. PBS *Frontline*, April, 2005, available at http://www.pbs.org/wgbh/pages/frontline/shows/architect/interviews/whitman.html.

56. Avlon, *Independent Nation*, 4.

EPILOGUE: IN HEAT

1. *60 Minutes*, June 8, 2005, CBS.

2. Peter Beinart, "The Rehabilitation of the Cold–War Liberal," *The New York Times*, April 30, 2006.

3. Fox News, November 24, 2006.

4. Samir Amin, *The Liberal Virus: Permanent War and the Americanization of the World*, translated by James Membrez (New York: Monthly Review Press, 2004).

5. F. E. Emery and E. L. Trist, *Towards a Social Ecology*, (Springer, 1975)

6. Corey Robin, "The Fear of the Liberals," *The Nation*, September 26, 2005.

7. *Diary of a Political Tourist*, written and directed by Alexandra Pelosi (2004; HBO).